THE JESUS MYSTERY

THE JESUS MYSTERY

✠

ASTONISHING CLUES TO THE TRUE IDENTITIES OF JESUS AND PAUL

LENA EINHORN

THE LYONS PRESS
Guilford, Connecticut
An imprint of The Globe Pequot Press

CONTENTS

CHAPTER 1

PROLOGUE

There were always historians who said it could not be done because of historical problems. There were always theologians who said it should not be done because of theological objections. And there were always scholars who said the former when they meant the latter.

John Dominic Crossan,
The Historical Jesus, 1991[1]

This story, if such it can be called, has been within me for many years; to be more precise, for twenty-five years. Yet I have not written it earlier, or in any other way attempted to give it form. One can well ask why, as it lies close to what I have previously worked with.

Some years ago my colleague Bengt Berg and I made a series of documentary films for Swedish Television that we called *From the Shadows of the Past*. The series, which consisted of three parts, dealt with some historical mysteries that researchers—with varying success—have devoted themselves to solving. We looked at the origins of the Finnish language and the Finnish myths, we looked at research on the origin of the Indo-Europeans, and we looked at the story of the Exodus out of Egypt and the origins of the Israelites. The last program, in particular, has great parallels with the issues raised in this book: they both concern central religious figures whose personal lives, despite their monumental roles in three world religions, to a great degree were ignored by contemporary history. Who actually was the newborn boy that Pharaoh's daughter is said to have found in the rushes (and, as Freud once asked, did she just "find" this boy with an Egyptian name)? Is there any equivalent to the Exodus, the flight of the Israelites from Egypt, in the otherwise fairly well documented Egyptian history? Is there any description at all of a people that could correspond to the Israelites? And is there, in Egyptian history, any equivalent to the person called Moses?

I am irresistibly attracted to the mysterious, or rather to the reality behind the mysterious. And above all I am tempted by that which has been hidden by time, by that which lies partly hidden in the obscurity of the past, but which lets some clues through to the present. I try, inasmuch as I have the opportunity, to unravel the past with all the means at my disposal: the actual existing, scientifically verifiable, historical knowledge we have of the time and the setting; the parallel tales or legends that are available, and which can shed light upon each other; the psychological inducements that may have formed the basis for the actions of the individuals. In short: the eternal—and sometimes dangerous—cliché that there is often a grain of truth in that which is indistinct, is what spurs me on in my curiosity. The question being, what is that grain?

And it is just such a fascination that I have long felt for Jesus of Nazareth. I have been fascinated by the reality behind the text, the historical person behind the stories and the religious concepts. I have long been astonished by certain circumstances that make the story of Jesus, or rather the search for the historical truth behind the story, so incredibly fascinating. But despite that, I have never written anything down. Despite that, I didn't include the story of Jesus of Nazareth in the series *From the Shadows of the Past*. Why not? Because it felt like a taboo.

Jesus arouses emotions in a way that Moses never has done—although both are religious personalities. There may be different reasons for this: Jesus, according to Christianity, is the son of God, and in accordance with the doctrine of the Trinity is himself God, while Moses, despite his prominent position in the Old Testament, has never been considered anything but a human being. Another reason may be the two-thousand-year-old religious tensions that have their origins in faith, or the rejection of faith, in Jesus as the Messiah. Also, one must consider Jesus' fundamental importance to the Christian believer; the close relationship between faith in him—as the son of God, resurrected from the dead—and the religious experience.

Nevertheless, the search for the historical Jesus is neither a new nor an unknown phenomenon. The first academic who seriously applied himself to the question was the German theologian and orientalist Hermann Samuel Reimarus, in Hamburg in the mid-eighteenth century. Reimarus, who avoided publishing his radical hypotheses about Christianity during his lifetime, had parts of his work *Apologie oder Schutzschrift für die vernünftigen Verehrer Gottes* [Apology or defence for the rational worshippers of God] published posthumously, between 1774 and 1778, the most important of which is considered to be the fragment entitled "The object of Jesus and his disciples." Reimarus, who was influenced by the rationalism of the Enlightenment, sought—as did, for example, his successor David Freidrich Strauss—to describe a Jesus "free from religious dogma." According to Reimarus, and many others in this first wave of research into the historical Jesus, Jesus was primarily a Jewish revolutionary who tried to seize power in Jerusalem, but failed in this attempt and was executed, and Reimarus suggested that it was not until after Jesus' death that his disciples created the myth of the resurrection and the picture of Jesus that forms the foundation for Christianity. Reimarus was not an atheist, however, but rather he considered that human beings could—with the help of their intelligence—achieve a religious faith that is more true than one that has its foundations in miracles and revelations.

This first major quest for the historical Jesus came to an end in 1906 when Albert Schweitzer published his monumental work about the history of the research about Jesus, *The Quest of the Historical Jesus*. And Schweitzer soberly points out the following: Reimarus and his followers were not driven by a "purely historical interest," but their express purpose was to promote rationalism, and they used "the Jesus of history as an ally in the struggle against the tyranny of dogma."[2] Perhaps the problem (or fascination) with the quest for the historical Jesus had always been precisely this: the quest was characterized by the wishes and needs of those who put forward the hypotheses. The quest was never "free." As Schweitzer writes: "Thus each successive epoch of theology found its own thoughts in Jesus; that was, indeed, the only way in which it could make Him live."[3]

Such projection still goes on in our day. The dilemma for all those who continue to search for the historical Jesus, and they are many (the current stage is often called "The Third Quest"), is that there is so little to go on. In effect, they only have one major source: the New Testament. As the American theologian Craig L. Blomberg writes: "Two somewhat opposite problems confront historians. On the one hand, they discover much less independent testimony to the life of Jesus than they might have expected concerning one who gave rise to such a major world religion. On the other hand, when they look just at Matthew, Mark, Luke and John, it seems as though there is too much testimony."[4]

Yet the situation is typical, and in that respect the story of Jesus does not differ from that of Moses: they are both religious leader figures of gigantic proportions, persons who according to the canonic sources have had an enormous influence on their surroundings—and yet they are persons who to a great extent seem to have slipped past the pens of contemporary historians. That is mysterious, but nevertheless typical. Because out of this comes the mixture of truth and myth that makes legend, that makes something that allows our imagination to act but which, all the same, is created from something real. The question is, what does this "real" consist of?

As I have indicated above, I have had my own thoughts about the real person, the historical figure, Jesus, for many years. I do not claim to compete with the many theologians and historians who for more than two centuries have devoted themselves to finding the person Jesus behind the biblical stories. Just as Albert Schweitzer pointed out, they are many, and the way they speculate is, to a considerable degree, colored not only by their motives, but also by their will to confront and overthrow. Most Christian theologians stay more or less "within the fold" when they regard and analyze Jesus the person. Others have, in some instances, presented spectacular theories. This is an exciting field, and if one starts to attempt to penetrate behind the tempting curtain that history had laid out, one is simply pulled in further. Jesus lived only two thousand years ago, thus in historical time, and in a geographic area that at the time was occupied by one of the most powerful empires in the history of the world, the Roman Empire. In addition, he was active at precisely the time when the culture and society of this area, Jewish Judea and Galilee, were approaching their fall, one of the major catastrophes in Jewish history. There are threads to pull, there is written history, there are parallel stories, there are descriptions of contemporary religious and social upheavals. The question is how they are connected. The question is who this Jesus of Nazareth really was.

A necessary condition if one is to examine the *historical* figure of Jesus is that one ignores—at least temporarily—religious faith, and possibly too the idea of Jesus as divine. Reimarus was aware of this when he wrote, and that is perhaps the reason his thoughts remained unpublished during his lifetime (while Strauss, who published his book *The Life of Jesus* within his lifetime, would later comment, "it has made my life a lonely one."[5]). Nevertheless, this is necessary if one wants to have a chance to find the historical person. Respect for what Jesus achieved, and for the religious experience associated with a belief in him, ought thus not become less. It didn't for Reimarus. And nor does it for all those theologians who nowadays devote themselves to studies of the historical person.

Most of the hypotheses I will present are not mine alone. It is evident that when you start to allow yourself to look at Jesus with "historical eyes," you will discover that many of those who have sought after answers have come to similar conclusions. But in some respects I will allow myself to be rather provocative in my conclusions, and in at least one respect I will present a hypothesis that I have never previously seen in print. It is with religious figures as with innovations: in approaching them you are so caught up in an established frame of mind that—even though you consider yourself to be thinking freely—you sometimes nevertheless don't dare pursue a thought to its conclusion. It is too much of a break with that which we have always learned.

CHAPTER 2

DID JESUS EVER EXIST?

The question whether he has ever existed, as a person of flesh and blood, has been one of the first to confront anyone seeking the historical Jesus, and theologians as well as other researchers, believers and nonbelievers alike, have devoted shelf upon shelf of literature to answering it—or rather to attempting to argue for their particular conclusion. It is decidedly not an easy question to answer; the only thing that they do all agree on is that there is only one "authorized," coherent description of a person who is unequivocally Jesus of Nazareth, namely the description presented in the New Testament.

The New Testament—or the Greek Testament, as it has also been called—was sanctioned by the Church, in the form we now recognize it, in the fourth century. But the various works that make up the New Testament were written long before that. The question is, when—and by whom?

The most important part of the New Testament is without doubt the four gospels. In these we find a description—large segments of which are concordant—of the life and work of Jesus, from his birth to the crucifixion and resurrection. The authors endeavour to describe Jesus' deeds in detail, although on the whole restricted to a period of his life: his final year, and above all the last week of his life. Two of the gospels, Matthew and Luke (but interestingly not what is probably the oldest gospel, Mark) also provide brief descriptions of Mary's pregnancy and the birth of Jesus. The descriptions in the gospels, at any rate in the three that were written first, are so similar that it is generally agreed that to a certain degree they are based on each other.

So, when were they written? And by whom were they written? By people who had known Jesus, perhaps even by some of his disciples? Or by other people?

All four gospels, with the possible exception of Matthew, were originally written in Greek, despite the fact that Jesus and his disciples spoke Aramaic. This need not actually be so strange, because Greek at that time was the *lingua franca* in the eastern part of the Roman Empire. Yet it is something to be noted. Another circumstance to be noted is that they were presumably written in a different geographic area than the one they describe (it is, of course, impossible to know for certain, but it has been suggested that Mark was written in Rome or Syria and Matthew in Syria, while Luke is considered to have been Greek himself and may have written in Rome, and the gospel according to John may have been written in Ephesus). Nor need this be strange, since the societies the gospels describe—the Judea and Galilee occupied by the Romans but inhabited, and in part administered, by Jews—were completely destroyed after the Jewish uprising against the Romans in the years 66 to 70 CE (Common Era). After this, the population was spread to the winds, which would presumably have included the people who might have had some connection with Jesus of Nazareth.

Yet it is precisely from the starting point of this time frame that one can most strongly question the role of the gospels as eyewitness descriptions of the life and work of Jesus—because none of them is regarded as having been written during Jesus' life. None of them is even regarded as having been written within thirty years of his crucifixion.

So how reliable are they as descriptions of a person said to have actually existed, Jesus of Nazareth? Let us look a little at the general facts that are presented in the gospels, those that you would also expect to be described in historical works from or about that time. Because there are a number of facts presented that can be checked against historical sources.

According to tradition, the birth of Jesus is the starting point for our calendar. To judge by the fixed points named in the gospels—that is, in the two gospels that describe the birth of Jesus—this event cannot have taken place at that time, as we calculate it today. Matthew claims, for example, that Jesus was born in Bethlehem "in the reign of Herod." Herod the Great is not unknown as a historical figure; he was the king of Judea. And we know almost exactly when he lived: from 74 BCE (Before the Common Era) to 4 BCE. This dating is primarily based on the information given by the Roman-Jewish historian Flavius Josephus (or simply Josephus, as he is often called). In other words, Jesus must have been born several years before our era if King Herod was still alive at the time of his birth.

Another fixed point that is named, this time in Luke, is that Jesus was born at the time when Augustus Caesar issued a decree "for a census to be taken throughout the Roman world." Luke goes on to write that this "was the first registration of its kind; it took place when Quirinius was governor of Syria." Not only Augustus Caesar but also Quirinius are historical figures. Augustus Caesar lived from 63 BCE to 14 CE. His life and reign thus coincided, at least in part, with the life and reign of King Herod. What is more problematic is that Quirinius—again according to Josephus—did not become governor in Syria until the year 6 CE.[1] In other words, Jesus could not have been born both when King Herod reigned and when Quirinius was governor. The theologian F. F. Bruce, and others, have nevertheless tried to argue in favor of these events having taken place simultaneously.[2] But their efforts are rather desperate, and for most people this contradiction in the times of events is hard to explain.

That the times given for the birth of Jesus do not exactly match our calendar is one thing, but the inability of the gospel writers to place correctly in history events that ought to have been commonly known in the area and at the time that are described is a greater problem. It indicates that these gospel writers perhaps were not so close to the center of events (or, possibly, that they deliberately constructed the epoch in which they want us to believe that Jesus was active).

Another possible indication of a lack of knowledge is that Mark, the author of what is considered to be the first gospel, does not seem to be particularly well informed about the local geography where the story takes place. Mark writes in 7:31, "On his journey back from Tyrian territory he went by way of Sidon to the sea of Galilee, well within the territory of the Decapolis." The problem is that both Tyre and Sidon lie on the coast of Lebanon, northwest of Lake Galilee—but Sidon lies directly north of Tyre! So one would hardly go through Sidon on one's way from Tyre to the lake, unless one had some errand in the completely opposite direction.

Matthew solves the geographical problem by writing that "Jesus then withdrew to the region of Tyre and Sidon"[3]. But Mark makes several other geographical mistakes: in 5, he writes, "So they came to the country of the Gerasenes on the other side of the lake," and a few lines later he describes how a herd of pigs "rushed over the edge into the lake." But Gerasa (now Jerash) is not anywhere near Lake Galilee, or any other lake. Gerasa lies about thirty miles southeast of Lake Galilee, and about as far northeast of the Dead Sea. But this time, too, Matthew comes to the rescue. He places the episode with the herd of pigs rushing into the lake in "the country of the Gadarenes," which is about six miles from the lake.[4] Luke, too, names the episode as having taken place in "the country of the Gerasenes," but the church father Origen (185–254 CE) suggests that this refers to a village by the name of Gergesa, right next to the lake.[5]

Of course, we do not know whether the explanation for the geographical mistakes lies in early misinterpretations or in faults when the gospel was written down. These small examples simply serve the purpose of illustrating what we already know: the gospels are not contemporary descriptions.

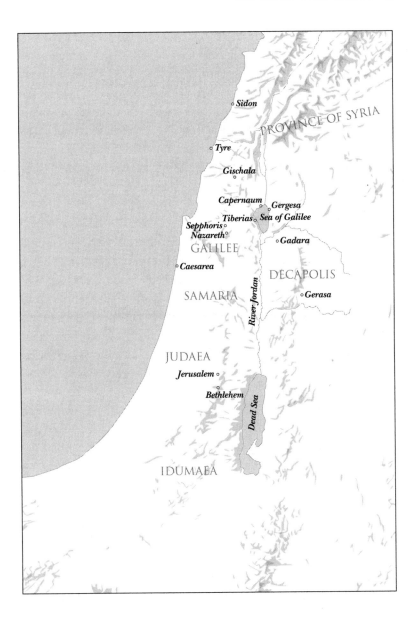

The oldest surviving fragment of any part of the four gospels is a piece of papyrus, the size of the palm of a hand, which is called P52. It was discovered in 1920 in Egypt, and each side has seven lines in Greek from what is regarded as a part of the gospel according to

John (18:31 to 33 and 18:37 to 38, respectively). The fragment is dated to about 125 to 160 CE, although earlier as well as later dates have sometimes been put forward.

It is also about the middle of the second century that we begin to find references to gospel texts in other works, and Irenaeus, a church father, names the four gospels around the year 185 CE. Even earlier (the year 96 CE is often named), Bishop Clemens of Rome had quoted some partly recognizable statements of Jesus, but without indicating that there were any formal gospels.[6]

Who wrote the four gospels that today make up the core of the New Testament? The answer is that we don't know who Mark, Matthew, Luke, and John were. It has been suggested that Mark was an interpreter or disciple of Peter, Jesus' leading apostle; that Luke was an assistant to the apostle Paul; and that Matthew and John were even disciples of Jesus. Church father Irenaeus—who lived in the second century—for example, claimed quite firmly that Jesus' disciple John lived in Ephesus at least until the year 98 CE.[7] He is said to have gained this information from Polycarpus, who in his turn is said to have been a disciple of John in Ephesus.[8]

But the arguments against Jesus' close associates having written any of the gospels are put forward just as forcibly. And when all is said and done, these four men will for the most part remain anonymous—with the possible exception of Luke. Luke is regarded as the author of not only the gospel bearing his name but also the Acts of the Apostles (which are also a part of the New Testament, and which describe the life and work of the apostle Paul and of Jesus' disciples after the death of Jesus). And in some verses of the Acts of the Apostles where he describes Paul's journeys, the author writes "we." Luke thus suddenly becomes a participant in the events described. If this is correct, then it is reasonable to assume that he did in fact know Paul. In addition, Paul names a Luke in some of his epistles. The gospel of John, too, ends with words that indicate that the author himself had been present, and had been a disciple of Jesus. But the last chapter of that gospel is considered by most commentators to be a later addition.

When were these stories written down? There is not an absolute consensus on this issue, but most Bible scholars today do agree that none of the gospels was written, or at least edited, before the year 65 CE—that is, they were created at least thirty years after Jesus was crucified. This conclusion is based on the gospel authors' obvious, or suggested, knowledge of certain historical events—primarily the destruction of Jerusalem—and their knowledge of each other's texts. The approximate dates that are usually given for the writing of the various gospels are:

Mark	ca. 68–73 CE
Matthew	ca. 70–90 CE
Luke	ca. 80–100 CE
John	ca. 90–110 CE[9]

So how do these gospels fit together? As mentioned above, three of the gospels—Mark, Matthew, and Luke—are regarded as having so many similarities with each other that they must partly be based upon each other, or on common sources. That is why they are called the *synoptic* (i.e. comparable) gospels. It is possible to line up long sections from the different synoptic gospels side by side and compare them almost word for word. The gospel that stands out is John, most likely the last to be written, which differs considerably from the other three.

The gospel of Mark was probably written first (despite the fact that Matthew comes first in the New Testament), and Matthew and Luke are seen as being based upon Mark to a great degree, even though there are sections common to these two that are not found in Mark. In order to explain the verses that are not found in Mark, it has been suggested that there is at least one more early gospel, a gospel that has not been found but which is said to have served as the original text for the particular sections in Matthew and Luke that are missing in Mark. This hypothetical gospel has been called "Q" (after the German word *Quelle*, "source"). Some Bible scholars create enormous structures around this Q gospel and date it to the 50's CE while others dismiss it as a futile attempt to give an earlier dating to the writing of the story of Jesus of Nazareth.

The time for the actual writing is significant not only because the reliability of a biographer increases the closer he or she comes to their subject. The actual point in time when these biographers finally seemed to have settled down to write, that point in time when the story of Jesus of Nazareth—a story more than thirty years old—was actually committed to writing, is of vital importance. It is a decisive date—for the story, for the setting it describes, and for the people described. Because in the year 70 CE, the world described in the four gospels was destroyed—absolutely, totally, and irreplaceably.

* * *

When the Roman Empire stood at the height of its power, it stretched from the Atlantic in the west to the Caspian Sea and the Persian Gulf in the east. During the reign of Augustus Caesar, it embraced almost the entire area surrounding the Mediterranean as well as large parts of western and central Europe. About 45 million people, perhaps one fifth of the population of the world, regarded the Roman emperor as their ruler.

One of the many areas that the Roman Empire had recently conquered was a relatively small province on the eastern shores of the Mediterranean, which they called Iudaea (after the central part of the province, Judea). It was a province that would come to create special problems for its Roman masters.

When the Jewish people had returned to Judea around 538 BCE from their exile in Babylonia, it had not been an easy homecoming. During the half-century that they had been exiled, not only had the Temple in Jerusalem been destroyed, but also much of the local infrastructure. And when they returned, it was not to a liberated country. King Cyrus of Persia, after conquering Babylonia, had given the exiled Jewish people living there the right to return to their country. But Cyrus continued to be their ruler.

Despite this, and despite the hardships that they had suffered, the Jews had learned something during their exile: how to manage without their Temple and their land, and how to retain their religious rites and traditions in a foreign environment. They had been hardened, and they would now make the best of the fact that they had been allowed to return home. One of the first things the Jews do after their return is to rebuild the destroyed Temple. And during the following century much of the religious life in the country will be reformed, under the leadership of the Jewish scribes Ezra and Nehemiah.

But in a political sense, life in Judea continues to be chaotic. In the year 331 BCE, Alexander the Great defeats the Persians, and Judea is by then already a part of his realm. When Alexander dies eight years later, an even more chaotic period starts, with a continuous change of rulers. Notwithstanding, the Jews are on the whole allowed to practice their religion. Alexander has lived according to the wise principle that if one wishes to rule over enormous land areas, one must keep the subjugated populations in good spirits. The Hellenist rulers who succeed him follow in general that same principle, and they allow the Jews to practice their unusual monotheist religion, and their religious rites. This state of affairs, however, comes to an abrupt end in the year 168 BCE.

Antiochus Epiphanes was unlike the earlier foreign rulers. For one thing, he was eccentric and dictatorial, but on top of that he could not understand why his subjects in Judea should be allowed to practice their own religion. So the year after his accession, Antiochus dedicates the most holy place of the Jews—the Temple in Jerusalem—to the Greek god Zeus. And as if that wasn't enough, he empties the Temple of its "secret treasures," he sets up an altar to Zeus on the Temple's large altar, and subsequently sacrifices pigs there. Furthermore, he forbids the practicing of the Jewish religion, and circumcision as well as the ownership of Torah scrolls are punishable by death. It is said that women who had their sons circumcised were punished by being crucified with their sons hanging from their necks.[10]

This is the final straw for the Jews. The first to strike back is an old priest in the village of Modiin, northwest of Jerusalem. His name is Mattathias. The revolt against Antiochus starts when Mattathias kills the first Jew who obeys Antiochus by coming to the village to make a sacrifice at the altar, and also kills the King's general accompanying the Jew, with a few of his soldiers. Mattathias then flees up into the hills with his five sons. This sparks a full-scale revolt which, after the death of Mattathias, will come to be led by his son Judah Maccabee (Judah the Hammer). And the incredible happens—within three years, Judah and his rebels defeat the foreign rulers. For the first time in many centuries the Jews are once again masters of their own land.

At the end of that year, the purified Temple is reconsecrated and a cruse with a little oil in it is found and lit on the altar. The oil is expected to last one day, but it burns for eight days. This is the "miracle" that has given rise to the Jewish holiday called Hanukkah. What Hanukkah really celebrates is the new freedom and independence from foreign rulers (Hanukkah, like Passover, is thus an independence celebration) but the liberated Jews wanted to create a religious holiday, so it was necessary to focus upon a "miracle," namely the oil that burned for eight days.

The new independence of the Jews lasts one hundred years. Not more.

The Jewish independence came to be characterized by bloody power struggles between various factions, interrupted by short periods of relative calm. Power rests with the relatives of Judah Maccabee, the so-called Maccabeans, but assassinations and revolts come one after the other. Finally, one of the competing princes, Aristobulus, simply bribes the Romans for assistance against his brother Hyrcanus. The Romans are more than willing to come to his rescue. In the year 63 BCE, a Roman army invades the Jewish nation. The Jews give up their land, the land they once had bewailed by the rivers of Babylon, practically without any resistance. This loss will come to mark the following hundred—and in fact two thousand—years of Jewish history.

At first, however, the population retains a quite considerable autonomy. The Roman Senate appoints the Idumuean Jew Herod as king of Judea in the year 40 BCE (he gains de facto control of Judea, Samaria, Galilee, and a large area east of the Golan Heights).

Herod (usually called Herod the Great, to distinguish him from later Herods) never won the approval of his people. He was to devote much of his life to, on the one hand, courting them like a beloved bride, and on the other, trying to frighten them into obedience. He himself could never forget the fact that he came from a converted people on his father's side and was a non-Jew on his mother's side, and he tried to compensate by marrying a Maccabean princess, Mariamne. Herod loved his Mariamne deeply, and yet he had her murdered. Because in Herod's life paranoia would always triumph over love. Before his life was over, he would murder his wife, her paternal grandfather, mother, and brother, as well as three of his own sons. Augustus Caesar, who had sanctioned the trial against two of the sons, is supposed to have said that he would rather have been Herod's pig than his son.

As a ruler, however, Herod was competent in many respects, which not even his unwilling subjects could deny. And in his assiduous courtship of them, he would not only build up the infrastructure in his country (and establish new towns), he would also make the Temple in Jerusalem into perhaps the most magnificent holy site in the Orient. Besides this, he saw to it that the Romans, on the whole, left their country alone.

But with the death of Herod the Great in the year 4 BCE, the autonomy breaks up. The realm is divided between three of Herod's sons—Herod Antipas is given Galilee and Perea, Archelaus is given Judea, Samaria, and Idumea, and Philip is given the areas northeast of Lake Galilee. But the sons' inability to retain control worries the Romans. Especially the son who has been granted the most symbolically important part, Judea, turns out to be unable to keep his subjects satisfied. Protests against the wilful Archelaus become so great that the Romans depose him in the year 6 CE and exile him to Gaul. But Archelaus is not replaced by another local vassal prince. Instead, the whole of his area is placed under Roman administration and connected to Syria—where the Quirinius named by Luke becomes governor. It is the beginning of the end of the Jewish state.

*

The Romans now establish a province consisting of Judea, Samaria, and Idumea and give it the name Iudaea. They appoint a governor for the province, a so-called *prefect* (later *procurator*) whose residence town is Caesarea. The prefect is a Roman, and from the year 26 CE, his name is Pontius Pilate. On a more local level, however, the Jews continued to some extent to administer themselves. The capital city, Jerusalem, is to a large extent run by the Jewish high priest and his council, the Sanhedrin. Beginning in the year 18 CE, the name of the high priest is Caiaphas.

But the power of the Jews over what was, until recently, their own country, and to which they had more or less invited the Romans, is now restricted all the more. The most important symbol for their attachment to the country—the Temple in Jerusalem—now stands as an empty promise of the reborn independence that did not last. One must look to Jewish history—the constant break-ups, the constant threats against their religious and physical existence, and their stubborn adherence to their distinctive religious character—to understand the feelings this arouses. It stirs up new religious movements in the country, not least among those who occupy themselves with apocalyptic thoughts—thoughts about the end of the world. And it brings to life one more concept: old religious ideas about a person, the Messiah, who shall come to liberate the people from all evil.

The word messiah—or *mashiach* in Hebrew—occurs thirty-eight times in the Hebrew Bible, (which roughly corresponds to the Old Testament). The word (which in Greek translation is *Khristos*) means "the anointed one," and it was a term that was originally used about some Jewish kings, priests, or prophets, but over time came to symbolize a presumptive ruler, anointed by the Lord, who would come and bring prosperity to the people of Israel. The more difficult the times were for the Jews, the more they placed their hope in this "prince of peace," as he is called in the Book of Isaiah. Especially during the Babylonian captivity, people hoped that a messiah would come and lead the Jews back to their homeland. There is nothing to suggest that a messiah figure was seen as a god, but possibly as someone sent by the Lord. According to some prophecies, a messiah must be of the clan of David.

The search for messiah figures, and the appearance of self-acclaimed ones, escalates with the march of the Romans into the realm of the Jews, during the first century BCE. And the presumptive messiah increasingly comes to be defined as a person who—apart from his creating peace on earth—shall reestablish the people of Israel and their land, restoring it to its position and condition in the time of King David. In some cases, the messiah figure is described as a military leader. This is the case in, for example, the Dead Sea scrolls (written between approximately the third century BCE and 68 CE). The "war scroll," describes, among other things, how the existing evil shall escalate, until, at the end of time, a final battle shall take place between "the sons of darkness" and the "sons of light." And in several fragments there is talk of a messiah figure (one of two or three) who shall come "with sword," a prince of the clan of David who shall defeat the powers of evil on earth and lead the people to the new time. Here one can notice the distinctly apocalyptic and eschatological features that mark much of the thinking from that time (and which are clearly present in the thoughts expressed by Jesus of Nazareth).

There were also a number of real-life self-proclaimed messiah figures during this turbulent period. One person who possibly had such aspirations was a rebel leader by the name of Judas the Galilean, a man mentioned by both Josephus and the gospel writer Luke.[11] Judas became legendary as the founder of the revolutionary and religiously inspired Zealots. The Zealots were a movement of action-oriented, and often violent, Jewish rebels, who partly modeled themselves after the leaders of the Maccabean uprising. The actions of the Zealots were directed both against the outer enemy, the Romans, and against those Jews whom the Zealots regarded as traitors.

Judas the Galilean started his activities in conjunction with an episode described in the New Testament: the tax-related census—

which, according to Luke, was ongoing at the time of Jesus' birth—in the year 6 CE. Initially, the Jews yielded to the requirements of the Romans, but, as Josephus writes, there was one Judas, "who, taking with him Zadok, a Pharisee, became zealous to draw them to a revolt, who both said that this taxation was no better than an introduction to slavery, and exhorted the nation to assert their liberty."[12] The Romans quashed the revolt, of course, but the Zealots eventually turned up again, later in history. Whether Judas regarded himself as a messiah or not is a matter of opinion. His religiously inspired leadership, with the aim of liberating the Jewish nation, speaks in favor of this theory.

A person who more clearly seemed to have messianic aspirations was the son (or grandson) of Judas, Menahem, who was one of the Zealot leaders of the Jewish revolt against the Romans in 66 to 70 CE. Menahem entered Jerusalem dressed as a king, went into the Temple dressed as a king, ordered the execution of the high priest, and then confronted the high priest's son, who, with the help of a great part of the population of Jerusalem, attacked Menahem and his men and forced them to retreat.[13]

One of the most famous of the aspiring messiah figures was a man by the name of Theudas, who is also mentioned by the gospel writer Luke in the Acts of the Apostles ("Some time ago, Theudas came forward, making claims for himself, and a number of our people, about four hundred, joined him."[14]). Josephus, too, mentions him, and in rather negative terms:

> Now it came to pass, while Fadus was procurator of Judea, that a certain sorcerer, whose name was Theudas, persuaded a great part of the people to take their effects with them, and follow him to the river Jordan; for he told them he was a prophet, and that he would, by his own command, divide the river, and afford them an easy passage over it; and many were deluded by his words. However, Fadus did not permit them to make any advantage of his wild attempt, but sent a troop of horsemen out against them; who, falling upon them unexpectedly, slew many of them, and took many of them alive. They

also took Theudas alive, and cut off his head, and carried it to
Jerusalem.[15]

One notable sentence in the above description by Josephus, is that of how Theudas promises to "divide the river." This, of course, either reflects an attempt to repeat Moses' feat of parting the Red Sea during the exodus of the Jews from Egypt, or how the River Jordan was stopped when Joshua led the Israelites to the Land of Canaan.[16]

And Theudas was not the only one to make use of such biblical parallels—perhaps primarily to Moses—in order to prove his elevated status and his capacity to liberate the Jews. Such deliberate allusions were made by many of those who claimed to be messiahs.

Another of the more renowned aspiring messiah figures from this time was a man called "the Egyptian." He made his appearance under another Roman procurator, Felix (ca. 52–59 CE), and according to the historian Josephus this Egyptian had certain similarities to Theudas—he calls them both "sorcerers" (*goês* in the Greek original)—but the Egyptian had a considerably greater number of followers. Josephus, in his book *War of the Jews*, describes the Egyptian as follows:

> . . . *for he was a sorcerer, and pretended to be a prophet also, and got together thirty thousand men that were deluded by him; these he led round about from the wilderness to the mount which was called the Mount of Olives, and was ready to break into Jerusalem by force from that place; and if he could but once conquer the Roman garrison and the people, he intended to domineer over them by the assistance of those guards of his that were to break into the city with him.*[17]

Josephus devotes quite some words to the Egyptian. In another of his books, *Antiquities of the Jews*, he describes how the Egyptian was defeated by the Roman procurator Felix:

> He [Felix] *also slew four hundred of them, and took two hundred alive. But the Egyptian himself escaped out of the fight, but did not appear any more.*[18]

Josephus tells, too, that the Egyptian said to his followers that the walls of Jerusalem would "fall on his command." Here, as well, we see a clear reference to the biblical stories, in this case how Joshua caused the walls of Jericho to fall.[19] The Mount of Olives also has a symbolic significance; the Bible says that it is here the Lord shall stand on the day of judgment.[20]

The number of aspiring messiahs seems to increase the closer one comes to the revolt against the Romans. According to Josephus, under the procurator just mentioned, Felix, there were an especially large number of characters who:

> . . . *were such men as deceived and deluded the people under pretense*
> *of Divine inspiration, but were for procuring innovations and*
> *changes of the government; and these prevailed with the multitude to*
> *act like madmen, and went before them into the wilderness, as pre-*
> *tending that God would there show them the signals of liberty.*[21]

So how does Jesus of Nazareth fit into this? To start with, we can note that he, as he is described in the gospels, shares a number of qualities with other proclaimed messiah figures at this time. For example, the gospel stories about Jesus are full of parallels to Old Testament history:

As mentioned above, the Old Testament states in a number of places that the king who shall come and save the Jewish people shall be of the clan of David. For example, "The days are coming, says the Lord, when I shall make a righteous Branch spring from David's line, a king who will rule wisely, maintaining justice and right in the land. In his days Judah will be kept safe, and Israel will live undisturbed."[22] And, indeed, according to the genealogical tables in both Matthew and Luke, Jesus descended from the clan of David.[23]

Jesus came riding into Jerusalem on a donkey, as the prophet Zachariah predicted that the King of Zion would do. And he is honored by the masses, according to Matthew as the "Son of David," and in Luke as "the King."[24]

Matthew and Luke write that Jesus was born in Bethlehem, despite his having grown up in the town of Nazareth in Galilee. According to the First Book of Samuel, Bethlehem is the home of David's family, and Micah, one of the twelve Books of the Prophets in the Old Testament, says, "But from you, Bethlehem in Ephrathah, small as you are among Judah's clans, from you will come a king for me over Israel, one whose origins are far back in the past, in ancient times."[25]

Matthew writes that Herod, having failed to find and kill the newborn infant Jesus, "gave orders for the massacre of all the boys aged two years or under, in Bethlehem and throughout the whole district."[26] Apart from the fact that no such decree from Herod is described in other historical sources, the association to the Old Testament is obvious: Exodus, the second book of Moses, describes the pharaoh's commandment that all newborn Hebrew boys shall be thrown into the Nile, which causes Moses' mother to hide her newborn child.[27]

Matthew also tells how the child Jesus is taken to Egypt, to escape the cruel Herod.[28] This too can be interpreted as a parallel to the story of Moses. In addition, Matthew cites the prophet Hosea: "Out of Egypt I called my son."[29]

As the famous American New Testament scholar E. P. Sanders notes in his book *The Historical Figure of Jesus*, "The gospels depict Jesus as saviour of the entire world, but he is a universal saviour who fits into Jewish salvation history."[30]

So the similarities with other aspiring messiahs are, at least in this respect, fairly obvious. In their descriptions of the life of Jesus, his biographers—the gospel writers—are at pains to point out parallels to the prophecies about the Messiah, and to earlier Jewish leaders who are described in the Old Testament. But is this Jesus of Nazareth—born around the year 1 CE, crucified around the year 30 CE—named by anyone other than the gospel writers? Are his life and work described by any of the contemporary historians who wrote about Iudaea and its political and religious troubles during this period?

*

In 1909, the American historian and freethinker John E. Remsburg published *The Christ: A Critical Review and Analysis of the Evidence of His Existence*. This book contains a table in which he lists forty-two historians who were active at the time of Jesus, or within the first century after him. And Remsburg writes thus: "Enough of the writings of the authors named in the foregoing list remains to form a library. Yet in this mass of Jewish and Pagan literature, aside from two forged passages in the works of a Jewish author, and two disputed passages in the works of Roman writers, there is to be found no mention of Jesus Christ."[31]

This has been one of the great historical dilemmas of Christianity: the New Testament describes a religious leader figure, Jesus of Nazareth, who not only is said to have had a large following, but was also supposedly perceived as such a great threat by the authorities that he was crucified in a process involving both Jerusalem's Jewish leadership and Iudaea's Roman prefect, a leader figure who then came to provide the foundation for one of the great religions of the world—and yet it is debatable whether any contemporary historian even mentions him.

So let us have a look at these contemporary historians. Which of them is sufficiently close in time and geography to the events described in the New Testament for us to expect them to confirm these events—if they actually took place?

The foremost portrayer of Judea and Galilee under Jesus' time is, without any comparison, the Jewish-Roman historian Flavius Josephus mentioned above. Josephus is considered to be one of the most important historians of antiquity, and he is the person who, almost single-handedly, conveyed the story of the long death struggle of the Jewish nation, and its final destruction around the year 70 CE. Yet, the remnant of the Jewish nation did not embrace Josephus' description, nor did they try to preserve it as a document of their own history. Josephus' four famous works, the content of which—despite certain exaggerations—has essentially been confirmed by historical research and archaeology, have instead primarily been handed down to posterity through Christian sources.

The reason is that contemporary Jewry regarded Josephus as a traitor.

Yosef ben Matitiahu, as Josephus was originally called, was born in Jerusalem in the year 37 or 38 CE, in a family with priestly and aristocratic ancestry. He tells us himself that the young Yosef was so wise, intelligent, and precocious that when he was only fourteen years old, Jerusalem's high priest consulted him on certain judicial problems, and he so thirsted for knowledge that when he was sixteen he devoted himself to the profound study of all three Jewish main factions—the Sadducees, the Pharisees, and the Essenes (toward the rebellious Zealots, the "fourth philosophic sect" as he calls them, he only feels contempt[32]). As these studies did not suffice, Yosef sought out a hermit, Banus, and lived with him in the desert for three years. In the year 57 CE, when he was nineteen years old, he returned to Jerusalem and joined the Pharisees, the most popular faction at that time. That, at any rate, is how he himself describes his youth.[33]

Others have their doubts as to the reliability of this history, not least because Josephus is negative towards the Pharisees in some of his writings. It is presumed that he either really did join the Pharisees, but for purely opportunist reasons—grounds which often seem to be close at hand for Josephus—or that in his autobiography he describes himself as a Pharisee only in order to retain good contact with the Jewish majority at the time the book was written. For Josephus had every reason to defend his good name before his own people.

Within a few years of the return of the young Yosef to Jerusalem, the rebellious feelings toward the Romans start to grow all the stronger in Judea and Galilee. It is above all the religious activists called the Zealots who step up not only the rebellious mood against the Romans but also intensify the internal conflicts within the

Jewish population. Josephus writes, "They also do not value dying any kinds of death, nor indeed do they heed the deaths of their relations and friends, nor can any such fear make them call any man lord."[34] The Zealots are fearless and fanatical, and they are beginning to influence the rest of the population.

In the late fifties or early sixties, the Roman procurator has some Jewish priests imprisoned and then sends them in chains to Rome. Yosef, who is acquainted with the priests, follows after them around 63 CE and seeks an audience with the emperor Nero himself to ask for their release. He gets in touch with Nero's wife Poppaea, who supports his cause and introduces him at the court. After two or three years, Yosef succeeds in gaining the release of his friends. This time spent in Rome not only strengthens the self-confidence of the young man, but also gives him a taste of the pomp and magnificence of the Roman court. This seduces him; it is something he will always remember with pleasure.

But when Yosef returns to his homeland, many things have happened: the year is 66 CE, and the Jewish revolt against the Romans has finally broken out. After decades of unrest and ill-feeling, after an all the more intensified movement of nationalistic messianism, this revolt was in the end unavoidable. As E. P. Sanders writes, "When the revolt finally broke out in 66, it is almost certain that many joined in because they believed that God was ready to deliver them."[35]

It had taken almost exactly one century, but now at least some groups among the Jews were ready to try to regain their independence by force.

Like other aristocrats and Jews with high positions within the Roman province, Yosef first was quite unsympathetic to the new revolt. But when they discovered that the rebels began to meet with success—they were able to repel the troops that the Romans sent to Jerusalem—a growing number of increasingly central Jewish groups started to ally themselves with the revolt. As did Yosef ben Matitiahu. Yosef was now appointed by the Sanhedrin, the supreme council in Jerusalem, to lead the fighting against the Romans in

Galilee. This task would demand not only qualities of military leadership, but also diplomatic skills, which Yosef was now considered to have. The reason was that some parts of Galilee had turned out to be very unwilling to join the revolt.

To start with, Yosef meets with certain successes, but he personally arouses animosity, and there is a rival militia led by a man by the name of John of Gischala. The two men waste a great deal of energy competing with each other, and partly as a result of this, the rebels fail to secure the old capital of Galilee, Sepphoris.

In the spring of 67 CE, Yosef's men are in the town of Jotapata, which controls the important road to Sepphoris. The Roman general Vespasian leads a massive attack against the rebel stronghold, and Yosef's forces are soon surrounded. For six weeks they stay in the fort at Jotapata and defend themselves against the Romans. But they are finally defeated, and most of them are killed. Yosef himself manages to escape the slaughter, and he finds forty other "persons of eminence" who had hidden in a hole nearby. He hides together with them. On the third day, they are discovered by the Romans. When the forty realize this, and that their leader Yosef also is considering surrendering himself to the Romans, they become furious. They demand of him that he should take his own life rather than surrender to the enemy. The situation becomes all the more threatening. It is now that Yosef makes his fateful decision (he describes himself in the third person):

> "And now," said he, "since it is resolved among you that you will die, come on, let us commit our mutual deaths to determination by lot. He whom the lot falls to first, let him be killed by him that hath the second lot, and thus fortune shall make its progress through us all; nor shall any of us perish by his own right hand, for it would be unfair if, when the rest are gone, somebody should repent and save himself." [36]

The others accept Yosef's decision, they are even overjoyed by it, "for they thought death, if Josephus might but die with them, was sweeter than life." So they start to draw lots, Yosef as well as the others. And the collective suicide begins—the man who last held the sword, is next in turn. In the end, all but two are dead. And, as he writes, "whether we must say it happened so by chance, or whether by the providence of God," Yosef is one of the two who are left at the end. He now turns to the other man (again, he describes himself in the third person):

> And as he was very desirous neither to be condemned by the lot, nor, if he had been left to the last, to imbrue his right hand in the blood of his countrymen, he persuaded him to trust his fidelity to him, and to live as well as himself.[37]

Such is the manner in which Yosef ben Matitiahu comes out of the hole alive, and surrenders himself to the Romans. This, according to many, monumental treachery has not only made Yosef ben Matitiahu the ultimate symbol for opportunism, it has also given rise to a mathematical problem, the Josephus problem, which is about how to work out who will be left alive after the collective suicide.

Yosef is taken to his conqueror, the Roman general Vespasian, and the general's son Titus. His life now hangs on a thin thread, despite the sympathy he receives from Titus. But Yosef ben Matitiahu knows what to do. He is a survivor—first and foremost. Before the amazed general he presents a prophecy that Vespasian will soon himself become the Roman emperor!

Yosef has learned how to communicate with the highest Roman authorities, and his conqueror lets himself be influenced by this educated man of the world who, to cap it all, brings him such a sweet prophecy. And why not? In Europe, a rebellion has broken out against Nero, the ruler of the Roman Empire. And besides, for several months a comet has been visible up in the heavens, and it looks like a sword. Vespasian simply can't ignore the man who stands before him and prophesies that he will soon be a great ruler.

Yosef is allowed to live. But he is arrested, and is sent to Jerusalem as a prisoner. There he witnesses the Roman siege. The following year Nero commits suicide. And one year after that, Vespasian is proclaimed emperor. Yosef's prophecy has been fulfilled.

Perhaps Yosef ben Matitiahu had simply wanted to save his own life. Perhaps he had higher ambitions. Whatever the reasons, he would now be richly rewarded for his prediction. Emperor Vespasian announces that Yosef is now a free man, and he is given his patron's name, Flavius, at least for posterity. Yosef ben Matitiahu becomes Flavius Josephus. The war against the rebels is now taken over by Vespasian's son Titus, and Josephus becomes his translator and friend. He stays in Jerusalem and shall come to witness how the city in which he was born and grew up, and the Temple that was at the very heart of the Jewish existence, are not only defeated but destroyed utterly. During the six-month siege, Josephus tries to mediate between the Romans and the Jews, and he tries to persuade his former comrades to capitulate before everything is destroyed. But he is hardly listened to. In the year 70 CE, the Jewish nation is crushed (although groups of Zealots hold out in small pockets for a further three years). And Josephus follows along with his friend Titus to Rome to be present when he makes his triumphant homecoming—immortalized in the Arch of Titus in Rome.

Flavius Josephus becomes a Roman citizen; he is granted an annual salary; he acquires some land in Judea, and he becomes a greatly respected person at the Roman court. But Josephus will not forget his origins. Some claim that he only wanted to defend himself and his actions, but that does not suffice as an explanation for the path that Josephus now chooses. He actually decides to devote the rest of his life to defending, explaining, and describing not only his own life and his own actions, but the history of the entire Jewish nation. In his own eyes, Flavius Josephus is and remains a loyal Jew who follows the laws of Judaism.

Josephus writes four major works: *War of the Jews*, written 75–79 CE; *Antiquities of the Jews* (a work of Jewish history from ancient times to the revolt against the Romans), published ca. 93 CE; *Against Apion* (a work about the enemies of the Jews); and the autobiographical *Life of Flavius Josephus*, written ca. 94–99 CE, possibly as an appendix to *Antiquities of the Jews*. Josephus evidently wanted to save not only himself from the ill will or forgetfulness of history, he wanted to do the same for the defeated Jewish people.

It is primarily *War of the Jews*, but also *Antiquities of the Jews*, that has proven to be such a rich source of knowledge about the Roman province Iudaea and its surroundings. It is in these books that Josephus tells about life and personalities in his home country. It is in these books he tells about procurators and revolutionaries, about high priests and aspiring messiahs.

So does he tell us anything about Jesus of Nazareth?

Jesus of Nazareth is mentioned twice in Flavius Josephus' books, both times in *Antiquities of the Jews*. One of the references, in Book 20 of the work, is brief and is about the killing of Jesus' brother James: "[High priest Ananus] assembled the Sanhedrin of judges, and brought before them the brother of Jesus, who was called Christ, whose name was James, and some others; and when he had formed an accusation against them as breakers of the law, he delivered them to be stoned." [38]

The other reference to Jesus is considerably longer, and it has been at the center of the debate over Jesus' existence for centuries. This reference occurs in Book 18 of the same work, *Antiquities of the Jews*:

> *Now there was about this time Jesus, a wise man, if it be lawful to call him a man; for he was a doer of wonderful works, a teacher of such men as receive the truth with pleasure. He drew over to him both many of the Jews and many of the Gentiles. He was [the] Christ. And when Pilate, at the suggestion of the principal men amongst us, had condemned him to the cross, those that loved him at the first did not forsake him; for he appeared to them alive again the third day; as the divine prophets had foretold these and ten thousand other wonderful things concerning him. And the tribe of Christians, so named from him, are not extinct at this day.* [39]

It is this paragraph that has been called *Testimonium Flavianum*, or the testimony of Flavius. The problem is: there is something that is not quite right about *Testimonium Flavianum*. Firstly, the text seems to be wedged in between two other paragraphs that deal with the revolutionary mood among the Jews, and which would flow much better if *Testimonium Flavianum* wasn't there. Secondly, apart from in this paragraph, there are no signs whatever in any of Josephus' productions that he was a believer in Christianity. In the above paragraph, Josephus describes Jesus as the Christ (messiah) whom one could hardly call "a man," and he tells that Jesus was resurrected from the dead. This is in effect a confessional text, which is hard to explain when one compares it with the rest of Josephus' works.

Although the debate about the authenticity of *Testimonium Flavianum* has been going on for several hundreds of years, not many Bible historians today are of the opinion that the text, in the form it is written, is authentic. It is considered to be a so-called interpolation, something that has been added to Josephus' works by a later scribe. This conclusion is strengthened when one looks at how Josephus was quoted by early church fathers.

As was mentioned above, the works of Josephus were not accepted by the Jews of antiquity. Josephus was regarded by his fellow Jews as a traitor and his work received attention outside of Roman circles only when Christianity started to be spread. The earliest preserved copies of *Antiquities of the Jews* date from around the tenth century, and although the work had been quoted considerably earlier than that, the earliest known to have done so were Christian church fathers. Two of these were Eusebius, bishop of Caesarea, who lived about 263–329 CE, and Origen, also one of the most important of the early church fathers, who lived about 182–251 CE.

In the year 324 CE, Eusebius wrote a work in which he describes Josephus' writings. In this he quotes *Testimonium Flavianum* almost word for word as it is known today.[40] But Origen, who wrote almost one hundred years earlier, in 240 CE, names the first considerably shorter reference—that about Jesus' brother James—but fails to mention *Testimonium Flavianum* entirely. And as if that wasn't enough, Origen wrote in one text "this writer [Josephus], although not believing in Jesus as Christ . . ." and in another text ". . . [Josephus] did not accept Jesus as Christ."[41] It has therefore been assumed that the version of *Antiquities of the Jews* that Origen read quite simply did not include *Testimonium Flavianum*.

Nor has Origen's text escaped suspicion. According to Origen, Josephus interpreted the destruction of Jerusalem and the Temple as the punishment of God for the Jews having executed James, the brother of Jesus.[42] Bearing in mind the very obscure presence of James in the works of Josephus—compared to the enormous amounts of text Josephus devotes to the destruction of Jerusalem—the connection between these two events does seem hard to explain (and we don't actually see it in the version we now have of *Antiquities of the Jews*).

Despite that, this short reference to the "brother of Jesus the so-called Christ" has found considerably more defenders than *Testimonium Flavianum*.

Although today very few scholars are prepared to accept *Testimonium Flavianum* as genuine, at least in its entirety, there are a number of leading Bible historians who are prepared to accept a somewhat modified version of the text (in their view, Josephus wrote *Testimonium Flavianum*, but the more confessional bits were added later). John P. Meier, Catholic theologian and author of the standard work *A Marginal Jew: Rethinking the Historical Jesus*, writes, for example, that he considers *Testimonium Flavianum* (albeit in modified form) to be of "monumental importance."[43] The Jesus scholar John Dominic Crossan can perhaps be regarded as representing the mainstream when he writes that "the problem here is that Josephus' account is too good to be true, too confessional to be impartial, too Christian to be Jewish."[44]

Why is there so much focus upon Josephus' two paragraphs about Jesus? Quite simply because they are just about all we have, if one ignores the gospels. And because Josephus *ought* to have written about Jesus. Put bluntly, if Jesus of Nazareth had been a person of importance during the time of the Roman presence in Judea and Galilee, then Josephus most certainly would have told us so.

There are two other significant Jewish historians from this period, although they are not as central to this story as is Josephus. One is Justus of Tiberias, a Jewish historian who lived in Galilee and was a contemporary of Josephus. He is also best known for having put forward, in his own description of the Jewish revolt, strong accusations against Josephus as a military leader. Justus' own texts have not survived. What we do have are descriptions of them, including one in a work by Photios, a patriarch in Constantinople in the ninth century. Photios has thus read Justus, and he reports that "he does not even mention the coming of Christ, the events of His life, or the miracles performed by Him."[45] From Justus of Tiberias it seems we won't be able to get any confirmation of the existence of Jesus.

The other significant Jewish historian, or rather philosopher, from this period is Philo Judaeus from Alexandria. Philo was born ca. 20 BCE and died ca. 40 CE. He came from the Egyptian city of Alexandria and his family became one of the most important Jewish families of that time. Among his influential relatives one can name his nephew Tiberius Julius Alexander, who abandoned Judaism and became Roman procurator over Judea from 46 to 48 CE.

Philo's philosophy came to be accepted with great enthusiasm by some of the early Christians, because his ideas to a certain extent seemed to touch on Christian ones. Nowhere, however, does Philo mention the existence of Jesus or his disciples, although he describes both the Essenes and Pontius Pilate.

In other words, from the historians who were active during or shortly after Jesus' lifetime it would seem we are not going to get any information, with the exception of the lines in Josephus' works, which have been called into question.

One possibility, of course, is that Jesus is one of the particular messiah figures that Josephus does actually name—for example, that he is the same as Theudas, or "the Egyptian"—and that the creation of myths, rumors, prejudices, or something else led to the content of the gospel writers' stories about this person differing to such a considerable degree from Josephus'.

While the first century following the birth of Jesus does not seem to offer us much information from non-Christian sources, things do start to happen at the beginning of the next century.

Cornelius Tacitus, who lived ca. 55–117 CE, is often considered to be the foremost historian of the Roman Empire. Toward the end of his life, he wrote a work, *Annales*, in which he describes the Julio-Claudian dynasty. In book 15, verse 44 of *Annales*, Tacitus describes the great fire in Rome in the year 64 CE, a fire that Nero himself was suspected of having started. And he writes:

> *Consequently, to get rid of the report, Nero fastened the guilt* [for the fire] *and inflicted the most exquisite tortures on a class hated for their abominations, called Christian by the populace. Christus, from whom the name had its origin, suffered the extreme penalty during the reign of Tiberius at the hands of one of our procurators, Pontius Pilate, and a most mischievous superstition, thus checked for the moment, again broke out not only in Judea, the first source of the evil, but even in Rome, where all things hideous and shameful from every part of the world find their centre and become popular.*[46]

This was thus written almost a century after Jesus lived. But unlike *Testimonium Flavianum*, this is hardly a confessional text. On the contrary, Tacitus expresses revulsion for Christianity (as he does for Judaism[47]). This fact naturally increases the probability of the text being authentic, or at least not a Christian interpolation. Tacitus does, however, make some mysterious mistakes: Firstly, he calls Pontius Pilate a *procurator*, which was admittedly the title the Roman governors would later be given. But it was not the title actually held by Pilate— he was a *prefect*. Another strange word is *Christus*. If Tacitus had come across the official Roman records when he described the Christians' history, he ought to have called Jesus by name (i.e., Jesus). "Christus" is a theological byname, and it means "the anointed" as does "messiah." In other words, it is believed that Tacitus in his historical description has here made use of the story that the Christians themselves have presented about their origins.

Most historians consider that these lines by Tacitus are authentic, and that Christian groups thus can be assumed to have been an important element in the life of Rome when *Annales* was written, ca. 116 CE. Perhaps it can also be an indication of their presence in Rome at the time of the great fire, in the year 64 CE.

Another Roman historian, Gaius Suetonius Tranquillus, writes in the year 120 CE, "He [Emperor Claudius] banished from Rome all the Jews, who were continually making disturbances at the instigation of one Chrestus."[48] What is interesting here is that Suetonius describes an event that took place as early as around the year 50 CE, during the reign of Emperor Claudius. The question is, however, whether "Chrestus" really refers to Jesus of Nazareth. Chrestus is said to have been a fairly common name in Rome at that time, especially among slaves. For that reason, it is very doubtful that this sentence has anything to do with Christians or Christ. But Suetonius too refers in the same work to the treatment of the Christians under Nero's reign—"Punishment was inflicted on the Christians, a class of men given to a new and mischievous superstition."—which he might possibly have taken from Tacitus, who wrote *Annales* some years earlier.[49]

Finally, we have Pliny the Younger, a Roman official and author, best known for his letters. Around the year 112 CE, Pliny, who was then governor of the province of Bithynia et Pontus by the south coast of the Black Sea, wrote a letter to the Roman emperor at the time, Trajan. In this letter, he asks for advice regarding how he should deal with the Christians, who refuse to pray to the emperor:

> *They stated that the sum total of their error or misjudgement, had been coming to a meeting on a given day before dawn, and singing responsively a hymn to Christ as to God, swearing with a holy oath not to commit any crime, never to steal or commit robbery, commit adultery, fail a sworn agreement or refuse to return a sum left in trust.*[50]

If one gathers together these non-Christian sources, the collected impression is undeniably that contemporary times had very little, or nothing, to say about Jesus of Nazareth. But the movement that had its starting point in him or his followers seems already at the beginning of the second century to have become so widespread, at any rate in Rome and Asia Minor, that it began to be regarded as a threat to the authorities, or at least as an irritation.

It does thus seem probable that Christianity quickly spread. The originator of this movement, Jesus of Nazareth, does nevertheless continue to elude those who try to find independent texts about his life and deeds.

There is, however, one additional non-Christian source that ought to be taken into account. It is not contemporary, but it is geographically close, and it is guaranteed free from Christian interpolations (which does not, however, guarantee its objectivity).

After the destruction of the Temple in the year 70 CE, the Romans expelled all Jews from Jerusalem. A large part of the population of the province had been killed—about one million dead is a figure that has been mentioned—and more than one hundred thousand Jews were taken to Rome as slaves. This was the start of the Jewish diaspora. And it could have been the end of the Jewish religion, if it hadn't been for a man by the name of Yochanan ben Zakkai.

Yochanan ben Zakkai was one of Jerusalem's religious leaders. He was said to be one of the youngest and most prominent of the disciples of the great rabbi Hillel, and it is told that he gave lessons in the shadow of the temple building. Ben Zakkai was a Pharisee, and during the siege of Jerusalem he was deeply involved in the discussions about how best to tackle the Roman forces. The Zealots led the opposition in the capital, and they said that they would die rather than surrender. Yochanan ben Zakkai, however, persevered in the view that life was always more important. He was a man who wanted to create peace "between nation and nation, between leader and leader, between family and family."[51] The Zealots refused to listen to him. Finally he made a decision that, if the information is correct, exhibits surprising similarities to the one Josephus made one year earlier: he fakes his own death. Yochanan ben Zakkai has his disciples smuggle him out of Jerusalem in a coffin. Once they reach the other side, they carry this coffin all the way to General Vespasian's tent outside the city. They put down the coffin, open the lid, and out climbs ben Zakkai. The rabbi asks to speak to the general, which request he is granted; he presents himself, and he tells that he has had a vision. In it he sees that Vespasian will soon be appointed Roman emperor. He quotes the words of the prophet Isaiah that "Lebanon with its noble trees will fall" but that "a branch will grow from the stock of Jesse."[52] And he now asks the general for permission to start a small religious school in the town of Yavne. Vespasian answers that if ben Zakkai's vision comes true, then his wish shall be granted.

One year later, Vespasian becomes emperor, and ben Zakkai is allowed to open his school. The story is so like that about how Josephus saves his life that one wonders if both can be true. But while Josephus came to be despised by his Jewish contemporaries, ben Zakkai came to be honored. The small school in Yavne developed into the new religious center of world Jewry. It was here that the great council, the Sanhedrin, found its new home. Here that they developed the rituals that a Jewry without its Temple would come to use. And it was within this religious center (which was later forced to move to Galilee) that—one hundred years later—the most important text of Judaism, after the Bible, started to be written down. When the Torah (i.e., the five Books of Moses) and the rest of the Bible had been written down in the centuries following the return from Babylonia, an important part remained that had not been committed to writing, namely the so-called "oral law" or the oral Torah. This, which was actually said to be just as old as the Torah, described how the written laws should be applied, and thus allowed in practice a certain development in the interpretation of the law. Stories and legends were later also gathered together in this oral Torah.

Now that the Temple lay in ruins, and the Jewish people had been spread to the winds, there was within the Sanhedrin a marked concern that the entire religion would be lost. This concern intensified after the final catastrophic Jewish revolt against the Romans, the so-called Bar Kochba revolt, in the year 135 CE. This is when they decide to start to write down the oral Torah as well. Roughly between 170 and 210 CE, this oral law was thus written down, and was given the name *Mishna*. During the following two or three centuries, there were rabbinical discussions around the Mishna, and these so-called commentaries were later written down, too, in the *Jerusalem Gemara,* ca. 400 CE, and the *Babylonian Gemara,* ca. 500–600 CE. Together, the Mishna and the Gemaras are called the Talmud.

As described above, the Talmud does not only consist of interpretation of law, but also of stories, often used to illustrate laws or words of wisdom. And it is in some of these stories that one finds references to a person, or persons, that many have interpreted as Jesus of Nazareth.

> *It was taught: On the eve of the Passover Yeshu was hanged. For forty days before the execution took place, a herald went forth and cried, "He is going to be stoned because he has practiced sorcery and enticed Israel to apostasy. Any one who can say anything in his favor, let him come forward and plead on his behalf." But since nothing was brought forward in his favor he was hanged on the eve of the Passover.*

The above can be found in the Babylonian Gemara, Tractate Sanhedrin 43a. It was thus written down about five hundred years after the death of Jesus, and represents discussions that took place between the rabbis during the period from 200 to 400 CE. But what is interesting is not only that the Talmud contains a number of references to a person who could easily be regarded as Jesus of Nazareth, but also that nowhere in the Talmud is there a denial of the existence of Jesus. This despite Christianity, when the Gemara was written down, having acquired a position of power in the Roman Empire, and the accusation that the Jews had killed Jesus had started to lead to persecution. The fact that the Talmud, despite this, does not deny the existence of Jesus has been regarded by many Christian theologians as proof that he must really have existed.[53] On the other hand, the religious opposition between Christianity and Judaism means that one cannot regard the Talmud as an unbiased source.

* * *

So that is the picture of the non-Christian sources as regards information about the person Jesus of Nazareth. They are brief, but perhaps not completely silent. As E. P. Sanders writes, "We have very little information about him apart from the works written to glorify him. . . . The more or less contemporary documents, apart from those in the New Testament, shed virtually no light on Jesus' life or death."[54] This is a gloomy conclusion that not even Sanders himself completely sticks to. For it is possible to try to fit some of the pieces of the puzzle together—not only with the help of the non-Christian sources, but also with the help of the officially sanctioned ones, those that we find in the New Testament.

The four gospels, Matthew, Mark, Luke, and John, were written down sometime between the destruction of Jerusalem and the beginning of the second century. Like so much that was written during that period, they are an attempt at recalling and committing to print memories from a lost epoch. Like the works of Josephus, they are written in exile, and *post factum*. But in the case of the gospels, they concern the memory of a single person and his immediate surroundings.

As we have already noted, the four gospels have a great deal in common, especially the first three: Matthew, Mark, and Luke. But because they are so similar, and evidently have their roots in the same sources—and each other—there is reason to prick up one's ears when one comes across differences. Because there are differences. And they mean something.

To start with, the four gospels are partly directed towards different readers. Matthew is regarded as being directed towards Jews, or Judaeo-Christians, who themselves have some connection with the land. The text seems to assume that the reader has a basic knowledge of Judaism, it continually refers to the Old Testament, and it even emphasizes that the message of Jesus is directed towards Jews, and no others ("These twelve Jesus sent out with the following instructions: 'Do not take the road to gentile lands, do not enter any Samaritan town; but go rather to the lost sheep of the house of Israel."[55]). Matthew argues against the Pharisees who represented the mainstream within Judaism after the destruction of the Temple, and the overall message is: Jesus is the Messiah we have all been waiting for.

Mark, on the other hand, is seen foremost as a gospel written for the Greek-speaking people in the Roman Empire. Jewish traditions are described and explained. At the same time, here, too, are many references to the Old Testament.

Luke is regarded as the most literary gospel, and it is written by a Greek for a non-Jewish public. From the very first, Luke makes it rather clear that he is not himself an eyewitness to the events he describes, but that he has "investigated the whole course of these events in detail" and that he now shall write "an orderly narrative" for his patron (a man whose name is given as Theophilus) "so as to give you authentic knowledge about the matters of which you have been informed."[56] Which sources has Luke used? Apart from his evidently having taken information from the other synoptic gospels (or at least Mark), and the other sources that Matthew has possibly used, it is a fairly common understanding that Luke seems to have read at least some of Flavius Josephus' writings.[57] It is worthwhile to bear this in mind: the gospel writers were not completely unaware of what the historians wrote—not even of what they wrote about the time when Jesus lived and was active. And if Jesus was mentioned, by name or in some other way, by Josephus, Luke presumably knew about it.

John, finally, differs radically from the three other gospels, not only as regards the facts he describes, but in the entire construction of the gospel. While the synoptic gospels are fairly concrete in their historical descriptions, John focuses upon certain scenes, and he is more meditative or metaphysical in tone. He is also the gospel writer who most clearly identifies Jesus as divine, as God himself. For whom, then, is the gospel of John written? Opinions vary. The beginning of the gospel is clearly intended to remind readers of Genesis, the First Book of Moses, but otherwise there are many Hellenist parallels in the gospel. Most theologians today consider the gospel of John to be the least reliable in a historical sense, although the fact that some of the material in this gospel is unique continues to create interest, and this material cannot always be dismissed.[58]

Besides these four gospels, there are the so-called Apocrypha, a number of texts that were written fairly early—and which sometimes remind us of the gospels—but which have not been recognised as part of the New Testament. These include the so-called gnostic gospels (the best known of these being the gospel of Thomas), which were found in Nag Hammadi in Egypt in 1945. The Apocrypha are considered in most instances to have been written later than the four gospels that are included in the New Testament: Mark, Matthew, Luke, and John.

As has already been mentioned, Mark, which is considered to be the first gospel, is sometimes rather awkwardly written. Not only because it muddles up geographical places, but also because it is written in a fairly disjointed manner. The later gospels have a tendency to correct the mistakes in Mark, or at least smooth over sensational information. They are, in other words, perhaps more touched up. But in this "dialogue" between the gospels, a lot of information can be gleaned. And it is undeniably interesting that the church fathers let this first gospel retain its small peculiarities. This is a sign of authenticity, as good as any.

For example, one can read in the gospel of Mark that Jesus' own family thought that "he is out of his mind," and that they "set out to take charge of him."[59] In Matthew and Luke, too, there is a description of Jesus' visit to his hometown, where his family lived, but here the rude comments are restricted to those from the public.[60]

In a similar manner, Mark chapter 6 says that the public in Jesus' hometown, when he comes to visit, ask, "Is he not the carpenter, the son of Mary, the brother of James and Joses and Judas and Simon?" And they go on: "Are not his sisters here with us?"[61] It is remarkable that Jesus here is not named as the son of Joseph. In a society where everyone is first named as "son of [father's name]," this can only mean that Mark—or those he quotes—is suggesting that Jesus was born out of wedlock (the public quoted here do not name anything about "the son of God" or a virgin birth, so that is hardly the explanation). But when the same event is described in Matthew they say instead, "Is he not the carpenter's son? Is not his mother called Mary, his brothers James, Joseph, Simon, and Judas?" [62] Jesus the carpenter has been transformed into Jesus the carpenter's son.

In the gospel of Mark, the disciples, too, are often described as not understanding the deeds of Jesus, and sometimes questioning them, even when others honor him. [63] This tendency of the disciples is played down somewhat in Matthew and Luke.

Another element—which admittedly is found in all four gospels, but perhaps most in Mark—is information that does not seem necessary for the telling of the story, and that could even confuse the reader, but which is nevertheless included. An example of this is the description of how Jesus is arrested. In the gospel of Mark, it says, "Among those who had followed Jesus was a young man with nothing on but a linen cloth. They tried to seize him; but he slipped out of the linen cloth and ran away naked." [64] Why tell about this young man and his cloth? What is the theological, or even personal, content? It seems to be irrelevant information, but precisely for that reason it is perhaps authentic.

So even if the gospels were written more than thirty years after Jesus' crucifixion, and even if the gospel writers themselves were not eyewitnesses, there is information in these gospels that has too authentic a tone to be constructed, or that creates such large problems for the early Church that nobody (one could reasonably argue) would add it if it had been made up. The latter category is called by some—for example John P. Meier—the "criterion of embarrassment." [65] This means that if, say, a story in the New Testament gives cause for embarrassment on the part of those who are telling it, then this may be a criterion for authenticity. One of the most embarrassing features in the gospels is, according to Meier, the descriptions of Jesus' relation to John the Baptist.

The gospel of Mark does not begin with the story of the birth of Jesus, or his family tree. The first eight verses in this gospel are about quite another person—namely John the Baptist. In the same way, Luke introduces his gospel by telling about how John the Baptist's mother becomes pregnant! Matthew manages to push the story of John the Baptist into chapter 3—where it of course belongs chronologically, as far as his relation to Jesus is concerned—after the story of Jesus' family background, birth, and the escape to Egypt. But it is remarkable that both Mark and Luke (and to some extent John) actually choose to tell the story of John the Baptist first, and in Luke's case by telling about John's mother's pregnancy. It can only mean that John the Baptist was considered to be of such decisive importance for Jesus' work that they were *forced* to name him before Jesus! Then all four gospels solve the dilemma that follows, by having John the Baptist declare that after him there will come somebody who is greater, "whose sandals I am not worthy to stoop down and unfasten."[66]

It is impossible to avoid the conclusion that John the Baptist, whoever he was, was a real person, and one who in his own day was far too well known to be overlooked, however embarrassing this fact was for the gospel writers. As historian Donald Harman Akenson writes, "The four gospels do everything they can to subordinate this embarrassing report, but there it sits."[67]

And if John the Baptist was a real person, there is every reason to believe that Jesus' relation to him was real too. Otherwise, why would they describe it?

To summarize, we can note that Jesus of Nazareth can hardly have been a person who was generally known in Iudaea during his lifetime, or important for the development of that society, because if he had been, he would have acquired a greater place in the contemporary historical descriptions. Now he doesn't seem to have had any place at all (if one accepts *Testimonium Flavianum* as an interpolation). An alternative explanation is that he was a person whom the gospels and the historians described in such different ways from each other that we don't recognise him.

What is quite clear, however, is that his teachings, within just a few decades, became widespread within the Roman Empire.

Has, then, this person Jesus ever existed? Even though the historical sources seem to lack conclusive evidence for this, there is altogether a great deal that would suggest that he did. I shall summarize some of the arguments that could support such a view:

The argument that must always be put forward in such a context as this is: What reason could there have been to "invent" a person like Jesus of Nazareth? It is one thing that he perhaps did not do exactly what the gospel writers say. But why make him up?

Another argument is the "criterion of embarrassment," which is described above, and the ways in which the gospels try to smooth over uncomfortable facts. Take, for example, the question of where Jesus was born: Matthew and Luke twist and turn like nobody's business in their efforts to place the birthplace of Jesus in Bethlehem, the town which—according to prophecies in the Old Testament—not only is said to have a connection to the clan of David, but also be where a messiah was to come from. If Jesus had never existed, there would be no conflict about suggesting Bethlehem as the birthplace— without all the shuffling. But what the gospel writers have to get around is that Jesus, in actual fact, seems to have more connection to other places, places that don't have any prophetic significance. Primarily he has a connection to Galilee. Luke claims that Jesus and Mary lived in the little town of Nazareth in Galilee, but were forced to go to Bethlehem to register for tax purposes (since Joseph came from the clan of David). Once there, Mary gave birth. Matthew, in turn, says that Joseph and Mary lived in Bethlehem, where Jesus was born, but that they then fled to Egypt, and after their return moved to Nazareth in Galilee. The gospel writers thus admit that Jesus' connection to Bethlehem is relatively weak, and they have to make an effort to place his birth there. In the same way that John the Baptist is "in the way" when trying to tell the perfect story, one could say that Galilee is "in the way." As some of the people Jesus meets while preaching say, "Surely the Messiah is not to come from Galilee? Does not scripture say that the Messiah is to be of the family of David, from David's village of Bethlehem."[68] If Jesus was somebody the gospel writers had made up, they would obviously not have placed him in Galilee. There is no prophetical value at all in making up this connection to Galilee, on the contrary, and thus it is probably true.

With similar reasoning, we can say that if the church fathers did not try to correct Mark's geographical mistakes (except by letting Matthew smooth over them), it is probably because Mark really made these mistakes when he wrote. An effort was made to keep the text as it was written, and this seems to imply a certain desire for authenticity.

What, then, can we say about the occurrence of texts outside the gospels and New Testament Apocrypha that provide some support for Jesus having existed? As regards non-Christian sources, aside from *Testimonium Flavianum*, it is mainly the Talmud that offers information about a person who seems to have some similarities to Jesus of Nazareth. The Talmud was written late, but it represents an oral tradition that has older roots, and it was written by people who had their origins in the same environment as Jesus of Nazareth. On the other hand, these people could have reason to argue against his teachings. All the more remarkable, then, that the Talmud does not deny the existence of Jesus.

We should, in this context, also mention the Koran. It was written down even later than the Talmud, in the seventh century, and quite a distance from the setting described in the New Testament. Jesus is, however, mentioned in the Koran, under the name Isa. And we cannot exclude the possibility that these references to some extent represent legends that do not originate in the New Testament. Jesus is described as a great prophet, and an apostle of Allah, but not as a God. With regard to more historical information, the Koran contradicts the gospels really only on one significant point: the crucifixion (something to which we will come back later)

There is, however, one more significant source of information about Jesus of Nazareth, one that we have not yet named. It is a Christian source, but one that is often overlooked. This, despite it being the only one that was quite definitely written before the destruction of Jerusalem.

*

What we know about the apostle Paul is, partly, the information he himself provides in the seven to fourteen letters by him that are included in the New Testament, partly what is written about him in the part of the New Testament called the Acts of the Apostles (and which in all likelihood was written by the same person who wrote the gospel of Luke).

Paul was born in the city of Tarsus in Cilicià, in what is now Turkey, and he was originally named Saul. He was born at roughly the same time as Jesus (his date of birth is often given at sometime between 3 BCE and 3 CE), and he was a Jew, of the clan of Benjamin. For some reason, and we have no explanation for it, Saul was born with Roman citizenship, which was an honor bestowed upon very few Jews in the Roman Empire. Yet he doesn't seem to have come from a family high on the social scale. Saul trained as a tentmaker. The religious leaning of the family was toward the Pharisees, and according to the Acts, Saul travelled to Jerusalem when he was young and in that city was taught by the great rabbi Gamaliel the Elder, the son or grandson of Hillel. What happened in the following years is not clear. But Saul seems to have found his religious home with Gamaliel

What is strange is that Paul states that it is on account of this schooling that he started to persecute Christians. "You have heard what my manner of life was when I was still a practising Jew; how savagely I pursued the church of God and tried to destroy it; and how in the practice of our national religion I outstripped most of my Jewish contemporaries by my boundless devotion to the traditions of my ancestors."[69] This account, which recurs a number of times in the letters and in the Acts, is strange for several reasons: firstly, Gamaliel and the Pharisees, as has already been mentioned in connection with Yochanan ben Zakkai, were a relatively pacifist party (as opposed to the Zealots), and, furthermore, at that time they were more distant from·those in power than, for example, the Sadducees. Furthermore, the Acts of the Apostles portray Gamaliel (who, here, just as in the Jewish tradition, is described as an influential Pharisee member of the Sanhedrin[70]) as a person with a positive attitude toward Jesus' apostles[71]. The other strange factor is the information that the Christians at this time were so many, or were such a great threat, that a faction among the Jews should find cause to persecute them, or even kill them—because if that had been the case, Josephus or Justus of Tiberias really ought to have mentioned it.

In the Acts, it is described that "Saul, meanwhile, was harrying the church; he entered house after house, seizing men and women and sending them into prison."[72] A little later, Saul, "still breathing murderous threats against the Lord's disciples," goes to Damascus, there too to search out and "to arrest [Christians] and bring them to Jerusalem."[73] But when he approaches Damascus something happens. Saul is suddenly surrounded by a blinding light from the sky:

> *He fell to the ground and heard a voice saying "Saul, Saul, why are you persecuting me?" "Tell me Lord," he said, "who are you?" The voice answered, "I am Jesus, whom you are persecuting. But now get up and go into the city, and you will be told what you have to do."*[74]

As Paul describes it, it is the resurrected Jesus he has encountered (although perhaps not in bodily form).[75] So this is after the crucifixion of Jesus has taken place, and because it is possible to provide approximate dates for a number of events in the life of Saul/Paul—on the basis of other fixed points named in, above all, the Acts of the Apostles—one can determine that the event outside Damascus took place within a couple of years after the crucifixion (the German theologian Martin Hengel has dated the experience outside Damascus to about the year 33 CE; another German theologian, Rainer Riesner, suggests that it took place as early as 31–32 CE[76]).

The event on the road to Damascus marks the start of Saul's conversion. He spends the following three years in "Arabia." What he does there is not described in the story. Regardless, Saul returns to Damascus after these three years, and then he goes to Jerusalem to meet Peter, Jesus' closest disciple. He also meets James, the brother of Jesus, but "I saw none of the other apostles." And Paul adds, "What I write is plain truth; God knows I am not lying!"[77]

After fifteen days, Saul journeys to his home district Cilicia, but "I was still unknown by sight to the Christian congregations in Judea." He does not return to Jerusalem until fourteen years later.

Saul, who eventually takes the name Paul, will come to be the one who spreads the Christian message out into the world, and one could say that he is the one who *de facto* creates Christianity. He spreads his message by traveling about in the countries around the Mediterranean, seeking out the local synagogues and preaching about Jesus. But when the Jews reject him, he speaks instead to non-Jews. His message is that the Messiah has come in the form of Jesus Christ, who died for the sins of humans, and he calls this Jesus the "Son of God" and "our Lord." He explains that the only path to salvation is to believe in this Jesus Christ. It is also almost the only demand. Paul greatly emphasizes the fact that Jesus has stood up from the dead, and in the letter to the Romans, he even says that Jesus "was proclaimed Son of God by an act of power that raised him from the dead"[78] (Paul, incidentally, does not mention any virgin birth, but rather that God sent his son "born of a woman" and that "on the human level he was a descendent of David"[79]). In his missionary work, Paul seems however to devote fairly little time to the person Jesus, or the events in Jesus' life.

Paul sets to work on his task in a frenzy of activity. And the success he achieves is completely incredible. The message spreads like a wildfire, and it is above all non-Jews who take it in. As bishop and New Testament scholar N. T. Wright writes, "How do we account for the fact that by AD 110, there was a large and vigorous international movement, already showing considerable diversity, whose founding myth . . . was a story about one Jesus of Nazareth, a figure of the recent past?"[80]

Paul doesn't just travel around in different countries. He also writes letters to the congregations he has founded. Some of these letters were kept, and they later came to be included in the New Testament. The letters are extremely personal and direct. Paul gives advice and praise, only to suddenly reveal himself to be a sometimes rather choleric missionary who gets angry when the congregations don't do what he tells them. For example, he devotes considerable energy to trying to get the new congregations to donate money to the congregation in Jerusalem. In other words, the content of these letters is often mundane and always rather personal.

The New Testament contains fourteen letters, which were originally assumed to have been written by Paul. The authenticity of one of them, the letter to the Hebrews, was questioned early on, and was rejected by Luther (among others), and a further six of the letters are today regarded as having been written by later disciples of Paul. Seven letters are however regarded as authentic (i.e., written by Paul). And it is interesting to note when they were written. Because the letters and the Acts of the Apostles are considered to contain enough information to provide an acceptable dating for much that happened in Paul's life, historians have settled on the following: The earliest letter, the First Letter of Paul to the Thessalonians, was written about the year 50 CE (although earlier datings have been put forward[81]). The last of the letters that are considered to be authentic were, according to the same method of dating, written about ten years later. In other words, Paul started to write his letters about two decades before the destruction of Jerusalem! Thus, while the gospel writers wrote down their stories more than thirty years after the crucifixion of Jesus, Paul, according to the commonly accepted chronology, waited only fifteen to twenty years.

Paul's letters are indeed of a different character than the gospels. They are more theological, there is more reasoning, and they are often about everyday matters, while the gospels are historical and narrative. Nor do Paul's letters contain very much information about the person Jesus. But they do contain some. And this seems to be fairly uncensored.

What may be confusing is that the gospels are placed before Paul's letters in the New Testament. This fact, and their content, give the impression that the gospels are eyewitness accounts while

the Acts of the Apostles and Paul's letters tell what happened afterwards. This is an illusion. Paul is probably much closer to the center of the events than the gospel writers. And whatever the
situation, these gospel writers seem to have been inspired by Paul
to write their stories. Not the other way around.

As Donald Harman Akenson writes about Saul/Paul, "He
is the nearest witness in time to the historical Yeshua [Jesus] and we
have to get as close to Saul as possible."[82]

CHAPTER 3

BIRTH AND CHILDHOOD

In those days a decree was issued by the emperor Augustus for a census to be taken throughout the Roman world. This was the first registration of its kind; it took place when Quirinius was governor of Syria. Everyone made his way to his hometown to be registered. Joseph went up to Judea from the town of Nazareth in Galilee, to register in the city of David called Bethlehem, because he was in the house of David by descent; and with him went Mary, his betrothed, who was expecting her child.

The Gospel according to Luke 2:1–5

The above story about the circumstances surrounding the birth of Jesus can be read in the New Testament, in the gospel of Luke. It tells us that Jesus was born at the same time as the census, and taxation, which were conducted under the leadership of Governor Quirinius. The same tax-related census, and the same governor, are also named by the historian Flavius Josephus in *Antiquities of the Jews*. And from that source we can conclude that Quirinius did not arrive in Syria until the year 6 CE.[1]

If one uses Luke as a source, Jesus was thus born—at the earliest—six years after our modern calendar begins. But if one uses Matthew, where King Herod is mentioned, as a source, Jesus would have to have been born *before* our modern calendar begins—because Herod (at any rate the most famous Herod, Herod the Great) died in the year 4 BCE. It is thus impossible that Jesus was born *both* during the era of Herod the Great and during that of Quirinius.

Most people take more account of the earlier date—presumably because the later date makes it virtually impossible to get the rest of the equation to work out, as there are certain other chronologically fixed points given in the gospels.[2]

So, in general, Jesus is regarded as having been born about the years 6 to 4 BCE.

Strangely, however, as mentioned above, the birth of Jesus is only described in two gospels, those of Matthew and Luke. The oldest gospel, that of Mark, completely bypasses this event. And neither can one claim that Matthew and Luke agree as to the circumstances—where the family lived before Jesus was born, and where they went afterwards. Most likely, these birth stories contain a great deal of mythology. The authors of the gospels do, after all, have to fit the birth of Jesus into the prophecies of the Old Testament about the arrival of the Messiah and his background—so he "must" be born in Bethlehem. But otherwise the information about the family's movements and places of residence is highly contradictory. And these contradictions surely mean something. In Matthew, for example, we can read the following:

> *After they* [the astrologists] *had gone, an angel of the Lord appeared to Joseph in a dream, and said, "Get up, take the child and his mother and escape with them to Egypt, and stay there until I tell you; for Herod is going to search for the child and kill him." So Joseph got up, took mother and child by night, and sought refuge with them in Egypt.*[3]

No such flight to Egypt is described in the birth story in the gospel of Luke. One may wonder why. At a first reading, the explanation seems simple: the gospel of Matthew was primarily directed towards Jews, and Matthew wanted to liken Jesus with Moses, who of course escapes the Egyptian pharaoh's killing of Jewish boys. That accounts for Egypt. This conclusion is strengthened by Matthew also writing that the family stayed in Egypt "to fulfil what the Lord had declared through the prophet: 'Out of Egypt I have called my son.'"[4] It should be noted here that the flight to Egypt is also described in some New Testament Apocrypha, but in the rest of the New Testament this residence is conspicuous by its absence. Perhaps, then, it is only a "messianic invention"?

Interestingly enough, however, the connection between Jesus and Egypt is actually found in a few other places outside the New Testament.

"There was a tradition that he had had something to do with Egypt." Thus writes Bible scholar R. Travers Herford in his book from 1903, *Christianity in Talmud and Midrash.*[5] And the tradition he refers to is none other than that which is expressed in the oral teaching of Judaism, the Talmud.

In the Talmud, there are a number of references to a person or persons who have been interpreted as Jesus. Different Bible researchers accord these references different status. One of the problems, as mentioned, is that the Talmud was written down several hundred years after the birth of Jesus. And to the extent that it touches upon Jesus, it presumably partly reflects a polemical attitude towards him. Another problem is that there is not just *one* name for the person who has been interpreted as Jesus. There are a number of different names.

Why? If Jesus is mentioned, why use pseudonyms and word games? Why do researchers have to occupy themselves with guessing games with regard to a person who, at the time the Talmud was written down, was definitely known under one name: Jesus of Nazareth?

*

The Talmud was put together between the years 170 CE and 600
CE—the Mishna first, then the Jerusalem Gemara and the Babylonian Gemara. But already in those days, life for the Jews had begun
to be colored by conflicts between Christianity and Judaism. The
so-called disputations, more or less voluntary debates between rep-
resentatives for Christianity and Judaism, started to become common as early as during the first centuries after Christ. At first, they
were decidedly rancorous and sarcastic, but, like the arguments between members of the same household, were essentially harmless.
Perhaps they weren't really so very different from the discussions
that continually took place in the Yeshivot, the rabbinic schools.

With the embracing of Christianity in the Roman Empire in
the fourth century, however, the debates are accompanied by bans.
In 553 CE, the Byzantine Emperor Justinian issues an order forbid-
ding the use of the Hebrew translation of the Old Testament in synagogues, and the study of the Mishna is totally banned. The
atmosphere hardens, and the disputations start to become dangerous occasions.

In 1240 CE, one of these disputations is transformed into a
frontal attack upon the Talmud.

Paris in the thirteenth century was a maelstrom of religious activity. Waldensians and Cathars had started to question the established
Catholic Church, and Pope Innocent III announced a violent cam-
paign against them in 1209 CE. Previous to that, the Bishop of Paris
had threatened with excommunication all laymen who took part in
theological discussions.

In the midst of all this, a flourishing Talmudic activity was
taking place on the right bank of the River Seine. After a sixteen-
year exile, the Jews had been allowed to return to Paris, and had
immediately established themselves in the area around Les Halles.
One of the most important Talmud schools in Central Europe is
now established here too. From 1224 CE, its leader, who also becomes the chief rabbi of Paris, is Yehiel.

Yehiel is a committed teacher who attracts students from all of Europe. Sometimes even Christian linguists from the other side of the river come to his school for special lessons in Hebrew. The school has a good reputation, although some of the discussions that take place in and around the Talmud school, and, in fact, all over Paris, do worry the already nervous religious establishment in the city. "It is absurd to discuss the Trinity on street corners," writes the Christian theologian Peter of Blois.[6]

Among the many students who come to Yehiel at this time, there is a young man from La Rochelle, called Donin. Donin turns out to be a very independent thinker—and a bold one, too. During his time at the school, he starts to express a strong dislike for the Talmud. Much could be discussed within these walls—and passionate argumentation around analyses of Talmud texts was what the students devoted themselves to every day. But a condemnation of the Talmud, which was considered to be just as sacred as the five Books of Moses, that was quite another matter. Yehiel would not tolerate it. The debate raged within the walls of the school for more than a year. Then Yehiel excommunicated his student, before the entire congregation.

This was an extremely cruel punishment. Excommunication meant total exclusion. Nobody would eat with Donin, nobody would receive him in their home. The young Donin was from now on *persona non grata*. He put up with this for ten years. Then he took his revenge.

In 1236 CE, under dramatic circumstances, Donin declared that he had converted to Christianity. He had himself baptised as Nicholas and joined the Franciscan Order. Then he embarked upon a journey. He travelled around France, visiting Anjou, Poitou, and Aquitaine, and he visited crusader soldiers. Dressed in his monk's habit, Donin preached against the Jews and Judaism, something which led to the burning of synagogues and the destruction of Torah scrolls. He demanded that the Jews should convert en masse. Five hundred went along with this, but three thousand who refused were massacred by the mob. And then, finally, in the year 1238 CE, Nicholas Donin made his way to Rome, and to Pope Gregory IX.

There he sought the pope's help to impose the ultimate punishment—a ban against the hated Talmud.

Donin presents to the pope thirty-five accusations against the Talmud for blasphemy, and proposes that all copies of the Talmud in the Catholic world be destroyed. Furthermore, he says that if it hadn't been for the Talmud, which, he claims, the rabbis hold higher than the Bible, the Jews would have long since converted to Christianity.

Gregory is angered by what he hears, as well as surprised. Up until then, the Jews had admittedly been blamed for not having accepted Jesus as their savior, but their books had never been accused of being blasphemous. Rather the opposite, the Hebrew Bible basically constituted the Old Testament of the Christian Bible. At the same time, the thing the monk claimed, that it was the Talmud which caused the Jews to stick to their teachings and withstand Christianity, was most upsetting.

The pope thought about this for all of one year. Then he decided to use all the power of the Church in a frontal war against this book of the Jews. In an encyclical dated June 9, 1239, he asks the rulers of seven western European realms to confiscate all the copies of the Talmud in their own country. And it should happen on one and the same day—the first Saturday in Lent in the following year. Donin himself is granted the honor of delivering the encyclical to the bishop in Paris, from where it is to be spread.

Only the French king, Louis IX—called "Saint Louis" on account of his piety—takes heed of the pope's request. On the morning of the Sabbath, Saturday March 3, 1240, all copies of the Talmud found in France are confiscated and transported to a monastery in Paris. Then follows a trial.

King Louis had a mother who was known to be a very determined woman. While her son was still an underage regent, Blanche of Castile had governed France herself, and indeed waged war against the heretic Albigensians in Languedoc. Now it was she who was given the task of sitting as the judge for the approaching trial against the Talmud. She probably made the decision herself; it is said that Blanche still to a considerable degree decided for her son.

On July 24, 1240, the court proceedings begin, and they are to take place in the royal palace. In the magnificent great hall, Queen Blanche makes her entrance and assumes her position on the dais. She is followed by the prosecutor, and he is no other than the person who is considered most suited and most familiar with the Talmud's blasphemous qualities: Nicholas Donin.

Four French rabbis—all leading figures within French Jewry—have been appointed to defend their holy scripture. The first to speak is Yehiel.

The situation could hardly have been more charged. The controversy, now almost two decades old, between the teacher and his obstinate, and severely punished, student had now led to the very Talmud being put on trial. Donin had achieved what he wanted, and the man who once had crushed him now sat there with his beloved book on the bench of the accused. Queen Blanche had every reason to expect an exciting battle.

Nicholas Donin had brought with him all the volumes of the Talmud to the trial. Now he lifted one of the volumes up high, so that everyone could see. Then he carried it towards the spectators so that they could discern the text. Next, he turned toward his former teacher and asked him whether he believed *everything* that was written in these more than four-hundred-year-old books to be true.

"Four hundred years?" roared Yehiel. "They are fifteen hundred years old!" Then he sarcastically asked his former pupil which part of the Jewish faith he wanted to discuss. Donin's answer came as a total surprise to the rabbi: He didn't want to discuss any articles of faith of Judaism at all. Nor did he wish to discuss the thirty-five accusations he had presented to Pope Gregory. Instead, explained the monk, the discussion would be about one, and only one, thing: the presentation of Jesus Christ in the Talmud.

The rabbi was astounded. The discussion would be about something quite different than what he had expected. He turned to the queen: "Lady, I beg of you," he said, "do not oblige me to reply. The Talmud is a holy book of venerable antiquity in which no one until the present has been able to discover a fault. Jerome, one of your saints, was familiar with all of our law. If he had found the least blemish in it, he scarcely would have allowed it to remain. Your doctors, and you have had many more learned than Nicholas these last fifteen hundred years, have never attacked the Talmud." Then Yehiel turned to the gathered: "Know further that we are prepared to die for the Talmud."

Now the Queen interrupts, and assures Yehiel that nobody is threatening the Jews, or their property. But the rabbi must answer the accusations concerning the Talmud.

It is Donin's turn to speak again. And he immediately returns to his accusation—that of how Jesus is treated in the Talmud. The monk reads aloud the sections he finds relevant, twenty in all, and translates them into French. When he has finished, he turns to the listeners: "See how this people insults your God. How do you allow them to live in your midst?"

Yehiel could not have expected this, and he was hardly prepared. But his answer is not long in coming: "There is nothing in those passages that Nicholas just read out that is about Jesus. They are about completely different people!"

Rabbi Yehiel is so sure of his case and he argues so well, that Donin now starts hurling abuse at him. Finally, Queen Blanche interrupts again: "Why do you spill your good odor?" she asks the monk. "The Jew, out of respect for you, has succeeded in proving that his ancestors did not insult your God, and yet you persist in trying to make him confess to blasphemies. Aren't you shamed by such maneuvers?"

Yehiel is declared innocent. But the Talmud is not. It is decided that there should be a retrial of the Jews' holy book, and this time it will take place before a Church tribunal. The second trial ends in quite a different manner than the first: The Talmud is declared to be "a tissue of lies," and is condemned to be consumed by fire.

The decision is not unanimous, and for two years the Archbishop of Sens manages to delay the execution of the verdict.

But after his death, in 1242, there is no longer anyone highly placed who is prepared to defend the Jews' holy book. In June, 1242, wagon upon wagon leaves the monastery in Paris where the volumes have been stored. And all the known copies of the Talmud in France are cast into the flames.[7]

This is the first time the Talmud is to suffer such a verdict. But it will not be the last. The Talmud will be burned many a time after this. And in 1554, the Vatican issues a papal bull in which it orders the removal of all Jewish books that contain text that can be interpreted as blasphemy against Jesus. Five years later, the Talmud is included in the *Index Expurgatorius*, a list of books that Catholics are forbidden to read, and later Pope Pius IV orders that the Talmud shall even be deprived of its name.

The first "censored" version of the Talmud is issued in 1578–1581 in Basle, and it forms the basis for most later editions. It has, however, been possible to re-create earlier texts, and thereby also the sections seen by some to refer to Jesus—the major common factor of which is that it is always a little unclear who they are about.

One of the explanations for this ambiguity is that the Talmud presumably from the very first was subject to a certain degree of self-censorship. As we have been able to note, it was not only Christian theologians who had been ill at ease with these sections. It had been just as awkward for Jewish scholars. And just like Rabbi Yehiel, Jewish scholars have time after time claimed that these sections are not about Jesus of Nazareth at all, but are about completely different persons.

It is a paradoxical fact that today it is above all Christian theologians who refer to the Talmud texts about Jesus (if it is indeed him they are about), for the purpose of proving that Jesus did in fact exist.

So what was actually written about Jesus—or the person who possibly is Jesus—in the Talmud?

Yeshu, Yeshu ben Pantera, ben Stada, Balaam, Peloni. As already touched upon, not just one, but several names in the Talmud have been associated with Jesus. The names that might well be regarded as most relevant in this context are *Yeshu ben Pantera* (*Pandira, Pandera,* or simply *ben Pantera,* which means "son of Pantera,") and *ben Stada* (son of Stada). And sometimes, as in the following lines, the authors of the Talmud confirm that these names refer to one and the same person:

> *And this they did to ben Stada in Lydda, and they hung him on the eve of Passover. Ben Stada was ben Pandira*[8]

A similar identification is made in another Talmud tractate:

> *Rabbi Eliezer said to the Sages: "But did not ben Stada bring forth witchcraft from Egypt by means of scratches [in the form of charms] upon his flesh?" "He was a fool, answered they, and proof cannot be adduced from fools. Was he then the son of Stada: surely he was the son of Pandira?".*[9]

What the above quote treats is the question of whether one may under any circumstances write on the Sabbath, for example by scratching one's skin. Ben Stada is taken as an example, as it is told that he took spells with him in a cut in his flesh. The example is rejected by the rabbis, because ben Stada is dismissed as a fool. As mentioned previously, one does not find words of praise about Jesus or his teachings in the Talmud (assuming one accepts that it is Jesus who is being referred to). But the question is whether, despite this, one can find fragments of historical truth.

As Travers Herford pointed out, there is "a tradition that he had had something to do with Egypt." The above lines from the Babylonian Gemara represent just one of several examples in the Talmud where it is stated that ben Stada had been in Egypt. It is also one of several examples where it is stated that he took spells with him from that country. In another place, one can read the following:

> *He who scratches on the skin in the fashion of writing is guilty, but he who makes marks on the skin in the fashion of writing, is exempt from punishment. Rabbi Eliezer said to them: "But has not ben*

*Stada brought [magic]-spells out of Egypt just in this way?" They
answered him: "On account of one fool we do not ruin a multitude
of reasonable men."* [10]

Rashi, the most famous Talmud commentator (he lived 1040–1105
CE, mainly in France), has explained the need to hide magic spells
by the fact that Egyptian magicians examined all who left Egypt to
check whether they were taking books on magic with them—the
Egyptian magicians did not want their craft to be spread outside the
country.[11] As is stated in another Talmud tractate, "Ten measures of
sorcery descended into the world; Egypt received nine, the rest of
the world one."[12]

It is, incidentally, remarkable that in the Revelation of John, the last
book in the New Testament, we can read the following lines about
one of the four horsemen of the apocalypse, the man on the white
horse, a person who is often interpreted as Jesus Christ.[13]

*His eyes flamed like fire, and on his head were many diadems. Written
on him was a name known to none but himself. . . . On his robe and
on his thigh was written the title: "King of kings and Lord of lords."* [14]

We have to use "if" a lot here. If we accept that "ben Stada" and
"Yeshu ben Pantera" refer to Jesus of Nazareth, then he does seem
to have some connection with Egypt—just like it says in the gospel
of Matthew. And if that is the case, he does seem to have acquired
a certain knowledge of magic there.

"The belief in magic, that is to say, in the power of magical names,
and spells, and enchantments, and formulæ, and pictures, and figures, and amulets, and in the performance of ceremonies accompanied by the utterance of words of power, to produce supernatural
results, formed a large and important part of the Egyptian religion."
This is how E. A. Wallis Budge puts it in his introduction to his classic work *Egyptian Magic*. "The belief in magic," he adds, "is older in
Egypt than the belief in God." [15]

Few realms have so clearly united politics and religion as the Egyptians did. At an early stage there developed a view of the kings'—the pharaohs'—role as a link between humans and the gods. This was the country where the miracle of the flooding of the Nile, and the renaissance of growth, was repeated year after year. With a sufficient faith in the gods and ritual actions to please them one could, as they saw things, rely upon life continuing and on the re-generating power of nature. And the pharaoh was quite simply a part of this ritual system. People saw the king as essentially always being the same person. It was the same divine essence that was just transferred from one individual to the next. In the same way that one learned that nature was cyclical to an almost completely reli-able degree, living and dying with the waters of the Nile, one also looked upon life itself as something cyclical: life and death were very close to each other. And this was manifested too in the way the pharaoh was regarded; mythologically, he had two sides: one was Osiris, who ruled over the realm of the dead; the other was Horus, who represented life. And these two forms made up a unit.

Two other phenomena that formed a unit in ancient Egypt were religion and magic. In Egyptian mythology, magic (or *heka* as it was called) was one of the forces that were used to create the world. In Egypt, priests were the main practitioners of magic, and they were often thus both magicians and spiritual guides. Their knowledge of magic was regarded as something given to them by the gods, and it was kept as a professional secret. The highest prac-titioners of magic were the priests who could read the most ancient texts that were kept in a secret place in the temples, a place called *per-ankh*, the House of Life.

The purpose of the magic was to transfer power from a "supernatural being" to a human, thereby giving the human the ca-pability to achieve superhuman results. In a tangible sense, it was often about protecting oneself from unforeseen events, from failed harvests, from enemies, from accidents or illness. Some parts of the day were considered to be more dangerous than others—for exam-ple, the night was a time when one could more easily meet with an accident—and to protect oneself, recourse to magic was often taken.

The role of magic in Egyptian society is mentioned in the Old Testament. In Exodus, the Second Book of Moses, we are told how God says to Moses and Aaron that if the pharaoh gives them a "sign," Aaron should take his rod and cast it down before the pharaoh. The rod would then be transformed into a "serpent." Moses and Aaron do as God has told them. "At this, Pharaoh summoned the wise men and the sorcerers, and the Egyptian magicians did the same thing by their spells. . . . But Aaron's staff swallowed up theirs."[16]

At the time in which Jesus lived, Egypt—like Judea—belonged to the Roman Empire. The country had indeed been a Roman puppet state for quite a long time, but after Cleopatra's suicide in the year 30 BCE, Egypt was incorporated into the Roman Empire, and would be governed by Emperor Augustus.

Yet much remained unchanged. Like the Hellenist rulers, the Romans—at any rate in the beginning—did allow much of the old Egyptian culture and religion to survive. The practice of magic was still widespread. But while magic had earlier been mastered and guarded only by the Egyptian priesthood, during the Roman times there were signs that certain individuals had managed to acquire this knowledge and practiced it for their own gain. In Egypt one was especially worried about foreigners taking the knowledge of various magical rites out of the country, which is just what Rashi's Talmud commentary points out.

And in the Gemara one can read that the man who was called ben Stada learned his magical skills in Egypt, and took them with him to the realm of the Jews.

The question whether Jesus, as he is described in the gospels, worked with magic, is one that has always given rise to discussion. The problem is that magic has been described as something negative within both Judaism and Christianity. As John Dominic Crossan says, "Religion is official and approved magic; magic is unofficial and unapproved religion."[17] Or, expressed in other words: Magic is the term that religious leaders use to belittle miracles carried out by the wrong sort of people. And where one crosses the line between "miracle" and "magic" can be most subtle. According to the Christian view, "magic" is most often something evil, while a "miracle" is most often something good. But the view of what is good and what is evil, what is supernatural and divine, and what is "sorcery" is, as Crossan points out, often a function of the observer's own basic attitudes.

The earlier a gospel is written down, the more it emphasizes Jesus' ability to carry out miracles. The gospel of Mark is full of miracles. And it is not uncommon in the gospel text that Jesus is indeed accused of magic when he carries out miracles: "The scribes, too, who had come down from Jerusalem, said, 'He is possessed by Beelzebul', and 'He drives out demons by the prince of demons,'" as it says in the gospel of Mark, chapter 3.[18] In the gospel of Luke, we can read something similar:

> He was driving out a demon which was dumb, and when the demon had come out, the dumb man began to speak. The people were astonished, but some of them said, "It is by Beelzebul prince of demons that he drives the demons out." [19]

According to the gospels, Jesus carried out faith healing, such as the exorcising of evil spirits, as well as "miracles of nature," such as walking on Lake Galilee or causing a storm to subside. And Jesus himself indicates that these miracles are a proof that he is "the one who is to come," the man for whom John the Baptist prepared the path.[20] The problem is that, for the disciples, these are not particularly impressive pieces of evidence, at least not as the gospel of Mark describes it. They regularly express doubt.

That Jesus could carry out miracles, or perform magic, depending on how you look at it, is stated clearly in all the gospels. Where he has learned this is not discussed. But we can note that these two aspects of the Talmud texts—the contact with Egypt and the knowledge of magical things—are to a certain degree echoed in the gospel texts (if we interpret "ben Stada" as Jesus).

There is yet another relevant Talmud story that deals with Egypt, in which the person concerned, at any rate in the Babylonian

Talmud, is called Yeshu (in one manuscript he is even called Yeshu the Nazarene).

In this story, Yeshu is fleeing to Egypt to escape an evil king who kills rabbis. He flees together with a well-known rabbi by the name of Yehoshua ben Perachyah. This rabbi later rejects him, and he does so "with both hands," which is criticized in the Talmud. The rejection takes place when the rabbi and his disciple come to an inn (the word for "inn," *acsania*, can also mean "inn hostess"):

> *Then he* [Yehoshua] *said, "How beautiful is this inn* [acsania]*!"*
> *Thereupon Yeshu observed, "Rabbi, her eyes are narrow." "Wretch", he*
> *rebuked him, "dost thou thus engage thyself."*

Yeshu subsequently tries in vain to be taken back into the rabbi's fold, but is briskly repulsed, "with both hands." The story ends with the words: "Yeshu practiced magic and led Israel astray." [21]

Does this Talmud story refer to Jesus? Something that doesn't agree at all is the date. Rabbi Yehoshua ben Perachyah and the king who is mentioned, Alexander Jannai, who did in fact order a massacre of Pharisaic rabbis, lived about one hundred years before the birth of Jesus. But there is a certain echo in the stories in the gospels. According to the gospel of Matthew, Jesus fled to Egypt to escape an evil king ("Herod"). And it is a fact that also Herod the Great, and even more so his son Archelaus, at times had violent clashes with religious Jews. [22]

Furthermore, something in this story from the Talmud is undeniably reminiscent of the parable of the prodigal son in the gospel of Luke. [23]

The Talmud is not an historical document, nor does it make any claims to be one. It is a collection of laws, anecdotes, and legends. So one must take any information that can be distilled from it with a pinch of salt. But one should probably not ignore it completely. And because the gospel of Matthew describes a connection with Egypt, which is possibly confirmed in the Talmud, there are indeed certain indications that Jesus could have lived there during a part of his life (and did not Josephus speak of an aspiring messiah who was called "the Egyptian"?).

At the same time, if one has the gospels as a starting point, it is not indicated that Jesus grew up and became an adult man in Egypt. The gospel of Matthew portrays the time in Egypt as fairly short, only lasting until the death of Herod. On the other hand, the New Testament describes how Jesus during his final year returns to his hometown of Nazareth, and he has obviously not been there for a long time. People at first do not remember him, and then remember him in relation to his parents (or at any rate his mother) and his brothers and sisters, in other words presumably as a child or youth. One possibility, of course, is that Jesus had returned to Egypt, or travelled to some other place, as a youth, and stayed there for some or all the time that is not described in the gospels. Because this is one of the peculiarities of the gospel narratives: with the exception of the birth stories in the gospels of Matthew and Luke, and a short visit to Jerusalem at the age of twelve, the life of Jesus up to his thirtieth year is completely unknown. He turns up, as if from nowhere, to see John the Baptist in the Judean desert.

But let us back up a little, and return to the gospels' birth stories. Because Matthew and Luke don't just restrict themselves to the birth of Jesus, they also describe his mother's pregnancy.

> This is how the birth of Jesus Christ came about. His mother Mary
> was betrothed to Joseph; before their marriage she found she was
> going to have a child with the Holy Spirit.

> —Matthew 1:18

What hides behind these words in the gospel of Matthew, and similar ones in the gospel of Luke, has made up something of a dividing line in the way of looking at the historic Jesus. It has either been assumed that Mary really did become pregnant through the Holy Spirit, or an alternative explanation for these lines has been sought—lines which, for that matter, are not to be found in the gospel of Mark or in the letters of Paul (i.e., the earlier sources). If one wishes to disregard the religious interpretation, a possible explanation is that the lines about the virgin birth are a way for the gospel writers to give Jesus divine qualities from the very time of his birth. Another possible explanation is that the virgin birth is a circumlocution for a real event, a real event that needed to be explained or explained away. The latter interpretation has followed along since the time the gospels were written down.

As mentioned earlier, both Mark and Matthew quote residents in Jesus' hometown in the same way when they identify Jesus, but with a decisive difference: in the gospel of Mark, Jesus is "the carpenter, the son of Mary"—his father is not named. In the gospel of Matthew, however, he is the "carpenter's son." It seems as if Mark does not even attempt to hide the fact that the inhabitants in Jesus' hometown seem to have regarded him as having been born out of wedlock (nor does Matthew, for that matter, hide the fact that Mary and Joseph did not live together when she became pregnant, and that Joseph even thought about abandoning Mary[24]). A similar intimation about illegitimacy can possibly be found in the gospel of John. Below is an excerpt from chapter 8, in which Jesus is speaking to "the Jews who had believed him" (but whom he nevertheless claims want to kill him):

> "I tell what I have seen in my Father's presence; you do what you have learned from your father." They retorted, "Abraham is our father." "If you were Abraham's children," Jesus replied, "you would do as Abraham did. As it is, you are bent on killing me, because I have told you the truth, which I heard from God. That is not how Abraham acted. You are doing your own father's work."
>
> They said, "We are not illegitimate; God is our father, and God alone."[25]

The above lines are open to interpretation. And when pronouncements such as this, or the one in the gospel of Mark, are made—such pronouncements that could be interpreted as implying that Jesus is an "illegitimate child"—they are always placed in someone

else's mouth. Besides, they are often contradicted by other statements. For example, in John 1, the disciple Philip says, "We have
found the man of whom Moses wrote in the law, the man foretold
by the prophets: it is Jesus son of Joseph, from Nazareth." And in
chapter 6, a group of Jews say, "Surely this is Jesus, Joseph's son!"[26]
It is, by the way, interesting how the gospels define certain groups
as "Jews." It is interesting for the simple reason that virtually all the
people in the settings Jesus finds himself, including the disciples and
Jesus himself, are Jews! They are in a Jewish country. Yet there is a
distinct expression of alienation, of being an outsider, about Jesus,
and just as distinct is the fact that this alienation is defined in relation to "Jews." In the lines above from the gospel of John, Jesus even
seems to distinguish between the ancestry of the Jews and that of
himself. The question is why.

Psychological interpretations are always tricky in a context
such as this. We are speaking of a religious figure, described in religious texts written down about two thousand years ago. Much
has been rephrased; much is rationalization. But if we really are
going to try to get at the reality that may lie behind the lines, psychology must be one of our tools. Even though it means venturing
out onto thin ice.

Because the thing is that intimations of illegitimacy are not
just found in the gospels; they are in at least two other sources. And
depending upon how much faith we put in these, they can possibly give us an explanation for the alienation Jesus felt.

The first source, yet again, is the Talmud. And just as in the case of
the stories of the magician who came from Egypt, there is deep dis-
agreement as to which, if any, of the many names who are claimed
to represent Jesus really do mean Jesus.

The earliest reference that, by some, is regarded as concerning Jesus is also the only one in the Mishna (the part of the Talmud
that was written down first): "Said Rabbi Shimon ben Azzai: 'I found
a roll of genealogical records in Jerusalem, and therein was written
Peloni is the illegitimate child [mamzer] of an adulteress.'"[27] The only
reason at all for suspecting that this concerns Jesus, is the use of the

name "Peloni." It can be compared with "John Doe" in American legal texts—i.e., a person whose name one deliberately does not provide. The name Peloni has been associated with Jesus, and the view has been put forward that the above Mishna quote is indeed about Jesus. Herford, for example, considers it "certainly probable that the reference is to Jesus." [28] But many scholars consider the assumption to be preposterous, or at the very least far-fetched. Shimon ben Azzai was, incidentally, a scribe who lived at the end of the first century and the beginning of the second century.

In the Gemara, which of course was put together later, there are a number of lines that concern "ben Pantera," "Yeshu ben Pantera," or "ben Stada." In general, the names turn up in texts that are about a person who is trying to lead the Jews away from their religion. And in some of them, this person's origin is touched upon. The one quoted most often is the continuation of the text that is given earlier in this chapter, about the man who came from Egypt (the word "ben," again, means "son of"):

> Rabbi Eliezer said to the Sages: "But did not ben Stada bring forth witchcraft from Egypt by means of scratches [in the form of charms] upon his flesh?" "He was a fool, answered they, and proof cannot be adduced from fools. Was he then the son of Stada: surely he was the son of Pandira?"
>
> Said Rabbi Hisda: "The husband was Stada, the paramour was Pandira."
>
> [Another said] "But the husband was Pappos ben Judah?—His mother was Stada." [Another said]"But his mother was Miriam the hairdresser?—It is as we say in Pumbeditha: 'S'tath da (lit., 'she has turned away from'—) her husband.'" [29]

Or the similar lines from tractate Sanhedrin 67a:

> And this they did to ben Stada in Lydda, and they hung him on the eve of Passover. Ben Stada was ben Pandira.
>
> Rabbi Hisda said: "The husband was Stada, the paramour Pandira."

> [Another said] "But was not the husband Pappos ben Judah?—
> His mother's name was Stada." [Another said]"But his mother was
> Miriam, the dresser of women's hair?—As we say in Pumbeditha: 'S'-
> tath da (lit., 'she has turned away from'—) her husband."" [30]

Miriam is the Jewish name for "Mary," and this can perhaps provide more credibility to the assumption that the above text is actually about Jesus. What is meant by "the dresser of women's hair"? The original Aramaic expression is *megaddela neshaia*, and the mother is thus called *Miriam megaddela neshaia*. What is interesting, is that Miriam, or Mary, is here given almost the same name as Mary Magdalene (or Mary from Magdala). To place Pappos ben Juda in the period is, however, harder, since he was a real person, a scribe, who lived at least a half-century after Jesus, and among other things is said to have locked his wife in the house to stop her from being unfaithful. [31] It is possible that Pappos ben Juda can here be serving as a metaphor for a deceived husband.

The text is full of puns. Here, for example, is an interpretation of what the origin of the name *Stada* might be. "*S'tath da*" means "to turn away from," and seems here to thus have the meaning "unfaithful" ("turn away from her husband"). This suspicion of adultery is also expressed clearly and unambiguously when it is written: "The husband was Stada, the paramour Pandira." Ben Stada and ben Pandira are here said to be the same person with two different names, which is explained by one of them designating him as son to his stepfather or mother, the other as son to his mother's lover.

Who then was this Pandira (Pantera, Pandera), the presumed lover? Many attempts have been made to explain this name. One suggests that the word can be derived from *parthenos*, which means "virgin" in classic Greek, and that ben Pandira would thus mean "son of a virgin." Herford comments upon this as follows: "the obvious appropriateness of a name indicating the alleged birth of Jesus from a virgin might make us overlook the improbability that the form *parthenos* should be hebraized into the form Pandira, when the Greek word could have been reproduced almost unchanged in a

Hebrew form. It is not clear, moreover, why [in the Talmud] a Greek word should have been chosen as an epithet for Jesus."[32]

The Greek has however attracted other interpretations of this name, and one suggestion is that it could derive from *pentheros*, which means "father-in-law," or quite simply from the name "Panter." But has this name, Pandira or Pantera, actually been used as a personal name? Yes, it does in fact seem to have been.

In 1859, an archaeological find caused quite a sensation among those who were engaged in research on the historical Jesus. In the German Rhineland, in a little village called Bingerbrück, work had been started on the extension of a railway line. During the excavation work, a number of gravestones were suddenly uncovered. To their surprise, archaeologists discovered the stones to be extremely old, from the first and second centuries CE to be more exact. On some of the stones, the inscriptions were still fairly legible. They were in Latin, and it was clear that some of the graves had been of Roman soldiers, presumably with quite a high rank. One particular stone gave rise to a lot of attention: the gravestone with its statue was about five feet high and about two and a half feet wide and portrayed an archer. The head, neck, and shoulders were broken off, but otherwise the statue was well preserved. And, most important of all, the greater part of the inscription remained. It read as follows:

Tib[erius] Iul[ius] Abdes Pantera
Sidonia ann[orum] LXII
stipen[diorum] XXXX miles exs . . .
coh[orte] I sagittariorum
h[ic] s[itus] e[st]

That is: "Tiberius Iulius Abdes Pantera from Sidon, sixty-two years of age, with forty years of service, a soldier in the First Cohort of Archers, rests here."

This archers' company is understood to have been stationed at Bingerbrück in the middle of the first century CE, and was based in Syria until about the year 6 CE.[33] In other words, this soldier—

whose surname was Pantera—seems to have lived at the right time, and at least close to the right place, to be able to have been the father of Jesus (and the supposition that soldier Pantera was a non-Jew, father of Jesus—and perhaps even lay in German soil!—came eventually to be used in a new Nazified theology[34]).

Could it be that they had found Jesus' biological father? Actually, they had no other evidence than the surname. Besides, Pantera was not unknown as a surname for roman soldiers. There are even other inscriptions found that bear this name[35] Nevertheless, here was proof that the name "ben Pantera"—son of Pantera—could actually refer to a personal name, at least a Roman personal name, rather than just be a play on words.

This, thus, was, what could be gleaned from the Talmud. To summarize, we can see indications, but no proof, that some Talmud texts refer to Jesus of Nazareth, and that they describe him as a man who has lived in Egypt where he supposedly learned "sorcery," that he was the illegitimate son of a woman by the name of Miriam, or Mary, that his biological father was called Pantera or Pandira, and that he was hanged at Passover time. This person is often presented as someone who leads the people of Israel astray. As for the two rabbis who are named in the Talmud texts above, we know that Rabbi Eliezer lived at the end of the first century and the beginning of the second (i.e., he was a contemporary of the authors of the gospels), while Rabbi Hisda lived in Babylonia from 217 to 309 CE.[36] To make it worse, the texts were written down two centuries after the death of Rabbi Hisda. So we are concerned with stories that, though they may be based on old traditions, would have had time to go through many changes before finally being written down. Having read the lines in the Talmud, we still stand there with much circumstantial evidence and different interpretations, and just as many question marks.

But the thing is: there actually is one other source in which these issues are discussed. And it was written considerably earlier.

We do not know very much about Celsus. What we do know is that he was a Greek philosopher, that he was a strong opponent of

Christianity—which he considered to be a movement created by sorcerers and magicians—and that he wrote his only known work, *Alethes logos* (*A Word of Truth*), between 175 and 180 CE. This work has not survived. The reason we know of it at all is that a certain Ambrosius, sixty years later, sent the work to his friend Origen—the church father mentioned earlier—so that he could write a refutation of Celsus' claims. The reason was that these claims had come to be regarded as so alarming that the Church did not want them to go unchallenged.

Origen is said to have hesitated a long time, but in the end he did agree to write a work that would entirely be concerned with disproving Celsus. And in this work, called *Contra Celsum* (*Against Celsus*) he did not just put forward arguments against Celsus, he came to quote word for word as much as perhaps 90 percent of Celsus' text. So it is in *Contra Celsum* that Celsus' words have been preserved. And when one reads these quotes, one can see why the church fathers felt compelled to go to a counter-attack. In book one of *Contra Celsum*, Origen quotes the following words from Celsus:

> *When she* [the mother of Jesus] *was pregnant she was turned out of doors by the carpenter to whom she had been betrothed, as having been guilty of adultery, and that she bore a child to a certain soldier named Panthera.*[37]

The context in which Celsus makes this statement is that he lets a fictive Jew argue with Jesus, and then put forward this message. Whether Celsus has gained his information from Jewish sources is not clear. But one can see that what was written down in the Talmud two hundred to four hundred years later is not a result of new ideas. They were already circulating in the year 175 CE. Here, too, we have concrete evidence about the following: The "ben Pantera" who is later described in the Talmud does indeed refer to Jesus of Nazareth.

Furthermore, Pantera is evidently a personal name, and this person—who is here claimed to be the biological father of Jesus—is reported as being a soldier.

*

The name of Pantera was so well known in the early Church that the conservative church father Epiphanius felt himself obliged, in the fourth century, to weave it into the family tree of Jesus by adding that a forefather to Jesus, by the name of James, had the surname of Pantera.[38] Several centuries later, church father John of Damascus writes that Mary's paternal grandfather was named Bar Panter.[39]

The person Pantera, he who was mentioned both by those who wrote down the Talmud and by the philosopher Celsus, was not somebody who could be ignored.

There is something else that Celsus confirms for us: according to legend, Jesus had some sort of connection with Egypt. In *Contra Celsum*, Origen writes the following:

> He [the fictive Jew] *accuses Him* [Jesus] *of having "invented his birth from a virgin" and upbraids him with being "born in a certain Jewish village, of a poor woman of the country, who gained her subsistence by spinning, and who was turned out of doors by her husband, a carpenter by trade, because she was convicted of adultery; that after being driven away by her husband, and wandering about for a time, she disgracefully gave birth to Jesus, an illegitimate child, who having hired himself out as a servant in Egypt on account of his poverty, and having there acquired some miraculous powers, on which the Egyptians greatly pride themselves, returned to his own country, highly elated on account of them, and by means of these proclaimed himself a God." Now, as I cannot allow anything said by unbelievers to remain unexamined, but must investigate everything from the beginning, I give it as my opinion that all these things worthily harmonize with the predictions that Jesus is the Son of God.*[40]

It is these lines from *Contra Celsum* that finally have convinced most Bible scholars that the "Yeshu ben Pantera" who is described in the Talmud does in fact refer to Jesus of Nazareth—which does not in any way necessarily mean that the stories that are presented represent what really happened.

At the same time, there are those who, despite the statement of Rabbi Hisda, do not want to accept that "ben Stada" and "ben Pantera" are the same person. These people include the Israeli professor Joseph Klausner and the British R. Travers Herford.[41] Herford writes that even if ben Stada seems clearly to be identified as Jesus of Nazareth, "the possibility remains that originally they were not identical," in other words that ben Pantera was Jesus, and ben Stada was somebody else. And Herford adds: "I venture to suggest as worthy of consideration, the hypothesis that Ben Stada originally denoted 'the Egyptian' [described by Josephus] who gave himself out to be a prophet, led by a crowd of followers to the Mount of Olives, and was routed there by the Procurator Felix . . . according to Josephus, the Egyptian himself escaped."

* * *

"A man of noble birth went on a long journey abroad, to have himself appointed king and then return." Thus begins a parable that Jesus tells in the gospel of Luke.[42] To read the gospels in light of the information—true or otherwise—that can be found in other sources is an exciting, but at the same time potentially deceptive, occupation. Sometimes it is simply a guessing game. But if we are to interpret the quite evident alienation that Jesus, according to the gospels, expresses, perhaps especially in relation to the Jews in the midst of whom he is living, it is undeniably tempting to take the tale of Pantera into consideration. Because if Jesus was born out of wedlock, it was considered a dreadful stigma. And on top of that, if he was the son of a Jewish woman and a Roman soldier, the stigma would be double. It was the Romans who provided the threat to Jewish life in Judea, and to be the child of a local woman and a Roman soldier must have been difficult indeed.

We do not know, but perhaps this is the explanation for the strong identification and empathy with the poor and outcasts that Jesus expresses, as in the parable of the laborers in the vineyard, which ends with the words: "So the last will be first, and the first last." Or in the parable of the wedding celebration: "The servants went out into the streets, and collected everyone they could find, good and bad alike. So the hall was packed with guests." When Jesus says to his disciples: "Whoever humbles himself and becomes like this child will be the greatest in the kingdom of Heaven," he is describing a powerful sympathy for the most vulnerable in society. And when he, as described in the gospel of Luke, tells of the prodigal son—the one who went away to a foreign country, lost everything, and then upon his return was welcomed into the arms of a loving father—perhaps he is speaking of his own longing.[43]

There are many explanations for the attractiveness of Jesus; he came at a time when the Roman Empire was ready for a religious conversion, and he offered a possibly more accessible variety of a religion, Judaism, which had already begun to gain adherents in the eastern parts of the Roman Empire. But one should not underestimate the incredible power of attraction that lay in the particular message that Jesus preached: even the weakest among us belong to the kingdom of Heaven. And you only have to pray for the forgiveness of your sins, and believe in me, to become a part of the congregation. As E. P. Sanders writes, "God's love of the outcast, even those not generally obedient to his will, is the theme of some of Jesus' greatest parables. . . . God is like a shepherd who goes in search of one lost sheep; God is like a good father, who accepts his prodigal son back with rejoicing."[44] The story about the prodigal son is central among Jesus' parables, and the regaining of a Father, who in this case is the greatest Father of all, God himself, is full of symbolism.

"Ask, and you will receive; seek, and you will find; knock, and the door will be opened to you."[45] The message is loving, forgiving, and irresistible. And perhaps it comes from a private trauma, a private wish to belong.

CHAPTER 4

ENCOUNTER WITH JOHN THE BAPTIST

It is a fact that the gospels describe a very short period of Jesus' life with great richness of detail, and above all they are concerned with his very last week. Otherwise they are virtually silent. If we disregard the two birth stories in the gospels of Matthew and Luke, there is only one reported event before Jesus' thirtieth year: in the gospel of Luke, it is told that when he was twelve years old he followed along with his parents to Jerusalem during Passover, a tradition that his parents kept up every year. On their way back to Nazareth, they discover—after a day!—that he isn't with them. They then return to Jerusalem, and after searching for three days they find Jesus in the Temple, where he is sitting among scribes and listening and asking questions, "and all who heard him were amazed at his intelligence, and the answers he gave." His parents are astonished, and Mary asks how he could cause them so much worry. Jesus answers: "Why did you search for me? . . . Did you not know that I was bound to be in my Father's house?" Then he goes home with them.[1] It may be of relevance here that a Jewish boy becomes *Barmitzvah* (confirmed into the Jewish faith) when he is thirteen years old, and spends all the previous year studying for this. Although the cere-mony as it is carried out today is a later phenomenon, during the time of the second temple there were similar initiation ceremonies. It is possible that something like that is what is described in the gospel of Luke.

And then there is silence. For almost twenty years.

Then suddenly, it seems, Jesus steps out of the shadows. Luke only writes: "When Jesus began his work he was about thirty years old." After this, Luke immediately lists Jesus' ancestry, almost as if he had just been born![2] The context in which Jesus appears is a meeting, a decisive meeting for his life as well as his work: He goes to "John by the Jordan valley" in order to be baptized.[3]

The person who is to baptize Jesus, and whose story intro-duces three of the four gospels—John the Baptist—is just as myste-rious a figure as Jesus himself. There have been many attempts to interpret who he really was.

"In the fifteenth year of the emperor Tiberius, when Pontius Pilate was governor of Judea, when Herod was tetrarch of Galilee, his brother Philip prince of Ituraea and Trachonitis, and Lysanias prince of Abilene, during the high-priesthood of Annas and Ca-iaphas, the word of God came to John son of Zachariah in the wilderness." Thus begins the third chapter of the gospel of Luke. With the generous times given here, it is possible to date the activ-ities of John the Baptist fairly well. Emperor Tiberius started to reign alone on August 19, in the year 14 CE. Using this as a starting point we can say that John the Baptist starts his preaching as late as 28–29 CE (some people, however, consider that this date can be put somewhat earlier, as Tiberius reigned jointly with Augustus for a couple of years before the latter's death). Whatever the circum-stances, we do have an approximate period of time within which to maneuver. And within this period of time, we do indeed find the tetrarch Herod Antipas ruling over Galilee, his brother Philip ruling over the areas north of Lake Galilee, Pontius Pilate ruling over Judea, and Caiaphas being the high priest in Jerusalem (with regard to Lysanias and Annas, a certain amount of reinterpretation is necessary if the text is to agree with other historical sources).

These are times of change. In the aftermath of a popular uprising, Archelaus has been deposed as ruler over Judea, and the Romans have transformed the Jewish vassal state into the Roman province of Iudaea, appointing a Roman prefect. From the year 26 CE, this prefect is called Pontius Pilate, a person who will come to be of decisive importance in Jesus' life. He will also come to be described by contemporary historians, above all with regard to his early days in the new country:

"But now Pilate, the procurator of Judea, removed the army from Cesarea to Jerusalem, to take their winter quarters there." Thus begins Flavius Josephus' description of Pontius Pilate's first confrontation with his Jewish population.[4] The cause for the confrontation was that Pilate ordered that the army, upon entering the holy city, was to carry standards on which there were images of the Roman emperor.[5] This was a rash decision. "Our law forbids us the very making of images," writes Josephus, "on which account the former procurators were wont to make their entry into the city with such ensigns as had not those ornaments. Pilate was the first who brought these images to Jerusalem, and set them up there; which was done without the knowledge of the people, because it was done in the night time." In the morning the Jews in Jerusalem are horrified to discover the new standards, and they come "in multitudes" to Caesarea, where they pray and plea of the unrepentant Pilate that he shall take away the standards with the images of the emperor. But Pilate refuses. Without the knowledge of his visitors, he has arranged for his soldiers to surround the place, and when the Jews yet again come to plea with him, he gives a signal to the soldiers to surround them, and subsequently threatens to have them executed if they do not immediately return home. "But," writes Josephus, "they threw themselves upon the ground, and laid their necks bare, and said they would take their death very willingly, rather than the wisdom of their laws should be transgressed; upon which Pilate was deeply affected with their firm resolution to keep their laws inviolable, and presently commanded the images to be carried back from Jerusalem to Caesarea."[6]

The tug-of-war between the Roman rulers and their Jewish population has thus already started. And in the religious ideas that now start to be promulgated, one can note that for many—at least spiritually—this is experienced as a struggle for life and death. This is a time when there are developments within Judaism toward increasingly apocalyptical thoughts—ideas about the end of the world and the day of judgment. The mood is perhaps not entirely unlike that which would appear within the Russian aristocracy in the years prior to the Russian Revolution: there was a feeling of approaching disaster, and one of the ways in which this was manifested was that people were attracted to charismatic religious leaders.

In Judea, as well as in Galilee, which still remained more independent, there arose at this time a swarm of different Jewish religious sects representing a variety of different shades. A Bible historian writes, "Try to conceive of a mental world so rich with ideas, prophets, factions, priests, savants, and god-drunk fanatics that it was the equivalent of a night-sky kept alight by thousands and thousands of fireflies, brief-lived, incandescent, luminous."[7] The Jerusalem Talmud states that the reason the Jewish people were sent into exile and their Temple destroyed was that in the years running up to this, there had been as many as twenty-four religious parties of "apostates."[8]

One of the most important of these fairly new groups was a mysterious sect of white-dressed men who lived in the Judean desert: the so-called Essenes. And this is a sect that later historians return to time after time in their attempts to find the historical context of Christianity.

According to Flavius Josephus and Philo, the Essenes were only four thousand in number.[9] But despite the insignificant number of members, and despite their what we would now regard as rather unusual expressions of Judaism, the Essenes were so central that even Flavius Josephus, who was rather conventional, spent several years in his youth trying to gain a deeper knowledge of their teachings. This group aroused his fascination:

These men are despisers of riches, and so very communicative as raises our admiration. Nor is there any one to be found among them who hath more than another, for it is a law among them, that those who come to them must let what they have be common to the whole order,—insomuch that among them all there is no appearance of poverty, or excess of riches, but every one's possessions are intermingled with every other's possessions.

Flavius Josephus, The War of the Jews, 2:8:3

* * *

It was when he was in the vicinity of Qumran that the young Bedouin boy Jum'a Muhammad Khalil discovered the two openings in the cliff. Since it was in this desert area close to the Dead Sea that he and his cousins often had to keep watch on the family's sheep, he knew the district fairly well. Jum'a Muhammad, who was a curious boy, knew that there had been some archaeological discoveries in the area, so when he saw caves he used to try to get into them to see if he could find any coins. These particular caves he could not remember having seen earlier. The openings were a little above the ground, and they were small, especially the lower one which was only big enough "for a cat to enter." On the off-chance, Jum'a Muhammad threw a stone into this opening. He suddenly heard something smash—the sound was like a clay pot breaking. He excitedly called his two cousins who were close by, Khalil Musa and Muhammad Ahmed el-Hamed (who was called edh-Dhib). After some debating, they came to the conclusion that they wouldn't be able to get through the lower opening, and besides it was getting dark. The three boys decided to make their way home, and return another day.

The next day the boys had to take their sheep to drink at the spring at Ain Feshkha, so they couldn't get back to the cave until two days later. And this time, only one of them went: Muhammad edh-Dib, the youngest boy. He went very early in the morning, while his cousins were still asleep.

Muhammad climbed in through the upper hole, which was just big enough for a thin person to get through. It was dark inside the cave, but when he had become accustomed to the weak daylight that found its way in, he could see about ten pots in the cave, lined up against the walls. Some of them were covered over. There were also lots of bits of broken pottery, because stones had fallen from the ceiling and presumably broken some of the pots.

Now, Muhammad edh-Dib felt really excited. There must be something in those clay vessels. He went up to the pots by the wall, the ones that were still in one piece. And he turned them over.

The feeling with which the young Bedouin boy left the cave that day cannot be called anything but disappointment. All except two of the pots turned out to be empty. One was filled with earth. And the last pot, one of the covered ones, wasn't filled with gold coins either. It contained three rolls of skin, two of which were wrapped in cloths.

A few days later, the older cousin Jum'a Muhammad took the rolls with him to a tent site near Bethlehem. They were hung on a tent pole for weeks—now and then taken down to be looked at. The rolls turned out to be full of strange lettering. When they finally ended up in the shop of a cobbler and antique dealer in Bethlehem called Kando, several of the rolls had been damaged. The year was 1947, and within a few months it was clear that the three Bedouin boys had found the first part of what was to become perhaps the greatest discovery for Bible research in modern times—the so-called Dead Sea scrolls.[10]

Eventually there would be more finds in several caves in the immediate area. The scrolls and fragments that were found turned out to be about two thousand years old and were written on goatskin, papyrus, and even copper. The discovery caused a sensation for many reasons: to start with, the scrolls contained the oldest copies of large sections from the Hebrew bible that have ever been found. All the books were represented, except the Book of Esther. And the researchers were delighted to find that those who had created the Torah and other Bible texts through the centuries had done so with great precision—the texts were virtually identical. Another point was that these were the first contemporary texts that had been found in the area where Jesus lived—a period that also comprised the absolutely final phase of the Jewish realm. And the people who started to interpret the texts in the scrolls were richly rewarded: the texts gave a juicy picture of the religious ideas and traditions that dominated among the Jews during this period, and they found to their surprise that these were incredibly more varied than had previously been understood. Some of the scrolls in Qumran specifically described the lives and ideas of the people who had lived there, close to the caves by the Dead Sea. And although this has begun to be disputed, most researchers are still agreed as to the interpretation that these people were Essenes, or at least a group among the Essenes.

The Essenes had some very special ideas. To start with, they were nearly all men, and they lived more or less like monks. Celibacy was an ideal, and although there were Essenes who did marry and then often lived in a wider area, the kernel of the sect consisted of men who lived entirely without women and in celibacy. They gained new members by adopting children, and by admitting men who were "wearied with the miseries of life," as the Roman historian Pliny the Elder writes.[11] (Philo, however, is quoted with the information that "Accordingly there is among the Essenes no mere child, nor even a scarce-bearded lad, or young man."[12]) The sect, which is believed to have existed approximately between 150 BCE and 70 CE, lived according to very strict and virtually ascetic rules. Death was welcomed, as the Essenes, according to Josephus, considered that "bodies are corruptible, and that the matter they are made of is not permanent; but that the souls are immortal, and continue for ever."[13] But, at the same time, the Essenes had a positive approach to life in other ways: they lay great emphasis on the equal value of all people, slavery was condemned, and everything was jointly owned. Yet it was a group that was fairly hierarchical, and that emphasized obedience and docility:

> *This is the rule for an Assembly of The Congregation: Each man shall sit at his place: the Priests shall sit first, and the elders second, and all the rest of the people according to their rank. . . . No man*

shall interrupt a companion before his speech has ended, nor speak
before a man of higher rank; Each man shall speak in his turn. And
in an Assembly of the Congregation no man shall speak without the
consent of the Congregation. . . . Whoever has interrupted his com-
panion whilst speaking [shall do penance for] *ten days. . . .*
Whoever has murmered against the authority of the Community
shall be expelled and shall not return.

From *"The Community Rule" (the Dead Sea scrolls)* [14]

The Essenes were deliberately isolationist. They were not allowed to eat food prepared by anyone outside the group; and although they clearly and distinctly confessed to Judaism they rejected the leadership at the time in the Temple in Jerusalem.

The Essenes were thus oppositional, in their quiet way, but at a time when opposition was the rule rather than the exception. Today they might appear to be very odd as a Jewish group (not least because they lived in celibacy, something which is not hailed as an ideal, much less a requirement, within any faction of Judaism today), but what the Dead Sea scrolls show us is just how diversified Judaism was before the destruction of the Temple, and perhaps above all during the century when the Romans occupied the area, when everybody felt that a catastrophe was imminent.

Much of the world of ideas of the Essenes was clearly apocalyptical. As has previously been mentioned, the so-called War Scroll describes with a dreadful richness of detail the impending war between good and evil, between the "sons of Light" (themselves) and the "sons of Darkness" (the Romans, but also other Jewish sects). And the Essenes also describe the waiting not only for one but two or three messiahs who shall lead the people towards the new age. Much would indicate that "the new age" does not imply total destruction, but rather a catastrophic series of events that are followed by something new, a liberation.

Almost as soon as experts started studying the newly found scrolls and fragments from Qumran, parallels were drawn to Christianity.

And perhaps above all to John the Baptist, the man who preceded Jesus Christ. Just like the Essenes, John, and sometimes Jesus too, spent time in the desert; just like them, Jesus, and as far as we can judge John too, were not married; their worlds of ideas had quite obvious similarities, and the Essenes also considered themselves to have certain powers and an ability to predict the future. Besides this, the Essenes—just like John the Baptist—seem to have practiced baptism (although for that matter all religious Jews do that, if one regards the cleansing bath in a *mikve* as something resembling a baptism).[15]

It is quite clear that the way of life and the world of ideas of the Essenes are not identical to the way of life and world of ideas of Jesus,[16] but it has been assumed that they could be precursors, and that John the Baptist may have come from their ranks.

So what do we know about John the Baptist? The four gospel authors do accord him an extremely prominent position, and they describe John as an eschatological preacher who lives in the Judean desert. "Repent, for the Kingdom of Heaven is upon you!" is his message, according to the gospel of Matthew. And when Sadducees and Pharisees come to the River Jordan to be baptised by him, his words are harsh: "Vipers' brood! Who warned you to escape from the wrath that is to come? Prove your repentance by the fruit you bear; and do not imagine you can say, 'We have Abraham for our father.'" When the people ask him what they should do, he answers, "Whoever has two shirts must share with him who has none, and whoever has food must do the same."[17]

One of the people who one day comes to John at the River Jordan is Jesus of Nazareth, who now enters the arena, sometime around the year 30 CE. Why does he come to John? The gospels are decidedly taciturn about that point, except in the gospel of Luke where it is suggested that Jesus and John are related.[18] But in a part of the Apocrypha this is discussed more thoroughly. In the gospel according to the Hebrews, which is only preserved in references and quotes from the early church fathers (and which is seen by some as the origin of the gospel of Matthew), one can read the following: "Behold, the mother of our Lord and His brethren said to

Him, John Baptist baptizes for the remission of sins; let us go and be baptized by him. But He said to them, what sin have I committed that I should go and be baptized by him? Unless, haply, the very words which I have said are only ignorance."[19]

Regardless of how it happens, Jesus does make his way to the River Jordan and John the Baptist. And it seems as if the meeting with the preacher by the river is to be decisive. According to the gospel of Matthew (but not Mark or Luke) John tries to dissuade him, saying, "It is I who need to be baptized by you." But the newcomer insists: "Let it be so for the present." He then steps down into the water and John carries out the ritual. It is when Jesus comes up out of the water that something remarkable happens: "The heavens were opened and he saw the Spirit of God descending like a dove to alight on him. And there came a voice from heaven saying, 'This is my beloved Son, in whom I take delight.'"[20] In the form it is here depicted, this experience can only be described as an experience of salvation.

After this meeting, Jesus goes out into "the wilderness," and he stays there for forty days and forty nights, fasting. He is subjected to temptations, but he withstands them. He is taken by the devil to the Temple wall in Jerusalem, where he is challenged to throw himself down in order to prove that he is the son of God. He is taken to a high mountain, and shown "all the kingdoms of the world in all their glory" if he will do homage to the devil. Jesus withstands all this, and then "the devil left him; and the angels came and attended to his needs."[21]

The gospels have very little to say in their descriptions about what happens when Jesus himself starts to preach. But in the synoptic gospels, at any rate, this seems to occur at the same time as the disappearance of John from the scene (in the gospel of John it is implied that both of them carry out baptisms for a while in parallel, and possibly in competition[22]). Why, then, does John disappear? The explanation given in the gospels is that he is imprisoned by the authorities: Herod Antipas, the tetrarch of Galilee and Perea, feels insulted when John expresses criticism of the tetrarch for having taken his brother Philip's wife as his mistress and then having married her.[23]

From his prison, John inquires as to Jesus' new activity, and he has his disciples go to Jesus to ask of him if he is "the one who is to come, or are we to expect someone else?" Jesus tells them to return and tell John about the miracles that he has carried out: "the blind regain their sight, the lame walk, lepers are made clean, the deaf hear, the dead are raised to life, the poor are brought good news." Then he speaks to the people about John, and presents him as his "herald," the one who has prepared the way for him. "I tell you, among all who have been born, no one has been greater than John; yet the least in the kingdom of God is greater than he is."[24] The balancing act between exalting John and yet subordinating him to Jesus is evident in all the gospels.

Eventually, John the Baptist disappears completely from the scene. Not only is he imprisoned, he is eventually executed, too, although it is not clear after how long. According to the gospels, the circumstances are rather macabre—sufficiently so to have fired the imagination through the centuries and given rise to literature as well as paintings and operas. It is told that Herod Antipas' new wife, Herodias, had been greatly enraged by John's accusations of immorality, and because of that had asked her husband to kill him. But Herod Antipas had hesitated, as he "went in awe of him [John], knowing him to be a good and holy man." And this awe increased after the tetrarch had an opportunity to talk to his prisoner.

But one day, Herodias suddenly sees her chance to take revenge: Herod Antipas is going to celebrate his birthday and has invited "his chief officials, and commanders and the leading men of Galilee." As part of the entertainment a dance is to be performed, and it is Herodias' daughter who is going to dance. It is a brilliant performance. Herod Antipas and his guests are so delighted that after the performance he calls his stepdaughter to come to him. "Ask me for anything you like and I will give it to you," he says. "Whatever you ask I will give you, up to half my kingdom." The girl then goes out to speak to her mother, and returns to her stepfather with the following wish: "I want you to give me, here and now, on a dish, the head of John the Baptist." The distressed tetrarch orders a soldier to go to the prison and chop off John's head. The soldier goes on his way, and "then he brought the head on a dish, and gave it to the girl; and she gave it to her mother."[25]

According to the authors of the gospels, then, John the Baptist was such an important person that the ruler of the country felt threatened by him, or at any rate was influenced by his words, and this led him to personally order his execution. The question is: is this apparently influential man, John the Baptist, described in any other relatively contemporary source?

It is interesting to note that Paul never mentions John the Baptist in his letters, although these were written before the gospels (although, later, in the Acts of the Apostles, there is a description of a meeting between Paul and some people who had been given "John's baptism," which he then is said to belittle).[26]

So what about the great contemporary historian, Flavius Josephus?

Actually, some of the course of events *is* described in detail in Josephus' *Antiquities of the Jews*: the story of Herodias and her relations with the two royal brothers is described at length. The daughter of Herodias is mentioned too—and she is given a name: Salome.

What, however, is *not* mentioned is John the Baptist's criticism of the new relationship. But there is another person in Josephus' text who does express this criticism: namely the father of Herod Antipas' first wife, who was called Aretas and was king of Arabia Petraea. Aretas was so angered when his son-in-law wanted to divorce his daughter that he started a war. And this war led to the destruction of Herod Antipas' army. Josephus ends his story with the words, "So Herod wrote about these affairs to [the emperor] Tiberius, who being very angry at the attempt made by Aretas, wrote to Vitellius to make war upon him, and either to take him alive, and bring him to him in bonds, or to kill him, and send him his head."[27]

The criticism that John the Baptist is said to have put forward about the relationship is here actually put forward by Aretas! And it is Aretas' head that is at risk. For the time being, John the Baptist is conspicuous by his absence.

But what is strange is that after the description of the acts of war between Aretas and Herod Antipas, there is the following paragraph in Flavius Josephus' story:

> *Now some of the Jews thought that the destruction of Herod's army came from God, and that very justly, as a punishment of what he did against John, that was called the Baptist: for Herod slew him, who was a good man, and commanded the Jews to exercise virtue, both as to righteousness towards one another, and piety towards God, and so to come to baptism. . . . Now when others came in crowds about him, for they were very greatly moved by hearing his words, Herod, who feared lest the great influence John had over the people might put it into his power and inclination to raise a rebellion (for they seemed ready to do anything he should advise), thought it best, by putting him to death, to prevent any mischief he might cause, and not bring himself into difficulties, by sparing a man who might make him repent of it when it would be too late. Accordingly he was sent a prisoner, out of Herod's suspicious temper, to Macherus, the castle I before mentioned, and was there put to death. Now the Jews had an opinion that the destruction of this army was sent as a punishment upon Herod, and a mark of God's displeasure to him.*[28]

Is this paragraph in *Antiquities of the Jews* really written by Flavius Josephus?

Unlike *Testimonium Flavianum*, which is Josephus' presumed text about Jesus, most people regard this piece about John the Baptist as genuine. There are several reasons for this: the differences between Josephus' text and the gospels are greater than one would expect if it were a Christian interpolation. In other words: if a Christian author had added this text at a later date, it would surely have named Jesus in relation to John the Baptist as well as the story of the dance of Salome and the desire of Herodias that John be beheaded. Another argument in favor of the text being genuine is that Origen refers to it in *Contra Celsum*, written in the third century.[29] Part of the circumstantial evidence against the authenticity of *Testimonium Flavianum* was indeed that Origen did not name this section when he referred to Josephus' text (despite naming the reference to Jesus' brother James).

The problem with Josephus' description of John the Baptist, however, is that it sticks out. When Josephus names similar figures—charismatic Jewish religious leaders who suddenly turn up and gain many supporters—such as "the Egyptian" or Theudas, he is scornful. He calls them "tricksters" and "sorcerers." But with John the Baptist, Josephus has an almost reverential attitude, although for that matter he reacts the same with the Essenes.

Another problem is that John the Baptist turns up from nowhere, and in a single paragraph he is fitted in between the story of how Tiberius orders Vitellius to punish Aretas, and the story of how Vitellius prepares this punishment! Josephus' description would have had a much more natural flow to it if the paragraph about John the Baptist was not included. This single paragraph seems not only to be somewhat out of place, but also far too "sudden." One would expect John the Baptist to have been described earlier in Josephus' text, if he really was so important that the people regarded the outcome of the war as God's punishment for his death. The lack of balance between the person's modest presence in Josephus' text, and the result that his execution has given rise to, is strange.

Yet another problem lies in the chronology. To start with, the section about John the Baptist comes after *Testimonium Flavianum*, that is, the section about Jesus. It ought to be the other way round (although of course it would be possible to explain this, if one considered *Testimonium Flavianum* to be a forgery). What could well be a greater problem, is that the many facts that Josephus provides us with, together with the information in the gospels, also allow us to put a date on the death of John the Baptist. And were one to rely on this information, John's death occurs in the year 36 CE, thus after the crucifixion of Jesus. In 1984, the French scholar Christiane Saulnier published a work in which she put forward a long line of argument that proposed that the wedding between Herodias and Herod Antipas could have taken place as early as between the years 24 and 28 CE, but her reasoning has met with criticism.[30]

In summary, one could say that the section about John the Baptist is regarded by many as being authentic, but there are aspects of it that arouse suspicion. And as in the other two paragraphs that touch upon Jesus in Josephus' work—*Testimonium Flavianum* and the paragraph about James the brother of Jesus—the one about John the Baptist is only found in *Antiquities of the Jews*. In Josephus' other major work that deals with this period, *War of the Jews*, these three people are not mentioned at all.

If we were to assume that the section about John the Baptist was *not* written by Josephus, but is a later interpolation, would that mean that John is not mentioned by Josephus? Bearing in mind how the authors of the gospels consider themselves "obliged" to describe John the Baptist, despite that this risked lessening the importance of Jesus, there is every reason to believe that John existed and probably was fairly well known. One possibility is that he was an important leader among the Essenes, and since Josephus does not specifically name the leaders of the Essenes at this time, perhaps John is "hidden away" in this section.

But there is yet another person in Josephus' books that there is perhaps cause to remember:

> *Now it came to pass, while Fadus was procurator of Judea, that a certain sorcerer, whose name was Theudas, persuaded a great part of the people to take their effects with them, and follow him to the River Jordan; for he told them he was a prophet, and that he would, by his own command, divide the river, and afford them an easy passage over it; and many were deluded by his words. However, Fadus did not permit them to make any advantage of his wild attempt, but sent a troop of horsemen out against them; who, falling upon them unexpectedly, slew many of them, and took many of them alive. They also took Theudas alive, and cut off his head, and carried it to Jerusalem.*[31]

In the above text by Josephus, apart from it being about a charismatic religious leader, there are a further two pieces of information that can make one think of John the Baptist, and one piece of information that contradicts this: it is undoubtedly interesting that Theudas and his supporters were staying by the River Jordan, because John the Baptist did the same. And like John's head, Theudas' head ended up on a platter that was carried in to the leader who had felt threatened by him. What doesn't agree, is this leader's name, Fadus. Fadus was the Roman procurator between the years 44 and 46 CE. Theudas seems, thus, to have been killed about fifteen years after John the Baptist. One should bear in mind that dating is sometimes one of Josephus' weaknesses, particularly when he describes events that took place before his time—sometimes he is even mistaken as to the duration of the reign of a Roman emperor. Yet, were Josephus to be wrong by fifteen years, and name the wrong procurator, that would be a rather serious mistake.

There is, however, a strange little section in the New Testament—in the Acts of the Apostles, to be more precise—that gives rise to certain question marks regarding the dating of Theudas' activities—or, alternatively, the dating of the activities of John and Jesus! In chapter 5 of the Acts of the Apostles there is a description of how a short time after the death of Jesus—i.e., in the early to mid 30s CE—the high priest has Jesus' apostles arrested. They are taken to the council and an interrogation is started, after which the following happens:

> . . . A member of the Council rose to his feet, a Pharisee called
> Gamaliel, a teacher of the law held in high regard by all the people.
> He had the men put outside for a while, and then said, "Men of Is-
> rael, be very careful in deciding what to do with these men. Some
> time ago Theudas came forward, making claims for himself, and a
> number of our people, about four hundred, joined him. But he was
> killed and his whole movement came to nothing. After him came
> Judas the Galilean at the time of the census; he induced some people
> to revolt under his leadership. . ."[32]

This meeting of the council thus took place shortly after the crucifixion of Jesus, which took place about the year 30 (if we are to believe the gospels). And at that time, according to the above text,

Theudas was already dead. Yet according to Josephus, Theudas died around 44–46 CE. So either Josephus gives the wrong date for Theudas' activities, or Luke makes a mistake when he writes that Theudas was dead when Jesus was crucified. Or Jesus was not crucified until after the year 44 CE!

It all becomes even more mysterious when Luke writes that Judas the Galilean came *after* Theudas. Because Judas' revolt started, according to Josephus, as early as the year 6 CE. Here, however, there is possibly a reasonable explanation: directly after Josephus has described Theudas and his death, he tells about the *sons* of Judas from Galilee having been killed, and he then mentions Judas too.[33] And because a number of researchers, having studied their writings, have come to the conclusion that Luke had probably read Josephus, it is possible that Luke inadvertently writes about Judas, instead of the sons of Judas.[34]

So, either Luke has made two mistakes, or Josephus has given the wrong time for the activities of both Theudas and Judas. Or Jesus of Nazareth was crucified much later than we think.

* * *

It is thus not possible to arrive at any certain conclusions as to who John the Baptist was; we can only try to fit the pieces of the puzzle together, as best we can. That John the Baptist was an Essene is perhaps the most attractive alternative. In the gospel of Luke, there is a description of how John, after his birth, "grew up and he became strong in spirit; he lived out in the wilderness until the day when he appeared publicly before Israel."[35] Perhaps John was one of the young boys who were adopted by the Essenes.

But we cannot dismiss the possibility that he was Theudas.

Whatever the circumstances, the meeting with John the Baptist marks the start of the period in Jesus' life that the gospels are really about. This period is short, it is extremely dramatic, and the events that now take place will come to form the foundations of the religion that has its starting point in Jesus of Nazareth: Christianity.

CHAPTER 5

THE PREACHER JESUS

"When he heard that John had been arrested, Jesus withdrew to Galilee," it is written in the gospel of Matthew. And it was in Galilee that Jesus started to preach and gather together disciples.

How long was Jesus active? For how long a time did he journey around with his disciples, performing miracles and preaching the word? It depends on which gospel we read. In the gospel of John, three Passovers are mentioned, and some commentators consider that a fourth can be fitted in between chapters 2 and 6. Using this as our starting point, it would mean that Jesus was active for between just over two and just less than four years. However, if we read the synoptic gospels, this period shrinks to perhaps a single year, or less. And almost all this time is spent in the Galilee of Herod Antipas.

The fate of Galilee differs partly from that of Judea. When the Romans in the year 6 CE throw Archelaus out of Judea, and replace him with a Roman prefect, his younger brother Herod Antipas still remains tetrarch of Galilee. In other words, during Jesus' time Galilee retains greater autonomy than Judea—albeit under Roman suzerainty.

The population of Galilee, like that of Judea, was at this time for the greater part Jewish. There were indeed groups of Greeks, Romans, and other non-Jewish peoples here, often concentrated in certain areas, but most of what we know—archaeological finds as well as Josephus' texts—suggests that non-Jews comprised a minority in Galilee.[1] Certain adjacent areas, such as Decapolis, the union of ten states that lay to the east of Galilee, were dominated by a non-Jewish population, however.

"The Galileans are inured to war from their infancy," writes Josephus, "and have always been very numerous; nor hath the country been ever destitute of men of courage, or wanted a numerous set of them; for their soil is universally rich and fruitful, and full of the plantations of trees of all sorts, insomuch that it invites the most slothful to take pains in its cultivation, by its fruitfulness; accordingly, it is all cultivated by its inhabitants, and no part of it lies idle."[2]

The most important towns in Galilee at this time are Sepphoris and Tiberias.[3] But according to Josephus, even the very smallest villages "contain above fifteen thousand inhabitants" (surely one of his many exaggerations).[4] Josephus mentions Capernaum—according to the gospel writers, one of the places at which Jesus stayed—and he calls it a "village."[5] He does not, however, mention Nazareth at all. The difficulty in finding Nazareth in early sources other than the New Testament is something that has long puzzled researchers. As Jack Finegan writes, "In the Old Testament Jos. 19:10–15 gives a list of the towns of the tribe of Zebulon . . . but does not mention Nazareth. Josephus, who was responsible for military operations in this area in the Jewish War . . . gives the names of forty-five towns in Galilee, but does not say anything about Nazareth. The Talmud also, although it refers to sixty-three Galilean towns, does not mention Nazareth."[6] The first time the name Nazareth turns up outside Christian sources is on a marble inscription that has been found in a synagogue in Caesarea, dating from about the year 300 CE.

Nevertheless, there are archaeological finds in Nazareth, and some of them date back to Roman times. The area was clearly inhabited, but the village's (it can hardly have been much more than a village) local importance must have been very limited indeed.

"He came to Nazareth where he had been brought up," one can read in Luke, "and went to the synagogue on the sabbath day as he regularly did." So after John the Baptist is imprisoned, Jesus sets off in the direction of home and, as far as we can tell, returns to his home village of Nazareth. When one reads the gospels, one gets the impression that Jesus has not been home for a very long time. But his return is not a success.

When Jesus goes into the synagogue, people seem at first to be uncertain who he is. But he stands up and starts to read from the Book of Isaiah: "He has sent me to announce good news to the poor, to proclaim release for prisoners and recovery of sight for the blind; to let the broken victims go free." Following which Jesus explains that this text has now been fulfilled. According to the gospel of Luke, people in the synagogue now begin to cheer. But then somebody asks: "Is not this Joseph's son?" Jesus' tone is now radically changed: "Truly I tell you, no prophet is recognized in his own country," he says, and then goes on to describe how earlier prophets have only been able to help strangers:

> There were indeed many widows in Israel in Elijah's time, when for three and a half years the skies never opened, and famine lay hard over the whole country; yet it was to none of these that Elijah was sent, but to a widow at Sarepta in the territory of Sidon. Again in the time of the prophet Elisha there were many lepers in Israel, and not one of them was healed, but only Naaman, the Syrian.

"These words roused the whole congregation to fury," writes Luke, "they leapt up, drove him out of the town, and took him to the brow of the hill on which it was built, meaning to hurl him over the edge. But he walked straight through the whole crowd, and went away."[7]

Jesus has tried to return home, as someone born anew, as a healer and helper. And he is brusquely rejected. This rejection by his home village is described in all the gospels, although at different stages. The gospels also describe his reception by his own family, above all after he starts to perform miracles: "When his family heard about it, they set out to take charge of him," writes Mark. "'He is out of his mind,' they said." This is followed by a description of how the scribes who have come down from Jerusalem accuse Jesus of being "possessed by Beelzebul." Jesus speaks to them, and meanwhile his family turns up: "They stayed outside and sent in a message asking him to come out to them. A crowd was sitting round him when word was brought that his mother and brothers were outside asking for him. 'Who are my mother and my brothers?' he replied. And looking round at those who were sitting in the circle about him, he said, 'Here are my mother and my brothers. Whoever does the will of God is my brother and sister and mother.'"[8]

This rejection of his own family in favor of his disciples and supporters is described in all the gospels.[9] It is very clear that Jesus replaces his family with disciples, and that he makes the equivalent absolutely inexorable demands on his disciples. This is particularly clear in the following famous section in the gospel of Matthew:

Whoever will acknowledge me before others, I will acknowledge before my Father in heaven; and whoever disowns me before others, I will disown before my Father in heaven. You must not think I have come to bring peace to the earth; I have not come to bring peace, but a sword. I have come to set a man against his father, a daughter against her mother, a daughter-in-law against her mother-in-law; and a man will find his enemies under his own roof. No one is worthy of me who cares more for father or mother than for me; no one is worthy of me who cares more for son or daughter; no one is worthy of me who does not take up his cross and follow me. Whoever gains his life will lose it; and whoever loses his life for my sake will gain it.[10]

Or the even more radical lines in the gospel of Luke:

*If anyone comes to me and does not hate his father and mother, wife
and children, brothers and sisters, even his own life, he cannot be a
disciple of mine.*[11]

The demands are evidently very severe, and yet they are essentially
rather like those that John the Baptist, or the Essenes, made. It is an
asceticism which borders upon mercilessness, and demands upon
obedience and servility that in our eyes seem cult-like. But they are
typical for many of the radical movements that came into being in
Judea and Galilee at that time. People were looking for an answer
to the catastrophe that was approaching, and spiritual leaders
placed increasingly hard demands upon themselves and their supporters in order to be able to conquer fate. (And although it is a
subject of debate just to what degree Jesus actually inherited this eschatological way of thinking,[12] he was in many respects typical of
his time.) He turned to the Jews in his own country ("I was sent to
the lost sheep of the house of Israel, and to them alone"), and he
proclaimed that a new era would come for this people: "The time
has arrived; the kingdom of God is upon you." That he chose
twelve disciples would also have a symbolic meaning for the people of Israel. "Truly I tell you: in the world that is to be, when the
Son of Man is seated on his glorious throne, you also will sit on
twelve thrones, judging the twelve tribes of Israel."[13]

Jesus thus tempted his disciples with the promise that in
exchange for total loyalty and devotion, they would be given a su-
perior place in the coming realm. But if we think that Jesus shows
a hardness or ruthlessness in the absolute demand for obedience,
this contrasts sharply with his message to all the people he meets:
You no longer need to follow the religious laws in every detail, you
are all welcome in God's fold regardless of how you have lived or
your position in society, and you are all forgiven your sins. Just as
long as you follow me.

As Sanders writes: "From the point of view of his followers
and sympathizers he offered an immediate and direct route to God's
love and mercy . . . He did not say to potential followers, 'Study with

me six hours each week, and within six years I shall teach you the true interpretation of the law.' He said, in effect: 'Give up everything you have and follow me, because I am God's agent."' [14]

At the same time, Jesus is not an opponent of the Jewish law. "Do not suppose I have come to abolish the law and the prophets," he says in the Sermon on the Mount. "I did not come to abolish, but to complete." [15] But he is clearly antagonistic, almost fanatical, towards the scribes who represent the more established Judaism—the Pharisees and the Sadducees—and he accuses them of exaggerated literalism (see, for example, the story of when the disciples pick ears of corn on the Sabbath [16]).

In fact, only in one regard is Jesus decidedly stricter than the Jewish law: when it comes to divorce. While the Jewish law allows divorce (at least if the man wants it), Jesus forbids this: "What God has joined together, man must not separate." It does, admittedly, say at one point in the gospel of Matthew that "if a man divorces his wife for any cause other than unchastity, and marries another, he commits adultery," but this exception for "unchastity" is not included in the gospel of Mark, which was written earlier. When some Pharisees ask why then Moses allowed divorce, Jesus answers: "It was because of your stubbornness that Moses gave you permission to divorce your wives." [17]

One may well ask why, if other laws are to be made more palatable, this particular one should be tightened up. We can only speculate on the reason. One possibility, of course, is that Jesus has adopted the strict attitudes towards sexuality and marriage that the Essenes, and perhaps John the Baptist too, applied. Another possibility is that he speaks from experience, on the basis of something that has affected his own life.

How does Jesus find his disciples? When he is so brusquely rejected by his home village (or possibly even earlier), Jesus makes his way to Capernaum by Lake Galilee. And he shall stay in the vicinity of this lake for the near future. One day he goes out on a walk: "Jesus was walking by the sea of Galilee when he saw two brothers, Simon called Peter and his brother Andrew, casting a net into the lake; for they were fishermen. Jesus said to them, 'Come with me, and I will make you fishers of men.' At once they left their nets and followed him." Later, on the same walk, he picks up two more disciples, the brothers James and John, fishermen too. These two worked with their father, Zebedee, but "at once they left the boat and their father, and followed him."[18] Jesus is evidently a very charismatic person, who alienates some people, attracts others, but leaves nobody unaffected. The gospels differ in their description of how Jesus gathers his closest disciples around him, but they do agree as to the final number: twelve. Twelve, like the number of Israel's tribes. And together they shall create the new Israel.

This was when Jesus' proper period of preaching started. He was a master at parables and metaphors, and to present his message he used metaphors from nature, the family, and society. When the disciples ask Jesus why he uses parables, he answers them, according to Matthew 13:10–14, in the following way:

"To you it has been granted to know the secrets of the kingdom of Heaven, but not to them. For those who have will be given more, till they have enough and to spare; and those who have not, will forfeit even what they have. That is why I speak to them in parables, for they look without seeing, and listen without hearing or understanding. The prophecy of Isaiah is being fulfilled in them: 'You may listen and listen, but you will never understand . . .'"

The above quote includes interesting information indeed. Because Jesus not only tells the disciples that the parables are necessary to make people understand his message. He is also saying that there is information, perhaps included in the parables, that ordinary people will never understand, that there are hidden messages, messages that only those who "know the secrets of the kingdom of Heaven" will grasp. This is strengthened by the following exchange, from Mark 8:15–21. Jesus has told the disciples to "be on your guard against the leaven of the Pharisees and the leaven of Herod." The disciples respond that they don't have any bread. Jesus then says:

"Why are you talking about having no bread? Have you no inkling yet? Do you still not understand? Are your minds closed? You have eyes. Can you not see? You have ears: can you not hear? Have you forgotten? When I broke the five loaves among five thousand, how many basketfuls of pieces did you pick up?" "Twelve," they said. "And how many when I broke the seven loaves among four thousand?" "Seven," they answered. He said to them, "Do you still not understand?"

What Jesus, in fact, is saying here, is that the obvious meaning of what he pronounces is not always the full meaning; there are several layers of interpretations to be made. This is, perhaps, something for Bible scholars to keep in mind.

But Jesus could also be direct and extremely clear. For the people who heard him list the "blessed" in the Sermon on the Mount—especially for those who felt themselves to be outsiders, to be belittled or helpless—this message must have been irresistible: "Blessed are the poor in spirit; the kingdom of Heaven is theirs. Blessed are the sorrowful; they shall find consolation. Blessed are the gentle; they shall have the earth for their possession." At the same time, he asks his listeners to treat their fellow humans with the same love and empathy that he offers them: "If someone in authority presses you into service for one mile, go with him two. Give to anyone who asks; and do not turn your back on anyone who wants to borrow." [19]

Praise and blame. Carrot and whip. Jesus offers total love, but he also makes total demands.

During the following year, Jesus and his disciples journey about in Galilee, "teaching in the synagogues, proclaiming the good news of the kingdom, and healing every kind of illness and infirmity among the people." The period where Jesus is a healer has now begun too. Where he learned to cure sickness and carry out other miracles is not told in the gospel texts. Nothing is said about him having learned this from John the Baptist. Yet it is apparent that very shortly after his return to Galilee, he starts to perform miracles. And he is successful, except in one place—in his home town of Nazareth:

"And he was unable to do any miracle there, except that he put his hands on a few sick people and healed them; and he was astonished at their want of faith."[20]

The miracles do seem in part to be a means for Jesus to prove his relation to God, something that he clearly expresses before the messengers sent out by John the Baptist (although he often refuses to carry out miracles when asked to). But these miracles do not seem to be the real purpose of his activities. The purpose is to "proclaim the good news of the kingdom," and to ask people to follow him. The miracles are a way of getting there—he can use them to help, he can use them to prove his power.

What then are these miracles? Jesus cures illnesses and drives out evil spirits. He calms storms and walks on water. He feeds five thousand men in the wilderness with just five loaves and two fishes.

But perhaps the most remarkable of his miracles occur on three occasions: bringing the dead to life. This is something that, it seems, he gets better and better at—or at least all the more convincing—each time he does it. Surprisingly, these three different incidents are described in different gospels. In the synoptic gospels we can read of a head of a synagogue whose young daughter has just died. Jesus goes to his home, and says: "The child is not dead: she is asleep." Then he takes her hand, and she gets up.[21] In the gospel of Luke, it is told how Jesus meets a widow in Nain, whose only son has just died. Jesus goes up to the bier and lays his hand on it. Then he says: "Young man, I tell you to get up." Then the dead man sits up and starts to speak.[22] But it is in the gospel of John that the last, and the most famous, of these "bringing the dead to life" miracles is described.[23] This takes place shortly before Jesus makes his entry into Jerusalem for his last week. And in this instance, the dead person who is to be brought back to life is already in his grave.

Jesus had returned to the River Jordan, to the place where he was first baptized by John. One day a message comes to him from dear friends, the sisters Mary and Martha who live in the village of Bethany, close to Jerusalem: their brother, Lazarus, also a friend of Jesus, is severely ill. The reaction of Jesus is completely atypical: "This illness is not to end in death," he answers, and

remains by the River Jordan. The writer of the gospel now emphasizes yet again just how fond Jesus is of the brother and his sisters,
as if to make quite certain that the reader understands just how remarkable it is that Jesus does not immediately set off to Bethany. He
stays by the River Jordan for two days, then he says to his disciples: "Let us go back to Judea." The disciples warn him and say that
he risks being stoned by the Jews (in the gospel of John, Jesus has
only shortly before this visited the Temple in Jerusalem, and there
been threatened by Jews who want to stone him). Jesus answers
that "anyone can walk in the daytime without stumbling, because
he has this world's light to see by." And then he explains the purpose of the journey: "Our friend Lazarus has fallen asleep, but I
shall go and wake him." The disciples answer of course: "Master, if
he is sleeping, he will recover." But now Jesus makes it clearer:
"Lazarus is dead." Then he says something mysterious: "I am glad
for your sake that I was not there, so that you may believe." The
only reasonable interpretation is that Jesus means that he has deliberately let Lazarus die, so that he can then bring him back to life,
and thereby make his disciples "believe."

Getting his disciples to "believe" in him has been shown to
have been a greater problem than Jesus had anticipated. Especially
in the gospel of Mark, it is clear that the disciples are often not particularly impressed by his miracles, or do not understand them, although the people around can be overwhelmed.[24] It is paradoxical,
because he does actually teach the disciples to perform miracles. Yet
evidently he must, at regular intervals, try to prove his capacity to
them, and perhaps to a wider circle. Succeeding in bringing Lazarus
back to life is, perhaps, a way for Jesus to prove that he is the person he says he is.

Now Jesus sets off with his disciples to Bethany. When they
finally arrive, they are told that Lazarus has been in his grave four
days already. Martha meets Jesus on the road and says to him:
"Lord, if you had been here my brother would not have died," upon
which Jesus answers her: "I am the resurrection and the life. Whoever has faith in me shall live, even though he dies; and no one
who lives and has faith in me shall ever die. Do you believe this?"

Jesus has raised the stakes higher than ever before. And in exchange for faith in him, he is offering eternal life. And indeed, Martha answers him: "I do Lord; I believe that you are the Messiah, the Son of God who was to come into the world."

Martha then goes home and tells her sister Mary that Jesus has arrived. Jesus stays outside the village and waits for Mary to come. When she does arrive, she too starts to accuse Jesus of letting her brother die. She throws herself down at his feet and weeps, and all the people around them weep too. Jesus weeps as well. "The Jews [yet again, one cannot but be surprised at the use of the word 'Jews' in an environment where almost everyone is a Jew] said: 'How dearly he must have loved him!' But some of them said, 'Could not this man, who opened the blind man's eyes, have done something to keep Lazarus from dying?'"

Jesus becomes upset, and goes to the tomb, "a cave, with a stone placed against it." He then says: "Take away the stone." Martha protests, and says that four days have passed and that there "will be a stench," but Jesus insists: "Did I not tell you that if you have faith you will see the glory of God?" The stone is removed, and Jesus looks upwards and thanks his Father: "I know that you always hear me, but I have spoken for the sake of the people standing around, that they may believe it was you who sent me." Yet again, Jesus expresses clearly and unambiguously that the purpose of the imminent miracle is to get the people around him to believe in him. Then he calls out: "Lazarus, come out."

Out from the tomb steps Lazarus, "his hands and feet bound with linen bandages, his face wrapped in a cloth." Jesus now says to those standing around that they shall free Lazarus from his wrappings so that he can walk. "Many of the Jews who had come to visit Mary, and had seen what Jesus did, put their faith in him." That is what it says in the gospel of John.

The situation is so like that which is to take place a short time later, with Jesus himself as the protagonist, that one could almost call it a full-dress rehearsal.

* * *

The resurrection of Lazarus is also at the center of one of the most controversial discoveries—if it actually is a discovery—with regard to texts about Jesus:

In the spring of 1958, a forty-three-year-old historian from Columbia University, a man named Morton Smith, found himself in the Kidron Valley near Jerusalem. Smith had been invited to the Greek Orthodox Mar Saba Monastery, built on one of the dramatic cliff walls in the valley, to catalogue the monastery's manuscripts.

Mar Saba was founded almost sixteen hundred years ago, and it is still one of the world's oldest monasteries still working. Today there are only ten or so monks in the valley, but from the very beginning about four thousand lived here. And the monastery library had, over the centuries, been filled with letters and manuscripts. Smith, who had visited the monastery as early as the 1940s, was enthusiastic about his new task.

However, after a few weeks of reading, the scholar's initial enthusiasm had been replaced by fatigue. Many of the manuscripts were indeed old, but they did not contain anything sensational. What had started off as a rather fast reading pace now became somewhat leisurely. But one day, Smith picks up a printed work, an edition from 1646 of a book by Isaac Voss, with the title *Epistolae genuinae S.Ignatii Martyris*. He turns the pages of the book furtively, and comes to the empty end pages. But to his surprise he discovers that they are not at all empty.

> . . . *One afternoon near the end of my stay, I found myself in my cell, staring incredulously at a text written in a tiny scrawl. . . . If this writing was what it claimed to be, I had a hitherto unknown text by a writer of major significance for early church history.*[25]

What was written down on these end pages was a letter, or rather a copy of a letter. And the author of the original was, at least according to this copy, one of the most important church fathers, Clement of Alexandria. Clement, who lived approximately between 150 and 215 CE, was a forerunner within Christian mysticism and he was Origen's teacher.

But what was even more astonishing than the author's name was the content of the letter. It was so amazing that when it was published for the general public, fifteen years later, Morton Smith was immediately accused of having found—or himself written—a forgery.[26]

The letter from Clement was directed to a person by the name of Theodore, and was an answer to a letter from him. Theodore had a problem, because he had heard from a group of "heretical" Christians who called themselves Carpocratians—and whose religious practices included sexual rites—that they based their beliefs on a secret version of the gospel of Mark. Because they claimed that this secret gospel of Mark had its origins in Alexandria, Theodore was now turning to Clement to ask him if he had heard mention of any such thing. Clement, in his answer to Theodore, expresses disgust for the Carpocratians but he does confirm that there actually is an alternative version of the gospel of Mark, a more "spiritual" gospel, intended only for those Christians who sought "perfection." This version, writes Clement, was handed over to the Church in Alexandria by Mark—and the Carpocratians had managed to get hold of it and had distorted it.

Because Clement evidently considers that Theodore is one of the people who have shown themselves worthy to receive the content of this more "spiritual" gospel, he continues the letter with two quotes from the gospel—one very short, the other considerably longer. He claims that the longer quote should be fitted in between verses 34 and 35 in chapter 10 of the known gospel of Mark. And if one reads this quote, one immediately realizes that it is a new version of the story of the resurrection of Lazarus, a story that up until then had only been present in the gospel of John. But this "new" version gives details that were definitely not in the gospel of John:

They came to Bethany. There was one woman there whose brother had died. She came and prostrated herself before Jesus and spoke to him. "Son of David, pity me!" But the disciples rebuked her. Jesus was angry and went with her into the garden where the tomb was. Immediately a great cry was heard from the tomb. And going up to it, Jesus rolled the stone away from the door of the tomb, and immediately went in where the young man was. Stretching out his hand, he lifted him up, taking hold of his hand. And the youth, looking intently at him, loved him and started begging him to let him remain with him. And going out of the tomb, they went into the house of the youth, for he was rich. And after six days Jesus gave him an order and, at evening, the young man came to him wearing nothing but a linen cloth. And he stayed with him for the night, because Jesus taught him the mystery of the Kingdom of God. And then when he left him he went back to the other side of the Jordan.

As mentioned previously, it took fifteen years before Smith's find—or forgery—became known to most Bible researchers. He had presented it at a congress as early as 1960, but it was not until 1966 that Morton Smith finished his first book on the subject, *Clement of Alexandria and a Secret Gospel of Mark*, and several more years passed before this found a publisher. But it was only when a slimmer and more popularly written book, *The Secret Gospel*, was published in 1973 that the discussion, or rather battle, suddenly flared up.[27]

What Morton Smith claimed to have found became for many people the "evidence" to confirm what many had suspected: that people they had intuitively connected with each other—Lazarus in the gospel of John, the young man in the linen cloth in the gospel of Mark, "the disciple he [Jesus] loved" (who is only mentioned in the gospel of John), and the "rich man" who is mentioned in several gospels—were indeed one and the same person.[28] With the "secret gospel of Mark" this seemed to be confirmed. And in the "new" text there was also a suggestion that Jesus had used mystical, possibly sexual, rites in his religious practices, something that Smith himself emphasizes in his interpretation of the text.[29]

The problem is only that the find is a little too neat to be true—and a little too "constructed" to be credible.

Smith, who was a respected scholar at Columbia University, was thus accused of having published a forgery. The problem for Smith was that although he had photographed the hand-written text he had found in the book by Voss, and published these photographs, the actual pages in the book had since then disappeared. It was said that the monks at the Mar Saba Monastery had ripped the pages out of the book to be able to keep them in a safe place, and now they couldn't be found.

But nor was it an original that Smith claimed to have found, but a copy made after 1646. And because there are several stages here—from the secret gospel to Clement, from Clement's letter to the person who copied the letter, from the copied letter to Morton Smith—it is probable that there never actually was any "secret gospel of Mark."

The discussion about the "secret gospel of Mark" continues to this day, more than ten years after Smith's death. What makes Smith's supposed "discovery" so appealing is that he manages, among other things, to link together a number of clues and of these create a unified picture. The gospels, and the Acts of the Apostles too, are full of small cul-de-sacs—evidently important people who turn up from nowhere, only to disappear again just as quickly. Lazarus is one of them. He appears in chapter 11 of the gospel of John, as somebody whom Jesus "loved dearly." Yet we have never heard of him before, and after they meet again in Bethany in chapter 12, a short while after Lazarus has been resurrected from the dead, we will never hear of him again.[30] In the next chapter, instead a new—evidently very important—person appears for the first time: "the disciple he [Jesus] loved." And he will stay around until the end of the gospel of John.[31] It is very easy to imagine that these two, Lazarus and the beloved disciple, are really the same person. In the same way, it is easy to come to such a conclusion with regard to the man in the linen cloth in Gethsemane and the disciple that Jesus loved: Since the gospel of Mark tells us that only one person among those closest to Jesus stayed behind when he was arrested, namely the young man with the linen cloth, and the gospel of John only tells of one disciple by the cross, the disciple whom Jesus loved, there has been much speculation about these two being one and the same person.[32] Perhaps it was so that for somebody in the seventeenth century, or somebody in the twentieth century, the temptation to confirm this was simply too great to withstand.

It is as if the gospel writers are playing with words; they give different individuals similar names or provide them with similar qualities, and it is up to the reader to try to draw conclusions from this. Such is the case with the many women who go by the name of Mary. Mary, or Miriam, was hardly a common name among Jews (at least if we are to judge by the occurrence of the name in the Old Testament and the Talmud). Yet Jesus surrounds himself with an abundance of Marys: Mary the mother of Jesus, Mary Magdalene, Mary the sister of Lazarus, Mary the mother of James and Joseph, the "other" Mary, Mary wife of Clopas, Mary the mother of John who was called Mark. And they all seem to have had a very close relation to Jesus or his disciples.

Who then are all these women with the same name? Let us begin with Mary "of Magdala." She is named for the first time in the following verses in the gospel of Luke:

> *After this he went journeying from town to town and village to village, proclaiming the good news of the kingdom of God. With him were the Twelve and a number of women who had been set free from evil spirits and infirmities: Mary, known as Mary of Magdala, from whom seven demons had come out, Joanna, the wife of Chuza, a steward of Herod's, Susanna, and many others. These women provided for them out of their own resources.*[33]

This woman, Mary Magdalene as she is also called, will come to be given an increasingly prominent place the longer the tale goes on, and also the more time passes after the writing down of the gospels. Mary Magdalene has often been regarded as the only woman that Jesus let get really close to him. There is a tradition in the Catholic Church, an idea that turns up as early as the third century, that she is identical with the "woman who was living an immoral life" who is mentioned in the previous chapter, a woman who kisses and anoints Jesus' feet, and thus "her many sins have been forgiven."[34] Pope Gregory I actually preached a sermon in the year 591 in which he identified Mary Magdalene not only with the "immoral" woman mentioned above, but also with Lazarus' sister, Mary.

Two of the Marys thus become one. And the circle can possibly be made even smaller: there is a theory that Mary Magdalene is identical with Mary, the mother of Jesus. To a certain extent this goes back to the Talmud texts we have already read, the lines that state that ben Pantera's mother was called *Miriam megaddela neshaia*.

Using modern psychology, one could perhaps speculate that one aspect of Mary becomes the madonna, the virgin, and the other the "immoral" woman.

The above verses from the gospel of Luke are of interest also for the way they shed light upon the company Jesus kept. Jesus surrounded himself with a number of different people. Which of them are disciples? There are evidently different levels. The very closest to Jesus are "the Twelve," the closest disciples (who are called apostles in the Acts of the Apostles), four of whom—Simon Peter, Andrew, James, and John—seem to be most close to him. But outside this circle, there are a large number—Paul refers to the "five hundred brothers" that the resurrected Jesus shows himself to. And when we read about how Jesus feeds "five thousand men" with five loaves and two fishes, these are evidently men who have followed Jesus to the "wilderness." Later he feeds "four thousand men" with seven loaves and some fishes, yet again in the wilderness.[35] The body of followers is evidently considerably larger than is often implied (and it can be worth remembering the word "wilderness," *ereimos* in Greek; it will come again into our story, as will the figure "four thousand").

As far as we can judge, Jesus and the disciples lived in a mainly male environment. In the gospel of John it is written, "At that moment his disciples returned, and were astonished to find him talking with a woman."[36] Perhaps Jesus did not communicate so often

with women, and he was not married (though this does not necessarily apply to his disciples[37]). Living in celibacy, or being an unmarried adult man, was certainly unusual in that environment. Yet
it does not have to be so strange if one sees it from the perspective
of, for example, the Essenes. Despite the fact that within the more
traditional Judaism marriage was regarded as something that was
absolutely desirable, and that today we do not know of any Jewish denominations that preach celibacy, there were in the time of
Jesus small Jewish groups that to a great extent were of a single sex
(i.e., male). It is possible that Jesus was influenced by them.

But at the same time, it is evident from the above lines that
there were women around Jesus, even though they were unable to
become disciples (and the disciples' astonishment at finding him
"talking with a woman" could be connected with the fact that the
woman in question was a Samaritan). Some of the women around
Jesus will also come to follow him on his last journey to Jerusalem,
and stay with him to the end.[38] It would seem that the women, to
a certain extent, supported Jesus and his disciples—"provided for
them out of their own resources," as it says in the gospel of Luke.

Whatever the circumstances, Jesus does seem to show
women great respect. And in the same way that he shows love toward the poor and the ill, he shows it too toward the women that
society otherwise despises most of all: "immoral women."[39]

Thus passes the year—or the years—as Jesus journeys around in
Galilee with his disciples, preaching the kingdom of God and carrying out miracles. He mostly avoids large towns, keeping to villages and rural areas. Jesus seems to meet with success and gather
many people around him, although he often comes into conflict
with "Pharisees and Sadducees," and it is even written that "the
Pharisees . . . began plotting . . . to bring about Jesus' death."[40]

Then one day Jesus decides to leave Galilee, and to make
his way to Judea and to the most holy town of Judaism, Jerusalem.
But before that, he starts to make predictions, predictions about his
own fate, predictions about his own death: "The Son of Man had
to endure great suffering, and to be rejected by the elders, chief

priests, and scribes; to be put to death, and to rise again three days afterwards."[41]

Why, one might wonder, does Jesus finally decide to make his entry into the city of Jerusalem, for what can only be interpreted as his ultimate clash with the Jewish establishment? If one is to believe the gospel of Luke, there is only one reason: "it is unthinkable for a prophet to meet his death anywhere but in Jerusalem."[42]

CHAPTER 6

ENTERING JERUSALEM

They were now approaching Jerusalem, and when they reached Beth-
phage and Bethany, close by the Mount of Olives, he sent off two of
his disciples. "Go into the village opposite," he told them, "and just as
you enter you will find tethered there a colt which no one has yet rid-
den. Untie it and bring it here. If anyone asks why you are doing this,
say, 'The Master needs it, and will send it back here without delay.'" [1]

Jerusalem is situated high up on a limestone plateau, at an altitude
of about 2,600 feet. The town seems in many ways to be out of
place—without contact with water, and at the edge of the desert. But
as a spiritual focal point one could hardly imagine a more apt site.
In the west lie the mountains of Judea, which seem to lead like a
staircase up to the holy city. Eastward lies the desert, which when it
reaches the Dead Sea after eighteen miles has sunk down to 1,300
feet below sea level. Seen from a distance, the town with its Temple
looks like a "snow-covered mountain glistening in the sun," as Josephus wrote. It is not hard to understand why the cliff that King
David, according to the Bible, bought from a Jebusite inspired his son
Solomon to build a temple here—or why legend places the Garden
of Eden in the vicinity of Jerusalem. The place and its surrounding

natural landscape fire our imagination. Besides, Jerusalem was an extremely well-chosen capital city from a military perspective. It was really only possible to approach the place from one direction. In the east, west, and south, deep ravines cut it off. And the thick walls made Jerusalem even more impregnable.

"By far the most famous city, not of *Judæa* only, but of the East." Thus the Roman historian Pliny the Elder described Jerusalem during Roman times.[2] After the Jews had returned from their Babylonian exile, around the year 538 BCE, much had happened. The town, which was destroyed by King Nebuchadnezzar fifty years earlier, had admittedly been reconstructed directly after the return, and eventually the Temple was too. But it was the despised King Herod, the Romans' vassal king, who, during the last decades, had restored Jerusalem to its former glory—or more. He built palaces and citadels, he built monuments and viaducts. And he extended and restored the Temple to—it was said—the same magnificence that King Solomon's Temple once had. All because the vassal king hoped that he would finally be accepted by his Jewish subjects.

The view from the Mount of Olives, straight across the Kidron Valley, was dominated by Herod's impressive Temple. It stood in the middle of a large platform, built up around the original cliff. Nobody knows for certain, but presumably it was the top of this cliff that was the "holy of holies," the part of the temple that only the high priest could visit, and only once a year.

In general, there were very strict rules about who could visit the various parts of the Temple, and when. There were several gates and courtyards, some that women could visit, others where only priests were let in, again others where non-Jews could come in. In one part of the Temple Mount, animals were sold to be sacrificed—lambs, goats, cows, doves—and that was where one also found the people who changed money. Every adult Jewish man was obliged to pay half a shekel every year in Temple tax, during the month of Adar.

On the Temple Mount there was another very important place, *Lishkat Ha-Gazith*, or the "hall of hewn stones." This is where the Jewish Supreme Council, the Great Sanhedrin, met. One theory is that during the period of the second Temple there were two different Sanhedrins: one that concerned itself solely with religious affairs—if so, it would have been this one that met in *Lishkat Ha-Gazith*—and one that functioned as the Jews' highest civil court, but which was also a political organ within the areas where the Romans allowed self-government. In that way, the Sanhedrin (at least in its political functions) in those days partly did the business of the Romans, and for that reason was regarded with a certain degree of suspicion by the population. During the time preceding the fall of Jerusalem, the Sanhedrin was probably dominated by Sadducees and the high priest was its chairman. There is however much to indicate that the religious power to a great degree lay with the Pharisees, and it is possible that a separate religious Sanhedrin was led by Pharisee sages.[3]

The high priest was thus perhaps primarily a political and administrative leader. During the years 6–15 CE, this high priest is called Annas. And in the year 18 CE the same position is shouldered by Caiaphas (possibly Annas' son-in-law) who retains the post until the year 36 CE, when he is dismissed by the Roman governor in Syria (incidentally the same year that Pontius Pilate is dismissed as prefect of Iudaea).

* * *

The Passover festivities are not far off on the day that Jesus comes to Jerusalem with his disciples. And it is surely no coincidence that he has chosen to make his entry into the holy city precisely at Passover.

To start with, this is the time of the year when Jews from all over the country go on a pilgrimage to Jerusalem. Jesus himself is said to have come there as a twelve-year-old during Passover, too. In *War of the Jews*, Flavius Josephus describes the "vast multitude" that gathers around the temple during this festivity to make sacrifices, and then to eat: "the number of sacrifices [lambs] was two hundred and fifty-six thousand five hundred; which, upon the allowance of no more than ten that feast together, amounts to two millions seven hundred thousand and two hundred persons [sic] that were pure and holy; for as to those that have the leprosy, or the gonorrhea, or women that have their monthly courses, or such as are otherwise polluted; it is not lawful for them to be partakers of this sacrifice; nor indeed for any foreigner neither, who come hither to worship."[4] In another place, Josephus says that the Jews in Jerusalem at that time of the year are "not fewer in number than three millions."[5] This is considered to be one of the instances where Josephus exaggerates, and a more moderate estimate would be somewhere between 300,000 and 400,000 people.[6] Tacitus, the Roman historian, in his turn writes that "I have heard that the total number of the besieged, of every age and both sexes, amounted to six hundred thousand," when the Romans attacked Jerusalem in the year 70 CE.[7] On that occasion too, it was Passover. And this is probably no coincidence either: Passover is the time of the year when there is the greatest risk that the Jews shall rebel. This is not only on account of the masses of people, but also because of the symbolic content of Passover—the festivity is celebrated in memory of the Exodus out of Egypt under the leadership of Moses, and the liberation from slavery under the pharaoh. In order to counter any possible attempts at rebellion, the Roman prefect often sent extra troops to the city during the Passover week.

In this we probably also find a reason for Jesus' choosing this particular time for his entry: the gospels have already linked Jesus and Moses, and bearing in mind that Jesus presents himself as the one who is going to lead the Jewish people in the coming realm, the kingdom of God, the choice of Passover is deeply symbolic. As is the way in which he makes his entry:

> *Daughter of Zion, rejoice with all your heart;*
> *shout in triumph, daughter of Jerusalem!*
> *See your king is coming to you,*
> *his cause won, his victory gained,*
> *humble and mounted on a donkey,*
> *on a colt, the foal of a donkey.*

We can read this in the Old Testament, in Zachariah, chapter 9. That is how a Messiah was expected to arrive. And that is how Jesus arrived: "So they brought the colt to Jesus, and when they had spread their cloaks on it he mounted it. Many people carpeted the road with their cloaks, while others spread greenery which they had cut in the fields; and those in front and those behind shouted, 'Hosanna! Blessed is he who comes in the name of the Lord! Blessed is the kingdom of our father David which is coming! Hosanna in the heavens!'"[8]

Like most pilgrims who came to Jerusalem at Passover, Jesus had set up camp outside the city, in his case at Bethany where Lazarus and his sisters lived. From there he rode into Jerusalem on a donkey, and to this place he returned with his disciples in the evening. During the day he had made a visit to the Temple, where, according to Mark 11, "he looked around at everything." This would be the first visit, but certainly not the last.

The next day, Jesus goes straight to the Temple. He does it purposefully, and seemingly to provoke:

> *So they came to Jerusalem, and he went into the temple and began to drive out those who bought and sold there. He upset the tables of the money-changers and the seats of the dealers in pigeons; and he would not allow anyone to carry goods through the temple court. Then he began to teach them and said, "Does not scripture say, 'My house shall be called a house of prayer for all nations'? But you have made it a robbers' cave." The chief priests and the scribes heard of this and looked for a way to bring about his death; for they were afraid of him, because the whole crowd was spellbound by his teaching. And when evening came they went out of the city.[9]*

One almost gets the impression that Jesus and his disciples make raids into the city. They come in, do something spectacular, and then leave again.

Every day, Jesus goes to the Temple. There he preaches and he teaches. And he continues to provoke: "As he taught them, he said, 'Beware of the scribes who love to walk up and down in long robes and be greeted respectfully in the street, to have the chief seats in synagogues and places of honour at feasts. Those who eat up the property of widows, while for appearance's sake they say long prayers, will receive a sentence all the more severe."' [10] Jesus also tells a parable that can only be understood as a threat to the priestly leadership in the Temple (whom he calls here the "tenants"; the "owner of the vineyard" is evidently God):

> "A man planted a vineyard, let it out to vine-growers, and went abroad for a long time. When the season came, he sent a servant to the tenants to collect from them his share of the produce; but the tenants thrashed him and sent him away empty-handed. He tried again and sent a second servant; but they thrashed him too, treated him outrageously, and sent him away empty-handed. He tried once more and sent a third; him too they wounded and flung out. Then the owner of the vineyard said, 'What am I to do? I will send my beloved son; perhaps they will respect him.' But when the tenants saw him they discussed what they should do. 'This is the heir,' they said; 'let us kill him so that the inheritance may come to us.' So they flung him out of the vineyard and killed him. What, therefore, will the owner of the vineyard do to them? He will come and put those tenants to death and give the vineyard to others."

Luke ends the description of the parable with the words: "The scribes and chief priests wanted to seize him there and then, for they saw that this parable was aimed at them; but they were afraid of the people." [11]

It is when he leaves the Temple this time, that Jesus—according to the gospels—predicts the destruction of the Temple: "These things that you are gazing at—the time will come when not one stone will be left upon another; they will all be thrown down." [12]

This evening, too, Jesus shall leave the city. And he goes with some of his disciples to the Mount of Olives, with a view of the Kidron Valley and the Temple. The disciples ask him: "Tell us when this will happen?" Jesus answers that they should not allow themselves to be misled by others who "come claiming my name." And he goes on:

> *When you hear of wars and rumours of wars, do not be alarmed.*
> *Such things are bound to happen; but the end is still to come. For*
> *nation will go to war against nation, kingdom against kingdom;*
> *there will be earthquakes in many places; there will be famines. These*
> *are the first birth-pangs of the new age.*[13]

In the gospel of Luke, there is a similar description from their day of arrival in Jerusalem. But here Jesus focuses more upon what is going to happen to the city: "For a time will come upon you, when your enemies will set up siege-works against you; they will encircle you and hem you in at every point; they will bring you to the ground, you and your children within your walls, and not leave you one stone standing on another, because you did not recognize the time of God's visitation."[14]

Yet again, it is hard not to be reminded of the individual that Flavius Josephus would call "the Egyptian," he who came to Jerusalem as a messiah to liberate the city from its rulers. There are differences (above all, "the Egyptian," according to Josephus, was active during the time Felix was procurator, and Felix was not appointed until the year 52 CE), but the similarities are nevertheless remarkable. And in Josephus' story too, the Mount of Olives features:

> *Moreover, there came out of Egypt about this time to Jerusalem one*
> *that said he was a prophet, and advised the multitude of the com-*
> *mon people to go along with him to the Mount of Olives, as it was*
> *called, which lay over against the city, and at the distance of five fur-*
> *longs. He said further, that he would show them from hence how, at*
> *his command, the walls of Jerusalem would fall down; and he*
> *promised them that he would procure them an entrance into the city*
> *through those walls, when they were fallen down.*[15]

* * *

It is now two days before Passover, and Jesus and his disciples stay for the time being in Bethany. It seems to be mainly a time of preparation. For example, it is told that a woman comes on a visit when Jesus sits at table. She breaks open a bottle of very costly perfume, and pours it over his head. Some of the assembled are angry at this waste, and scold the woman. But Jesus reproves them: "Leave her alone. Why make trouble for her? It is a fine thing she has done for me. . . . She has anointed my body in anticipation of my burial." [16]

The closest disciples are now gathered around Jesus. But one of them suddenly leaves toward the city: "Then Judas Iscariot, one of the Twelve, went to the chief priests to betray him to them." [17] It seems to concern a major conspiracy, because, as it is told in the gospels, the high priest and the scribes now plan to seize Jesus and kill him. [18] The conflict, in the form it is described, seems to be entirely between Jesus and the Sanhedrin. The Romans are not mentioned, in contrast to the story of "the Egyptian" where the Roman army is portrayed as the opponent. On the whole, the Romans are not an important element or an express opponent in the stories in the gospels. It is the Jews, and above all the Jewish establishment, that stands in focus. This is remarkable in part because this was the period before the great uprising against the Romans, and most of the aspiring messiahs who showed themselves spoke of saving their people from the oppression of the Romans and reestablishing their own country. And in many ways, that is just what Jesus does too!

One can possibly see a parallel to the conflict between Jesus and the Jewish establishment in the Essenes, who also clearly distance themselves from the Jewish establishment, and to a certain extent disassociate themselves from the Temple in Jerusalem. It is, of course, relevant that the new Temple, with all its splendor, was built by a king who paid homage to the Romans. And the high priest sat there at the discretion of the Romans. Thus perhaps both the Temple and its leadership lost some of their respect and holiness.

"Now on the first day of Unleavened Bread, when the Passover lambs were being slaughtered, his disciples said to him, 'Where would you like us to go and prepare the Passover for you?'" [19] It has evidently been decided that, in honor of the celebration, they are going to spend the evening in the holy city. Jesus gives two of his disciples instructions for how they shall find the room where they shall all sit: "Go into the city, and a man will meet you carrying a jar of water. Follow him." And the disciples do indeed meet a man with a water jar, and he leads them to a house where a room has been prepared for them on the upper floor.

That evening Jesus and his disciples have their Passover meal. This meal is central, although the different gospels give it very different amounts of space—Mark gives it one fifth of a chapter, while John devotes all of five chapters to this meal. In fact, the earliest author of them all, Paul, also describes this meal. He brings it up in a letter to the congregation in Corinth: "On the night of his arrest the Lord Jesus took bread, and after giving thanks to God broke it and said: 'This is my body which is for you; do this in memory of me.' In the same way, he took the cup after supper, and said: 'This cup is the new covenant sealed by my blood. Whenever you drink it, do this in memory of me.'"[20]

Paul's description is very like that which is given in, for example, the gospel of Luke.[21] It is so similar that one may wonder whether Luke, who is presumed to have written at least twenty years after Paul, could have read Paul's letter.

In all the texts, it is quite clear that here Jesus is preparing his own sacrifice: "Take this; this is my body." And in the same way that a lamb is sacrificed and eaten at the Passover celebration, Jesus treats his imminent death as a sacrifice that, in this case symbolically, is taken as food.

There do not seem to be any provocations on this day, unless something happens on the Mount of Olives, something that the gospels don't tell us about. Because after the meal, during which Jesus predicts that he shall be betrayed by one of his disciples, they do, in fact, return to the Mount of Olives. They stop in Gethsemane, on the slopes of the Mount of Olives, to keep watch and wait for Jesus to be arrested. And this is clearly stated: Jesus is expecting to be arrested, and he is prepared to meet his enemies: "The hour has come. The Son of Man is betrayed into the hands of sinners."[22]

The whole week in Jerusalem has been like a preparation for this moment.

A great crowd of people "sent by the chief priests and the elders of the nation" with swords and cudgels, come to arrest him. And it is his disciple Judas Iscariot who betrays him, by giving him a kiss. "Judas, would you betray the Son of Man with a kiss?" Jesus asks him.[23] The betrayal is total. And it will become even worse. Because it is not only Judas who abandons his master at this moment. As it is written in the gospel of Mark: "Then the disciples all deserted him and ran away."[24] The only person, according to the gospel of Mark, who stays behind and "who had followed Jesus," is the man with the linen cloth. Nor do the disciples return to the trial or the crucifixion. All that is written is that Peter, when Jesus was arrested, followed after him at a distance, but upon being asked about Jesus, he denied his master.

It is hard to understand this in any other way than that the disciples, to the very last, retain their doubts as to Jesus being the person he has claimed to be—the doubts that Jesus has gone to so much trouble to dispel.

So why was Jesus arrested?

The question can in fact be put in two ways: What was the reason for the high priest finding cause to have Jesus arrested? In what way was he a threat to the establishment?

But also: What was Jesus hoping to attain? Why did he carry out his series of provocations in Jerusalem?

Let us start with the first question: In what way was Jesus a threat? If we are to believe the gospel writers, Jesus never really challenged the Romans. Nor did he attack Herod Antipas, the Jewish ruler of Galilee, appointed by the Romans. Jesus' only express enemies are the "Pharisees and Sadducees"—who represent traditional Jewry, and the Jewish religious establishment. And he primarily attacks them on the basis of legal texts.

Can this be the reason for his arrest? That is hard to believe. Discussions about the Torah and the Talmud were what a practicing

Jew devoted himself to in the rabbinical schools. There were of course limits as to how far criticism was allowed to go—as we have noted, in medieval France Donin was excommunicated—but a questioning of texts would hardly lead to arrest or execution. And at the time that we are now talking about, the century before the destruction of Jerusalem, there were more different schools of Judaism than ever before. For example, the Essenes were not arrested for condemning the leadership of the Temple. On the contrary, they were regarded as an established, albeit strange, form of Judaism.

So what did the threat consist of? If we read, say, the gospel of Mark, we are presented with a series of conflict situations around Jesus, first in Galilee and later in Jerusalem.[25] Jesus does some good deeds, or encourages his disciples to look after themselves, and is strongly criticized for this. In every case, it is the Pharisees who are portrayed as the opponents, and for each conflict situation the antagonism escalates. Bible scholar E. P. Sanders writes, "The reader of Mark is invited to believe that a series of good deeds by Jesus led the Pharisees to want to kill him."[26]

Of course, it is not as simple as that. But the conflict situations are probably a key nevertheless. Because what many Bible researchers think is that it was precisely those provocations that Jesus carried out in Jerusalem—primarily in the Temple—that caused the authorities to experience him as a threat. Not least, the accusations put forward against Jesus at the trial would suggest this.[27] As Mark Allan Powell writes in his book about research concerning the historical Jesus, "Most historians believe that some such incident [when Jesus overturned the tables in the Temple] did occur; indeed, most think that it provided the immediate cause for Jesus' crucifixion."[28] This was Passover time, a time of rebellion, and Jesus did exactly the same as the rebels (for example Menahem, who would come later) would come to do: he went straight into the Temple and created a tumult.

Then we come to the next question: Why did Jesus carry out these provocations? What was he hoping to achieve with them? And why did he predict, time after time (Mark, 8:31, 9:31, 10:32,

10:38–40, 12:1–12, 14:3–9, 14:24, 14:26–27; Matthew, 16:21–23, 17:22–23, 20:17–19, 23:37–39, 26:28, 26:30–32; Luke, 9:22, 9:44–45, 12:49–50, 18:31–34, 20:9–15, 22:19; John, 12:1–8, 12:20–43, 14:1–31), his own death?

He predicts his own death to such a degree that one wonders whether the crucifixion, in fact, was a part of the purpose of the provocations. Few established historians are prepared to go so far, but there are some, such as the prominent Jesus researcher bishop N. T. Wright, who claim that Jesus' death could have been part of the plan.[29]

This is a provocative thought, and one that, according to Sanders for example, would lead to the conclusion that Jesus was "weird."[30] But Sanders' conclusion is based, in that case, on the assumption that Jesus acted irrationally. And perhaps he did not.

What did Jesus of Nazareth want? What can we gather from his words and actions during the short time he was active?

"The time has arrived; the kingdom of God is upon you. Repent, and believe the gospel." Thus it is written in the gospel of Mark 1:15, and it summarizes rather well Jesus' view of what is to come. It was an eschatological message—the world as we know it will come to an end. But it was not therefore a negativist message; that which is coming next, namely the kingdom of God, is better than what we have now.

So what would the "kingdom of God" be, in real terms? It is not always clearly expressed, but one could possibly summarize it like this: At the moment, the kingdom of God is a kingdom in heaven, and is thus distanced from human life as we know it. But this kingdom shall soon come to the Earth—albeit through a revolutionary event which will temporarily create destruction—and the kingdom of God will thus be consistent with continued life. In this coming kingdom, society shall continue to exist, but humanity shall then live according to the will of God, in peace, mutual understanding, justice, and affluence. The kingdom of God thus provides hope in a hopeless time, and guidance for the future.

What is the role of Jesus in this? He himself speaks of the Son of Man: "But in those days, after that distress, the sun will be darkened, the moon will not give her light; the stars will come falling from the sky, the celestial powers will be shaken. Then they will see the Son of Man coming in the clouds with great power and glory."[31] It is the Son of Man who shall lead humanity toward the new age. Does Jesus mean himself when he says the Son of Man? Yes, in many sections this is perfectly clear ("Judas, would you betray the Son of Man with a kiss?").[32] The parallel term, the "son of God," is only used by others about Jesus (although he does, in parables—such as the one about the vineyard—indirectly refer to himself as the son of God).[33] And what is decisive for the ability of humans to achieve salvation is to *have faith* in him, Jesus, as this savior, this Son of Man: I shall lead you there. Have faith in me and you shall reach it.

The coming age seems, in some ways, to be already present, in the vicinity of Jesus and manifested in his deeds. He is, one might say, preparing for the coming age. And he creates a microcosmic kingdom of God around himself.

Why Jesus preaches that "the kingdom of God is upon you," we can only speculate. He obviously had a powerful vision of a changed world, with societies where the weak would become strong, the oppressed would be rehabilitated, and the poor would become prosperous. And he wanted to be the one who not only would lead humankind there, but he also undertook to take the pain of humans along the way. "If anyone is thirsty let him come to me and drink. Whoever believes in me, as scripture says, 'Streams of water shall flow from within him.'"[34]

For Jesus to achieve his goals, it is thus completely decisive to be able to get people to believe that he is the person he claims to be. This is complicated, because for the people around him he appears as a man of flesh and blood. How can a man come "in the clouds with great power and glory"? Jesus must somehow go through a transformation, leave the earthly, human figure he just now appears in. At the same time, he must at last try to get people to understand that even now, in his evidently human form, he has powers that ordinary people do not have.

To die, yet to show himself alive, is the ultimate way for Jesus of Nazareth to prove that he is the one he claims to be. And, perhaps, that he is something more than the legendary John the Baptist: "'In the same way the Son of Man is to suffer at their hands.' Then the disciples understood that he meant John the Baptist."[35]

To create tumult around the Jewish establishment might certainly lead him part of the way—Jesus stands out as a leader figure, a person with ideas and ambitions, a man who confronts the establishment. But that is not enough: as a local provocateur he can never hope to become a leading light—or leader—for humankind. He must do something more spectacular than that.

CHAPTER 7

THE TRIAL

At this stage of the story of Jesus, three people turn up who shall come to be of decisive importance for his fate. These are the two high priests Annas and Caiaphas, and the Roman prefect Pontius Pilate. All three are described in historical sources.

Annas (Ananus, Hannan, or Hanin), the son of Seth, is described by Flavius Josephus as one of the most successful of the high priests in the Roman province:

> Now the report goes that this eldest Ananus proved a most fortunate man; for he had five sons who had all performed the office of a high priest to God, and who had himself enjoyed that dignity a long time formerly, which had never happened to any other of our high priests.[1]

The office of high priest had changed with the shifting fate that the Jewish nation had undergone. According to the scriptures, Aaron, the brother of Moses, was the first of the high priests of the Jewish people, and until the fall of Jerusalem, in the year 70 CE, eighty-three different men were said to have held this office.[2] From the beginning, the office of high priest had been a purely religious function, but it would gradually become a political one too. And the office, which was passed on from father to son, was held for life. But the hated Antiochus Epiphanes—the ruler who was the cause of the Maccabean uprising—had among his many acts of interference with Jewish religious practices taken it upon himself to dismiss the high priest. And this gave rise to a new tradition. When the Romans marched into Judea, and King Herod was put on the throne, the office of high priest served at the pleasure of the secular rulers. In fact, it now became these very rulers—be they Romans or Roman vassal kings—who chose the high priests, and dismissed them when they were dissatisfied. At the same time, they did however let the high priest retain a certain political power. Though now this political power was power as a Roman favor.

Another, newer, tradition that was followed, was that these high priests were usually Sadducees. The Sadducees were a Jewish party the members of which, at least according to Flavius Josephus, were conservative, privileged, and went to considerable lengths not to offend the Romans. According to Josephus, "The Sadducees are able to persuade none but the rich, and have not the populace obsequious to them, but the Pharisees have the multitude on their side."[3]

Annas became high priest in the year 6 CE, and he was appointed by Quirinius (or Cyrenius), the Roman governor of Syria. Josephus writes, "and when the taxings were come to a conclusion . . . he [Quirinius] deprived Joazar of the high priesthood, which dignity had been conferred on him by the multitude, and he appointed Ananus, the son of Seth, to be high priest."[4]

Josephus gives us very little information about what actually happened during Annas' term of office and how he carried out his duties. He simply writes, as mentioned previously, that Annas is "favored" and retains his office for an unusually long time.

Finally, however, Annas is dismissed too, and this time it is a Roman prefect who interferes:

He [Tiberius] *was now the third emperor; and he sent Valerius Gra-*
tus to be procurator [or prefect] *of Judea, and to succeed Annius*
Rufus. This man deprived Ananus of the high priesthood, and ap-
pointed Ismael, the son of Phabi, to be high priest. [5]

Now, high priests are dismissed one after the other, and in three
years four different men—five including Annas—hold this office. It
is the last of these high priests who is the famous Joseph Caiaphas,
the high priest who will come to be so central in the story of the
passion of Jesus.

Interestingly, there do seem to be archaeological tracks left
by Joseph Caiaphas. At the end of December, 1990, some men were
doing road construction in a park in Abu Tor, on the outskirts of
Jerusalem, when they suddenly came across a chamber under the
ground. Archaeologist Zvi Greenhut, from the Israel Antiquities Authority, was immediately summoned. The subsequent excavations
revealed twelve so-called ossuaries, chests made of limestone containing bones. These two-thousand-year-old chests turned out to
hold skeletal parts from sixty-three different individuals, and several of the chests had an inscription that immediately caused quite
a stir among the country's archaeologists: "Caiaphas" was written
there. But it was the most exquisitely decorated bone chest that
seemed to confirm that the grave belonged to the Caiaphas family
known from history: on this chest, which was fifteen inches in
height and thirty inches long, there was an inscription in Aramaic
that read *Yehosef bar Kaiafa'*—"Joseph, son of Caiaphas." [6]

Just like Annas, Caiaphas will come to hold his office a long time:
eighteen years. According to the gospels, Caiaphas does not, however,
seem to have been alone in this office. Both Luke and John describe
some sort of joint leadership together with the old high priest, the "favored" Annas. We can read in the gospel of Luke the phrase, "during
the high-priesthood of Annas and Caiaphas." And in the gospel of
John is written that Annas was "the high priest for that year." [7]

Is there anything to support this "joint leadership" in sources
outside the New Testament, such as in the writings of Josephus? No,

there does not actually seem to be. Despite the fact that Annas' family continues to be of importance, Josephus does not say that Annas himself continues in this office. This does not, however, mean that a joint leadership of high priests was unheard of. Josephus himself mentions one example:

The high priest Jonathan assumes a decidedly important place in the books of Flavius Josephus. He is appointed in the year 36 CE, directly after Caiaphas, and is himself one of Annas' sons. However, after only one year, Jonathan is dismissed. But he evidently still has influence, because he is later again offered the post of high priest, which he declines, on the grounds that he is "satisfied with having once put on the sacred garments." [8]

Nevertheless, Jonathan does turn up again in Josephus' writings, and is then indeed called "high priest." In one section, which is about the troubles during the rule of Procurator Cumanus (48–52 CE), Josephus mentions "Jonathan and Ananias, the high priests." [9] These two high priests obviously rule jointly. Ananias, son of Nebedaios, is probably the same high priest as the one mentioned in the New Testament in connection with the apostle Paul. [10] By that time, however, his joint regent Jonathan is dead, murdered by the Zealot rebels some time after the year 52 CE. [11]

But now it is about twenty years earlier, and Caiaphas is high priest. Alone, or together with Annas. Depending on which source we rely on.

Caiaphas starts in his office in the year 18 CE, as the last of the high priests to be appointed by Gratus before he leaves his post as prefect eight years later. "When Gratus had done these things," writes Josephus, "he went back to Rome, after he had tarried in Judea eleven years, when Pontius Pilate came as his successor." [12]

In the year 26 CE, both Joseph Caiaphas and Pontius Pilate are thus in place—in the posts they shall hold when Jesus of Nazareth is tried in court. Ten years later, both of them will have been dismissed. If we are to believe the gospels, the trial against Jesus thus takes place some time between the years 26 and 36 CE.

The stage is now set for what shall come to be the symbolically decisive event in the history of Christianity.

What actually happens when Jesus is arrested, there on the slopes of the Mount of Olives? When Jesus goes to meet his adversaries, near Gethsemane, these adversaries—according to the synoptic gospels—consist of "a great crowd . . . sent by the chief priests and the elders of the nation."[13] It would thus seem as if it is the Sanhedrin that is responsible for the confrontation that takes place on this night.

But one of the gospels, that written by John, does actually to a certain extent give us another picture. Here it says that "the Jewish police" are accompanied by "the troops [speira in Greek] with their commander."[14] This has been interpreted as meaning that Roman soldiers were there too, to arrest Jesus. As the Bible researcher F. F. Bruce writes, "The Johannine account, according to which the officers of the Sanhedrin were accompanied by a speira . . . has been taken to mean that Roman soldiers were also present, members of the cohort on duty in the Antonia fortress, for the Greek speira is the proper equivalent of Latin cohors, which in Judea . . . would be an auxiliary cohort with a paper strength of 760 infantry and 240 cavalry."[15] .

A strength of "760 infantry and 240 cavalry"? That is a force of one thousand soldiers! The perception that what is described is indeed such a force is strengthened by the Greek word that the gospel of John uses about the "commander": chiliarchos. The word means "leader for one thousand" (chilioi: "thousand"; archos: "leader").

If this is correct, then we are presumably not dealing with the arrest of a single person. Rather, what we seem to be looking at is some kind of battle, there on the slopes of the Mount of Olives!

The trial of Jesus is started, according to the gospels, immediately—so quickly that they perhaps do not even wait until the next morning. And this trial is not really one trial, but several.

To judge by the descriptions in the New Testament, Jesus is something of a hot potato for the various authorities—the religious and civil, the Jewish and Roman—and he is sent between them, because none of them wants to carry the full responsibility.

This is interesting information, and something might lie behind this unwillingness to "deal with the case." But a little more about that later. For the time being, we will stick to the gospels and they evidently give us slightly different descriptions of the course of events.

The shortest descriptions are to be found in the gospels of Mark and Matthew. There, the trial consists of only two stages: one before the religious, Jewish authorities—the Sanhedrin—and one before the civil, Roman—Prefect Pontius Pilate. It is remarkable that a simple crime case should be taken up at such a high level, and if this is correct it presumably was no simple crime case.

What all the gospel writers do agree upon is that it is the religious authorities that have the case presented to them first:

> The troops [Greek: speira] with their commander, and the Jewish
> police, now arrested Jesus and secured him. They took him first to
> Annas, father-in-law of Caiaphas, the high priest of that year.[16]

Only John describes this—that Jesus is first taken to Annas. According to the gospel of Matthew he is instead taken directly to Caiaphas, and the other two gospel writers tell us that Jesus is taken to "the chief priests, elders and scribes." That is where the first interrogation takes place, and in the gospels of Mark and Matthew, witnesses are interrogated too:

> Many gave false evidence against him, but their statements did not
> tally. Some stood up and gave false evidence against him to this effect:
> "We heard him say, 'I will pull down this temple, made with human
> hands, and in three days I will build another, not made with hands.'"[17]

When one reads these gospels, and they are the oldest ones, it seems quite clear that the original accusation is about the threat to "pull down the temple," which would amount to some kind of insurrection. Both Mark and Matthew state that it is not until the council has failed to get consistent statements from witnesses on that point, that the high priest asks the question: "Are you the Messiah, the Son of the Blessed One?"[18] Jesus' answer, which can be interpreted as confirmation, then, according to Mark and Matthew, forms the basis for the new accusation: blasphemy.

Luke, however, focuses directly on the question whether Jesus regards himself as the Messiah, while John is unclear on that point ("The high priest questioned Jesus about his disciples and about his teaching."[19]).

After this, Jesus is taken to the Roman ruler of Judea, Pontius Pilate, who is also in the city. Why is Jesus taken to him? The gospel writers on the whole agree as to the reason: The council wants to have Jesus executed, and such a verdict can only be given and carried out by the Romans.

With that the whole assembly rose and brought him before Pilate. They opened the case against him by saying, "We found this man subverting our nation, opposing the payment of taxes to Caesar, and claiming to be Messiah, the king of the Jews." Pilate asked him, "Are you the king of the Jews?" He replied, "The words are yours." Pilate then said to the chief priests and the crowd, "I find no case for this man to answer."[20]

Pilate, according to all the gospels, is clearly unwilling to condemn Jesus. According to the gospel of John, Pilate tries to pass the responsibility for the decision over to the members of the Sanhedrin: "Take him yourselves and try him by your own law." Luke, instead, writes that Pilate tries to send Jesus to the tetrarch of Galilee, Herod Antipas, who is in Jerusalem at the time.[21]

When Pilate nevertheless is finally forced to make the decision himself, he makes a last attempt to have Jesus freed. And it is rather dramatic:

At the festival season the governor used to release one prisoner requested by the people. As it happened, a man known as Barabbas was then in custody with the rebels who had committed murder in the rising. When the crowd appeared and began asking for the usual

favor, Pilate replied, "Would you like me to release the king of the
Jews?" For he knew it was out of malice that Jesus had been handed
over to him. But the chief priests incited the crowd to ask instead for
the release of Barabbas. Pilate spoke to them again: "Then what shall
I do with the man you call the king of the Jews?" They shouted back,
"Crucify him!" "Why, what wrong has he done?" Pilate asked; but
they shouted all the louder, "Crucify him!" So Pilate, in his desire to
satisfy the mob, released Barabbas to them; and he had Jesus flogged,
and then handed him over to be crucified.[22]

The above extract from the gospel of Mark, which ends with the
decision to have Jesus crucified, contains many very important and
paradoxical pieces of information. Let us start with the item that Pilate always used to liberate a prisoner at Passover: the gospels agree
as to this, but non-testament sources do not seem to give much
support for it. As F. F. Bruce writes: "The Barabbas incident consti-
tutes a problem which still awaits its solution. We have no certain
reference outside the Gospels to the release of a prisoner to the people each Passovertide."[23]

Who, then, was this Barabbas? It is interesting to note that
it is the gospels themselves that point us in the direction of the answer: In John, chapter 18, Barabbas is called a "robber." The word in
the original Greek text is *leistés* (ληστής). And *leistés* is a term that is
often used in descriptions from this period. But when Flavius Josephus writes *leistés* (plural: *leistai*) he does not mean an ordinary robber. He means a rebel, usually in the sense of "a Zealot rebel" (i.e.,
someone from the most violent of the groups that came to turn
against the Romans, often in a wider sense called the "Zealots").
Sometimes Josephus uses the word *Sicarii* instead of *leistai*. This
means "knife-men" or "dagger-men," from the Latin *sica* which
means a dagger. In *Antiquities of the Jews*, for example, he describes the
murder of the high priest Jonathan in the following manner:

"[Procurator] Felix also bore an ill-will to Jonathan, the high priest
. . . wherefore Felix persuaded one of Jonathan's most faithful friends,
a citizen of Jerusalem, whose name was Doras, to bring the leistai

upon Jonathan, in order to kill him; and this he did by promising to
give him a great deal of money for so doing."

The same story is told in *Wars of the Jews* in the following manner:

"There sprang up another sort of leistai *in Jerusalem, which were*
called Sicarii, who slew men in the day time, and in the midst of the
city; they did this chiefly at the festivals, when they mingled themselves
among the multitude, and concealed daggers under their garments,
with which they stabbed those that were their enemies. . . . The first
man who was slain by them was Jonathan the high priest."[24]

As Josephus describes it, these *Sicarii* were completely fearless, and
they were even prepared to kill their opponents inside the Temple.[25]
He also describes their daggers: "They made use of small swords
[*xiphidion*], not much different in length from the Persian *acinacae*,
but somewhat crooked."[26]

Of interest is that the statement that there were *Sicarii* or *leis-*
tai in the Temple finds an echo in the New Testament. In all three
synoptic gospels, Jesus says on his visit to the Temple when he over-
turns the tables, "Scripture says, 'My house shall be called a house
of prayer,' but you are making it a robbers' cave."[27] The original
wording for "robbers' cave" is, in all three gospels, "a cave for *leistai*."

Josephus is no admirer of these *Sicarii* and *leistai*, these different sorts of Zealots. He writes that "God, out of his hatred of
these men's wickedness, rejected our city."[28] But history would be-
stow upon them a certain heroic status. It was the Zealots who led
the revolt against Rome in the years 66–70 CE—the revolt that Josephus himself then joined—and it was the Zealots who, all alone, resisted the Roman army right up until the year 73 CE on the
mountain of Masada by the Dead Sea.

It should be pointed out that Josephus starts to use the term *Sicarii*
for the first time after the arrival of Felix as procurator of Iudaea,
in the year 52 CE. And he is quite clear about the *Sicarii* appearing

first in that period.[29] But what about the term *leistés*? Barabbas was, according to the New Testament, a *leistés*. Does Josephus describe *leistés* or *leistai* before the year 52 CE? Yes he does—but not during the time Jesus was active! If one reads carefully through Josephus' works, one will find that he does mention *leistai* now and then, up until the time Judas from Galilee starts his revolt against the tax, in the year 6 CE. After this—and during the *whole* of Jesus' lifetime—this word, *leistai*, is completely absent in the writings of Josephus. Although one can read in Josephus' works that the people sometimes protested furiously against the various deeds of Pilate, this does not seem to have been in the form of rebel activity.

The word *leistai* does, however, suddenly turn up again when Fadus becomes procurator, in the year 44 CE. And it becomes really frequent with the appointment of Cumanus in the year 48 CE. The reason for this is that the Jewish vassal king Herod Agrippa dies in the year 44 CE, after which the entire Jewish nation is placed under Roman administration. This unleashes intensive rebel activity, and an armed conflict between Samaritans and Galileans. Josephus himself writes, "and after this time all Judea was overrun with robberies."[30]

The only mention Josephus makes about "robbers" (*leistai*) being in any way active during Jesus' lifetime is that in one place he writes that a certain person, active in the fifties CE, had "ravaged the country for twenty years together."[31] And it is not only Josephus who indicates the relative lack of rebel activity during the life of Jesus. The historian Tacitus expresses this quite succinctly when he writes, "Under Tiberius all was quiet."[32] Tiberius was emperor between 14 and 37 CE.

But from the year 44 CE and thereafter, Josephus names *leistés* or some form of that word on as many as fifty-seven occasions in *Wars of the Jews*, and on twelve occasions in *Antiquities of the Jews*.

Yet again, one has reason to reflect upon whether the incidents that are described in the New Testament might have taken place much later than we believe.

Barabbas is thus called a *leistés* in the gospels, as are the two "robbers" who are crucified with Jesus. We can read in the gospel of

Mark, "Two robbers [leistai] were crucified with him, one on his right and the other on his left."[33] In the gospel of Matthew, too, they are called leistai.[34] Luke is the only one to use another word: kakourgos, which means "criminal."[35]

That Barabbas and the others really are rebels is also rather clearly stated. For example, in the gospel of Mark we read, "As it happened, a man known as Barabbas was then in custody with the rebels who had committed murder in the rising."[36]

But which rebels?

And which rising?

If one reads the gospel of Mark, one does not see any descriptions of any uprising. *Unless, of course, he is describing that which took place on the Mount of Olives in connection with the arrest of Jesus!* Mark writes of "the rising"—in the definite form—as if we would know which one he meant. And because the only disturbances he describes are the ones that take place when Jesus is arrested, those are presumably the ones he means. And it would, in that case, be there that "rebels" have been active. This would then explain why—according to the gospel of John—a force of troops up to one thousand strong would be necessary to arrest Jesus on the Mount of Olives.

We cannot know for sure, but it is not an entirely unreasonable interpretation to assume that Jesus is to be crucified together with other men who had been active during the same disturbances where he himself was present—on the slopes of the Mount of Olives. The fact that they were crucified on either side of him is also an indication that they belong together. And perhaps it is not a coincidence that Jesus, when he is being arrested, says to the crowd, "Do you take me for a robber [leistés], that you have come out with swords and cudgels to arrest me?"[37] Yet again, the word leistés turns up in this context! It is hard to believe that this is a coincidence. The gospels contradict, in part, such a conclusion when they describe how Jesus lets himself be arrested without a fight, and in the description of his fundamentally non-violent personality. Yet it is interesting to note that a violent incident is described there on the Mount of Olives:

> *At that moment one of those with Jesus reached for his sword* [Greek original: *machaira* = dagger or sword, often somewhat curved[38]] *and drew it, and struck the high priest's servant, cutting off his ear. But Jesus said to him, "Put up your sword. All who take the sword, die by the sword. Do you suppose that I cannot appeal for help to my father, and at once be sent more than twelve legions of angels? But how then would the scriptures by fulfilled, which say that this must happen?"*[39]

According to the gospel of John, the man who draws his dagger or sword is none other than Jesus' closest disciple: Simon Peter.[40]

And there is yet another interesting piece of information, this time in the gospel of Luke. During the last supper, just before they all set off to the Mount of Olives, Jesus urges his disciples to take money with them:

> *"Whoever has a purse had better take it with him, and his pack too; and if he has no sword [Greek: machaira], let him sell his cloak to buy one. For scripture says, 'And he was reckoned among transgressors,' and this, I tell you, must be fulfilled in me; indeed all that is written of me is reaching its fulfilment." "Lord," they said, "we have two swords here." "Enough!" he replied.*[41]

Jesus himself might not have offered any violent resistance—he seems, as it is described, to almost voluntarily accept his fate—but those around him appear to be more prone to violence.

It is also interesting to note that one of Jesus' disciples is actually referred to as "Simon who was called the Zealot."[42] And another of the disciples, the one who betrays him, is called Judas Iscariot. One of the interpretations for the name "Iscariot" is that it comes from *Sicarii* (singular form: *Sicarius*; Greek form: *Sikarios*).[43] The letters in the name in Greek are the same, except for the ending: Ἰσκαριώθ (Iskariôth) and σικάριος (Sikarios). In the Latin Bible, he is called Judas Scarioth.

But, as mentioned earlier, the *Sicarii* do not appear until the year 52 CE. At least if one is to believe Josephus.

* * *

There is yet another feature that is mysterious in the story of Barabbas. In the text about him in the gospel of Matthew, we can read:

> *There was then in custody a man of some notoriety, called Jesus Barabbas. When the people assembled, Pilate said to them, "Which would you like me to release to you—Jesus Barabbas, or Jesus called Messiah?"* [44]

So here Barabbas is not just called Barabbas. He is called *Jesus* Barabbas. Is that a coincidence? Let us have a closer look at the name.

The name *Barabbas* actually consists of two parts: *bar*, which (like *ben*) means "son of," and *Abba*, which means "father." The rebel Barabbas' name is thus, according to this gospel, "Jesus, son of the father"!

One interpretation of this is that Barabbas and Jesus were in reality the same person. What would be the purpose? One possible explanation is of course that somebody who has written down the story, somewhere along the line, has not understood that the two names really concern one and the same person. But it has also been suggested that there was a purpose behind this play on words, that the gospels have created a division into two (and a non-existent tradition of freeing a prisoner) almost like a parable. It is postulated that the purpose would be to create a choice for the reader: do you want to choose violence or will you turn the other cheek? [45]

Or perhaps it is about Jesus' own dilemma? And maybe one ought to consider how Jesus' own words are reported just after he has told the story, in the Temple, of the tenants and the vineyard. In the gospel of Luke, we can read thus:

> *But he looked straight at them and said, "Then what does this text of scripture mean: 'The stone which the builders rejected has become the main corner-stone'? Everyone who falls on that stone will be dashed to pieces; anyone on whom it falls will be crushed."* [46]

But in the gospel of Mark, the same statement is recorded as follows:

"Have you never read this text: 'The stone which the builders rejected has become the main corner-stone. This is the Lord's doing, and it is wonderful in our eyes'?" [47]

Are Jesus and Barabbas the same person? What would that then mean? That Jesus is set free? That he is set free and not set free?

It is, of course, possible that Barabbas is exactly what he is made out to be: a *leistés*, who happens to have the given name of Jesus, and a surname that is not at all unreasonable. Abba is, apart from meaning "father," a name, and somebody could very well be called "Jesus, son of Abba."

* * *

The people reject Pilate's offer to release Jesus, and instead choose to have Barabbas released. Pilate now feels obliged to sentence Jesus, and he sentences him, reluctantly, to first be flogged and then crucified.

So who was this Pilate, the man with the final responsibility, but who—if we are to believe the gospels—did everything he could to avoid punishing Jesus?

"He was a man of very inflexible disposition, and very merciless as well as very obstinate." Thus wrote Philo of Alexandria in his description of the Roman prefect.[48] Pilate had made a serious blunder before the Jewish population almost immediately after his arrival—when he attempted to bring in the emperor's standards to Jerusalem. And he would continue to make clumsy mistakes. Josephus describes, for example, how Pilate decides to have an aqueduct, a water canal, built to Jerusalem and he uses "sacred money" (i.e., the temple tax) to finance it. "However," writes Josephus, "the Jews were not pleased with what had been done about this water; and many ten thousands of people got together, and made a clamor against him, and insisted that he should leave off that design." It ended with Pilate ordering his soldiers to attack the crowd, and many people were killed.[49]

In their fear of rebellion, the Roman prefects and procurators came to react so violently that they eventually—several decades later—provoked precisely that which they feared: rebellion. When Pontius Pilate, in the year 36 CE, was recalled to Rome, it was because he—yet again—responded to a presumably fairly harmless manifestation with violence.

On this occasion, it was a religious leader in Samaria who had aroused Pilate's concern. The person in question had incited large crowds to go to Mount Gerizzim, the Samaritans' sacred mountain, where he promised to show them some holy vessels that Moses was said to have buried there. But when the crowds gathered at the foot of the mountain, bringing with them tools, and made ready to climb, a large force of soldiers turned up, sent out by Pilate. These attacked the crowds, and many people were killed. After this, the highest council of the Samaritans made contact with the governor, Vitellius, to express their anger. And Pilate was sent home to Rome to explain his actions. He never came back.[50]

We have, in other words, two very contradictory characterizations of this Pontius Pilate: in the descriptions of Josephus and Philo, he is portrayed as an unusually clumsy, inflexible, and cruel ruler, with little conscience or feeling for his subjects. Philo writes that Pilate's time in power was marked by "His corruption, and his acts of insolence, and his rapine, and his habit of insulting people, and his cruelty, and his continual murders of people untried and uncondemned, and his never ending, and gratuitous, and most grieving inhumanity."[51]

And yet this is the man who, according to the gospels, not only does everything to avoid having to execute Jesus—he even washes his hands when he cannot avoid sentencing him:

When Pilate saw that he was getting nowhere, and that there was danger of a riot, he took water and washed his hands in full view of the crowd. "My hands are clean of this man's blood," he declared. "See to that yourselves."[52]

How can we get this to fit together? Can it really be correct that such a cold and cruel ruler would take pity on a Jewish aspiring messiah, and possibly a rebel? Is someone lying here, or can there be a logical explanation for this contradictory behavior by Pilate?

Christian mythology has it that Pilate himself converted to Christianity, albeit after the death of Jesus, being influenced in this by his wife, Claudia Procula. The gospel of Matthew also mentions her influence: "While Pilate was sitting in court, a message came to him from his wife: 'Have nothing to do with that innocent man, I was much troubled on his account in my dreams last night.'"[53] In some Christian faiths, both Pilate and his wife have consequently been made into saints. But no such conversion has been registered in any more official historical writing, or in the gospels. The Church Father Eusebius of Caesarea quotes in the fourth century some Greek historians who are said to have written that Pilate, shortly after his return to Rome, fell into displeasure under emperor Caligula, and committed suicide. But no conversion is mentioned.[54]

One interpretation of the contradictory descriptions has been that those who put the gospels together wanted to remain on a good footing with the Romans and thus made an effort to portray Pilate in a good light. Thus, according to this interpretation, Pilate's benevolence towards Jesus was just a reconstruction after the event.

This, of course, is perfectly possible. But there is yet another story that perhaps can shed some light upon this issue. It comes from the Talmud. The beginning of the story has already been quoted earlier, but here is the whole thing:

> *It was taught: On the eve of the Passover Yeshu was hanged. For forty days before the execution took place, a herald went forth and cried, "He is going to be stoned because he has practiced sorcery and enticed Israel to apostasy. Any one who can say anything in his favour, let him come forward and plead on his behalf." But since nothing was brought forward in his favour he was hanged on the eve of the Passover.*
>
> *Ulla retorted: "Do you suppose that he was one for whom a defense could be made? Was he not a Mesith [enticer], concerning*

whom scripture says, 'Neither shalt though spare, neither shalt
though conceal him?'
With Yeshu however it was different, for he was connected with
the government." [55]

What is interesting about this Talmud quote is, of course, the final
comment: "for he was connected with the government." What does
this mean? The comment was supposedly made by a rabbi by the
name of Ulla, who lived at the end of the third century and the beginning of the fourth century. Ulla tries to explain the seemingly
unreasonable behavior of making such a great effort to defend a
man who "practiced sorcery and enticed Israel to apostasy." And
then he produces this remarkable explanation: "for he was connected to the government."

We cannot know if Rabbi Ulla had proper substantiation of
this when he made the claim. It is undoubtedly astonishing that a
Jewish spiritual leader, and perhaps rebel, from a little village in
Galilee should be "connected to the government." But there are in fact
two sources that could support this remarkable claim. One is the
New Testament, according to which the otherwise so ruthless Roman
prefect does everything he can to avoid having to execute Jesus. An
explanation of Pilate's contradictory behavior could, of course, be
that Jesus was privileged in one way or another, or that the Romans
for some reason wanted to protect him. The question is, why?

Let us look a little at how different people in the Roman Empire were
treated and regarded by the authorities. At that time, a person who
grew up under Roman rule could belong to one of three groups:

At the very bottom, were the slaves. These were regarded
as property, and they had no rights whatsoever. The slaves were
usually, though not always, foreigners: prisoners of war, captured
seamen, people who had been purchased as slaves in the provinces,
and so on.

The next group were the people who lived in countries occupied by Rome, such as Iudaea. They usually had a sort of "partial citizenship."

At the top were the people who had Roman citizenship. Such a citizenship could be gained in one of the following ways:

* Children of a Roman citizen, and born within a legal marriage (*connubium*) automatically gained Roman citizenship at birth.

* A freed slave, or the child of a freed slave, gained Roman citizenship.

* Soldiers who belonged to the Roman auxiliary troops gained citizenship after completing their service. Citizenship was inherited by their children.

* Some individuals gained Roman citizenship by virtue of their considerable contribution to the Roman state.

* Some individuals, and they were few in number, could buy Roman citizenship. This was very expensive.

So what distinguished a Roman citizen from somebody who only had "partial citizenship"? Roman citizenship brought with it certain duties but also a number of privileges: a citizen had, for example, the right to vote (*suffragium*), and the right to enter into a legal agreement (*commercium*). And there were the rights that consisted of the citizen receiving a more just—and lenient—treatment by the legal system. If the Roman citizen was in one of the provinces, he could always request to be sent to Rome for his trial. Nor could a citizen be tortured or condemned to death by a provincial court.

And if a Roman citizen did happen to be condemned to death, he was almost never crucified. The only exception was high treason or desertion during war.[56]

Is this where we should be looking for the explanation of why Pilate did not want to condemn Jesus to death? And of why the crime was finally high treason? Is this where we should be looking for the explanation of why Jesus was "connected to the government"? Could he have had Roman citizenship?

And if so: how had Jesus managed to acquire this Roman citizenship?

We do not know, because we cannot know. But it is undeniable that the story of the Roman soldier Pantera comes to mind here. Assuredly, it was probably not a "legal marriage" in which Jesus was born, if we are to believe the words of Celsus about Jesus' origins. But if Jesus had a Roman soldier as father, this might perhaps explain Pontius Pilate's reluctance to have him executed. And if it is correct, as Celsus writes, that the name of this Roman soldier was known, then he was probably a person of consequence.

There are thus three things that could support the thesis that Jesus for some reason is protected by the Romans: the gospels' description of Pilate's reluctance to have Jesus executed; the Talmud tractate in which it is stated that Jesus "was connected to the government"; and, finally, Celsus' statement about Jesus being the son of a named Roman soldier.

Yet Jesus is eventually taken to Golgotha—at least if we are to believe the gospels. But what happens there?

CHAPTER 8

ON WHETHER JESUS DIED ON THE CROSS

The theory that Jesus did not die on the cross, but arranged his own simulated death, has been around for at least two hundred years—and has given rise to discussion just as long. In German, the theory was called *Die Scheintod-Hypothese*, in English the Swoon Theory. The person who came to be most associated with the theory from the beginning was the German theologian, H. E. G. Paulus. In three works, published from 1800 to 1842, Paulus put a great deal of effort into interpreting all the miracles described in the New Testament by providing them with natural explanations.[1] Paulus, who was a rationalist like Reimarus, embraced the moral and spiritual content of Jesus' teachings and deeds, but considered that all the miracles that were described had rational explanations. And, as regards the crucifixion—and above all that Jesus rose again and showed himself alive—H. G. Paulus thought that the simplest explanation for this was that Jesus never actually died on the cross, but was taken down alive, albeit unconscious.

The idea was not new; at least two earlier works had presented a similar hypothesis. And in the subsequent debate there were contributions from many of the era's most important theologians, such as Schleiermacher, Gfrörer, Hase, Strauss, and Keim.[2]

So where did this idea come from? The reason for the development of *Die Scheintod-Hypothese* was of course that its advocates wanted to rely on the text in the gospels, and still come up with reasonable explanations. The debaters, who were often theologians, were thus fundamentally conservative with regard to the New Testament. Their dilemma, one could say, was that they nevertheless wanted to be able to ally themselves with the rational ideas of the time. Such intellectual efforts were, and are, of course not something that either a literal believer or a person who dismissed the gospels as fiction needed to bother with. The problems arise when you want to accord the gospels historical importance—and yet do not believe in miracles.

The Swoon Theory was not the only "rational" theory that was presented to explain the resurrection. Among the other theories, there are those that claimed that it was not Jesus who was crucified, but somebody else; that Jesus was crucified and died, but the disciples then stole the body from the grave and pretended that Jesus had risen again; and that the resurrection was a vision or a hallucination on the part of the observers.

What spurs on the imagination in the entire story of the crucifixion of Jesus is, of course, its very complexity: Jesus, one could say, lives twice and dies (or rises up into heaven) twice. He lives and then dies on the cross, after which he rises again and becomes alive, after which he suddenly disappears from humanity again. Whether one believes in the divinity of Jesus or not, there is something in the story that arouses our imagination. A completely made-up story seldom makes use of such twists and turns.

The Swoon Theory lives on into our own days. Among the twentieth-century authors who, in one form or another, have put forward this theory, one can note George Moore, Frank Harris, Ernest Brougham Docker, D. H. Lawrence, Robert Graves and Joshua Podro, Hugh J. Schonfield, Donovan Joyce, J. D. M. Derrett, Holger Kersten and Elmar R. Gruber, Michael Baigent, Richard Leigh and Henry Lincoln, Barbara Thiering, Gérald Messadié, and Helmer Linderholm.[3]

And the fact that it is the Swoon Theory that is so tenacious might have its explanation in certain details that the gospel stories provide us with.

Let us first start by looking at the crucifixion as a method of execution.

Crucifixion is a very old form of execution, and it is one of the most painful. According to some theories, crucifixion was invented by the Persians, but it came to be used in other countries too, relatively frequently from about the sixth century BCE. The Romans may have learned about crucifixion in Carthage and made use of it to execute rebels, slaves who rose up against their masters, pirates, other non-Roman criminals, and particularly hated enemies. As a rule, Roman citizens did not risk having to suffer this the most degrading and cruel of execution methods.

What made crucifixion so exceptionally cruel was the time it took for the crucified person to die. In general at least twelve hours, but often two, three, or even four days under unendurable pain. There are different opinions as to what was the most common cause of death. Some say it was suffocation—although volunteers who have been hung up with their hands outstretched on a cross have not shown any problems with breathing—others say it was dehydration in connection with other complications (the crucifixion was often preceded by lashing), leading to traumatic shock or hypovolemic shock (i.e., shock due to loss of blood).[4] In most cases, however, death was hastened by breaking the legs of the victim, which led to traumatic shock. This was considered an act of mercy.

In some circumstances, the condemned prisoner was nailed onto the cross; in other instances he or she was tied. There were different types of crosses, too: some of them looked like the Christian cross, a long upright pole with a horizontal bar—*patibulum*—a little way down from the top. A *titulus*, a sign with the condemned person's name and crime, was often fastened above his or her head. Sometimes, the horizontal bar was fixed right at the top of the pole, and sometimes the victim was set up on two poles that formed an X. Crucifixion on a single pole is described too (this is probably the quickest method of execution by crucifixion, and the one that most likely would lead to suffocation, if the arms are stretched straight up). The seat (sedile), which was often placed on the cross to take some of the weight off the arms, had no other function than to prolong the pain. Regardless of the construction, the principle was the same: maximum pain for a maximum period. And the ultimate aim was most often to terrify the spectators, and pacify them. In War of the Jews, Josephus describes how, during the siege of Jerusalem, Titus' soldiers tried to persuade the Jewish rebels to surrender by crucifying up to five hundred Jews every day along the walls of the city:

> So the soldiers, out of the wrath and hatred they bore the Jews, nailed those they caught, one after one way, and another after another, to the crosses, by way of jest, when their multitude was so great, that room was wanting for the crosses, and crosses wanting for the bodies.[5]

After death, the body of the crucified person was left hanging on the cross and animals started to eat the corpse. Burial was not allowed. There do seem to have been exceptions, however: Josephus writes (at least in the versions that have reached us) that since burial was so important to the Jews, sometimes the bodies were taken down before sunset and buried.[6] However, it cannot have been particularly common to allow the bodies of those crucified to be buried. Within the territory of the old Roman Empire from that time, the remains of only one crucified person have been found. They were discovered in 1968 in a bone chest, bearing the inscription Yehohanan ben Hagakol. Inside were the bones of a man who had obviously been crucified, approximately between the years 1 and 70 CE. His heels had been pierced through with a nail, on which traces of the wood of an olive tree were found, and his legs had been broken.[7] Otherwise, no other finds from that period and in that area have been documented.

Among the Romans, at least, crucifixion was considered such a cruel form of execution that it was eventually abandoned in

the fourth century, during the rule of the christianized Emperor
Constantine.

So, what happened when Jesus of Nazareth was crucified?

The descriptions in the gospels of the last hours of Jesus
are quite in agreement. But the gospel of John provides a little extra
information. Since this gospel was probably the last to be written
down, it is considered to be the least reliable. But when it comes to
the crucifixion, some of the information that John adds is of the
"seemingly irrelevant" category—information that does not seem to
be necessary for the telling of the story but is included nevertheless. So it deserves to be mentioned.

But let us start with the three other gospels, the synoptic
ones. They describe how Jesus is first taken into the *Praetorium*, the
imperial guard's large hall, where they "called together the whole
cohort."[8] This refers to the same *speira*, the same cohort, that has
been described earlier, six hundred to one thousand soldiers. They
taunt Jesus and beat him, put a crown of thorns upon his head and
dress him in a red cloak, mockingly calling him "the king of the
Jews," then put his own clothes back on and take him out for the
long, degrading walk along Via Dolorosa to Golgotha. Normally,
the person who was to be crucified would have to carry his own
patibulum to the place of execution, so that everybody should see
what was going to be done to him, but Jesus is relieved of some of
his burden, at least according to the synoptic gospels: "A man called
Simon, from Cyrene, the father of Alexander and Rufus, was pass-
ing by on his way in from the country, and they pressed him into
service to carry his [Jesus'] cross."[9] Why the soldiers forced a by-
stander to carry the horizontal bar, which took some of the burden
off Jesus, is not explained in the gospel texts.

When they finally come to Golgotha, someone gives Jesus
a glass of "wine mixed with myrrh" (according to Mark) or "wine
mixed with gall" (according to Matthew). But "after tasting it he
would not drink."[10] What was this drink? As far as we can tell, it
was some form of anaesthetic. Harold and Alma Moldenke, authors
of the book *Plants of the Bible*, write: "Wine mixed with myrrh was

given to Jesus just before the Crucifixion to lessen the pain, just as in the days before anaesthetics, intoxicating drinks were poured into the unfortunate patients on the eve of big operations."[11] And in a Talmud tractate we can read: "When one is led out to execution, he is given a goblet of wine containing a grain of frankincense, in order to benumb his senses, for it is written, Give strong drink unto him that is ready to perish . . . The noble women in Jerusalem used to donate and bring it."[12]

Why did Jesus refuse this drink? To remain alert? Neither Mark nor Matthew comment upon this.

Now Jesus is crucified, and on either side of him the two *leistai* meet the same fate. On the *titulus* that is fastened above Jesus' head it says, according to the gospel of Mark, "the King of the Jews." There is a description of how people shared his clothes between themselves. And on the ground below, people insult Jesus with the words: "So you are the man who was to pull down the temple, and rebuild it in three days! Save yourself and come down from the cross."[13] Now begins the long, drawn-out pain.

How long does Jesus hang on the cross?

> It was nine in the morning when they crucified him. . . . At midday a darkness fell over the whole land, which lasted until three in the afternoon; and at three Jesus cried aloud, "Eloï, Eloï, lema sabachthani?" which means, "My god, My God, why have you forsaken me?" Hearing this some of the bystanders said, "Listen! He is calling Elijah." Someone ran and soaked a sponge in sour wine and held it to his lips on the end of a stick. "Let us see," he said, "if Elijah will come to take him down." Then Jesus gave a loud cry and died; the curtain of the temple was torn in two from top to bottom. When the centurion who was standing opposite him saw how he died, he said, "This man must have been a son of God."[14]

The above verses, which are from the gospel of Mark, contain much and very important information. All three synoptic gospels have, on the whole, the same content, with the important difference that Matthew and Luke do not state at which time Jesus is hung on the cross, only the time that he dies. The earliest gospel, that of Mark, does give both times, however. And from this, we can determine that Jesus only hanged for six hours on the cross before he expired. This should be compared with the twenty-four, forty-eight, or seventy-two hours that it normally took. Some lines later in the gospel of Mark, it is pointed out how unusually quick this was: "Pilate was surprised to hear that he had died so soon, and sent for the centurion to make sure he was already dead."[15] This information is also missing in the gospels of Matthew and Luke.

The "centurion" mentioned above is undeniably of interest, as he is evidently the highest ranking soldier there. Mark portrays this Roman officer as being very sympathetically inclined towards Jesus ("This man must have been a son of God"). All three gospels point out this sympathy, although according to the gospel of Luke, the centurion's words are: "Beyond all doubt, this man was innocent."[16] Astonishing words from the man who is responsible for his crucifixion.

So, what actually occurred when Jesus expired? This information, too, is provided in the above verses: "and at three Jesus cried aloud, 'Eloï, Eloï, lema sabachthani?' which means, 'My God, My God, why have you forsaken me?'" As if at a given signal, somebody (who?) runs off and fills a sponge with "sour wine," and then puts this against Jesus' lips. Immediately afterwards, Jesus stops breathing. This is an extremely atypical death. That someone cries out at all just before he dies on the cross is remarkable. This has led some commentators to come to the conclusion that Jesus died of a "ruptured heart," i.e., a burst heart muscle, which is usually the result of the muscle having been weakened by a heart attack.[17] It is possible, of course, but is it probable?

What all advocates of *Die Scheintod-Hypothese* claim, is that there was something in the liquid that Jesus drank just before he expired, something that made him lose consciousness but not his life. There are a number of suggestions as to who it was who put this drink up to Jesus' lips, but the synoptic gospels do not themselves give us any clues: in the gospel of Matthew, we read about "the bystanders," and that "one of them" fetched the sponge. In the gospel of Mark, the description is almost the same: "some of the bystanders," and "someone" ran and soaked a sponge. One theory that has often been put forward is that Jesus in some way had made an agreement with the Romans about a faked execution—which would account for the sympathetic officer. Another is that it was some of Jesus' close associates, perhaps together with the above-mentioned officer, who arranged it all.

That is as much as the synoptic gospels tell us. So can the gospel of John contribute any more information? The text in the gospel of John is often formulated differently, and is quite often more detailed, than that in the synoptic gospels. That applies here, too. According to John, at the place of execution, there are some people who are very close to Jesus: "His mother was standing with her sister, Mary wife of Clopas, and Mary of Magdala." There too is another person who is often mentioned in the gospel of John: "the disciple whom he [Jesus] loved." John writes:

> Seeing his mother, with the disciple whom he loved standing beside her, Jesus said to her, "Mother, there is your son"; and to the disciple, "There is your mother"; and from that moment the disciple took her into his home. After this, Jesus, aware that all had now come to its appointed end, said in fulfilment of scripture, "I am thirsty." A jar stood there full of sour wine; so they soaked a sponge with the wine, fixed it on hyssop, and held it up to his lips. Having received the wine, he said, "It is accomplished!" Then he bowed his head and gave up his spirit.[18]

Who put the sponge to his mouth? Here, one definitely gets the impression that it is one of the named women or the beloved disciple, i.e., one of those people closest to Jesus. It can be worth recalling the theories that draw parallels between Lazarus and "the disciple whom Jesus loved."[19] It is a fact that Lazarus is mentioned a number of times up to chapter 12 in the gospel of John, and then disappears from the text, while "the disciple whom Jesus loved" turns up for the first time in chapter 13. Furthermore, in the gospel of John similar words are used about the feelings Jesus has for Lazarus and those he has for the beloved disciple—the words *phileo* ("like", "love") and *agapao* ("love") are used about both.[20] It was, after all, only a short while before that Jesus had woken Lazarus from the dead. Perhaps these two "awakenings" from the dead have the same main characters—Jesus and Lazarus—but in reversed roles. The sister of Lazarus was called Mary, but we do not know who "Mary wife of Clopas" was (although Hegesippus, a Greek Christian author who lived during the second century, mentions that a brother of Joseph was called Clopas.[21] This makes it probable that "his mother's sister" and "Mary wife of Clopas" are the same person). Again, it is remarkable that there are so many women called Mary around Jesus.

The gospel of John contributes further information:

> *Because it was the eve of the sabbath, the Jews were anxious that the bodies should not remain on the crosses, since that sabbath was a day of great solemnity; so they requested Pilate to have the legs broken and the bodies taken down. The soldiers accordingly came to the men crucified with Jesus and broke the legs of each in turn, but when they came to Jesus and found he was already dead, they did not break his legs. But one of the soldiers thrust a lance into his side, and at once there was a flow of blood and water. This is vouched for by an eyewitness, whose evidence is to be trusted. He knows that he speaks the truth, so that you too may believe.[22]*

Here are at least two new pieces of information: the two other crucified men, the *leistai*, had their legs broken, so that they would die quicker. But Jesus was spared this fate, because "he was already dead." This meant that Jesus' body was intact when it was taken down from the cross (and, of course, if he was still alive, he was in better condition to survive). Furthermore, the quick death cannot be explained by his having his legs broken (and nor is there any mention of leg-breaking in the other gospels). But then John writes: "one of the soldiers thrust a lance into his side," an action that produced "blood and water." And to emphasize that this really took place, the gospel writer adds: "This is vouched for by an eyewitness, whose evidence is to be trusted. He knows that he speaks the truth, so that you too may believe." It is interesting that John includes this information, because it is not probable that a dead person would start to bleed particularly much after being pierced. After all, the heart has stopped pumping. Certain old Bible manuscripts have another version of Matthew 27:49, where the lance is mentioned and it says that Jesus was pierced by it *before* he was dead. But otherwise, it is only in the gospel of John that there is a reference to a lance. Kersten and Gruber point out in their book that in the original Greek text (of both John 19:34 and the relevant manuscript of Matthew 27:49) it does not say that the lance went into his body. The Greek word ἔνυξεν (*enuxen*) rather implies a jab or a poke with the lance, and the text ought to be translated, "poked him in his side." It was not until the later Latin translation that it was said that the lance "opened up" his side.[23]

To summarize, there is a great deal that is atypical about how Jesus dies on the cross: it happens far too quickly, and without his legs being broken. He is far too strong just before the moment of death, and capable of talking as well as shouting. And it is striking that three of four gospel writers find reason to mention that Jesus accepts a drink just before the moment of death.

How likely is it that someone could survive a crucifixion, albeit one that has been interrupted? It has evidently happened. Flavius Josephus gives us an example from his own life:

> And when I was sent by Titus Caesar with Cerealius, and a thousand horsemen, to a certain village called Thecoa, on order to know whether it were a place fit for a camp, as I came back, I saw many slaves crucified, and remembered three of them as my former acquaintance. I was very sorry at this in my mind, and went away

with tears in my eyes to Titus, and told him of them; so he immedi-
ately commanded them to be taken down, and to have the greatest
care taken of them, in order to accomplish their recovery; yet two of
them died under the physician's hands, while the third recovered.[24]

It is considered that the Romans actually from the beginning regarded crucifixion as a method of punishment more than a method
of execution.[25]

What happens then, after the Romans have judged Jesus to be dead?
Now a new person is introduced into the story: Joseph of Arimathaea. We know very little about this Joseph; the gospel writers give
us extremely limited information. The gospel of John describes him
as "a disciple of Jesus, but a secret disciple for fear of the Jews." In the
gospel of Luke he is described as "a member of the Council, a good
and upright man, who had dissented from their policy and the action they had taken." In the gospel of Mark, Joseph is depicted in a
similar manner as "a respected member of the Council, a man who
looked forward to the kingdom of God," while the gospel of
Matthew has Joseph as "a wealthy man" who had become a disciple of Jesus.[26] So what does this Joseph of Arimathaea do?

[Joseph] *bravely went in to Pilate and asked for the body of Jesus.*
Pilate was surprised to hear that he had died so soon, and sent for
the centurion to make sure that he was already dead. And when he
heard the centurion's report, he gave Joseph leave to take the body. So
Joseph bought a linen sheet, took him down from the cross, and
wrapped him in the sheet. Then he laid him in a tomb cut out of the
rock, and rolled a stone against the entrance. And Mary of Magdala
and Mary the mother of Joses [Author's note: Joses was the
name of one of the brothers of Jesus] *were watching and saw*
where he was laid.[27]

Thus Jesus is not left on the cross, but is given a burial. And just
like Lazarus, he is put in a tomb hewn out of the rock, and a large
stone is rolled in front of the opening.

The synoptic gospels have nothing more to add about the actual burial. But the gospel of John does. And it is strange information indeed. Kersten and Gruber write in their book that "We have come to know the author of John's texts as the unknown person who wanted to communicate the mysterious events of the Crucifixion and burial of Jesus in a hidden way."[28] One definitely gains such an impression when one reads the following lines in the gospel of John, about what took place when Jesus was buried:

> *So Joseph [of Arimathaea] came and removed the body. He was joined by Nicodemus (the man who had visited Jesus by night) who brought with him a mixture of myrrh and aloes, more than half a hundredweight. They took the body of Jesus and following Jewish burial customs they wrapped it, with the spices, in strips of linen cloth.*[29]

"More than half a hundredweight" equals more than fifty-six pounds. And from the original Greek we can see that the weight of the spices was about seventy-five pounds! What did they need seventy-five pounds for? The Egyptians used myrrh and aloe for making mixtures of herbs for embalming purposes, but the Jews did not embalm. And the only reason Jews might possibly use myrrh and aloe in this context is as ingredients in aromatic oils.[30] But seventy-five pounds!

This does not, however, mean that the combination of myrrh and aloe is unknown. It is even known in large quantities. Myrrh and aloe were two of the most effective substances for healing wounds and providing disinfection in ancient times.

Myrrh, which is taken from the resin of the commiphora tree, has been used for hundreds of years to treat cuts and inflammation. Hippocrates prescribed it, and the Romans are said to have used it for respiratory infections and skin infections, to name just a few. It has also been shown that myrrh provides a certain degree of pain alleviation.[31]

Aloe vera, in turn, was regarded right up into the nineteenth century as one of the most effective treatments for burns.

The active ingredient was extracted from the leaves of the plant with the same name. Apart from aloe being seen as effective for healing wounded tissue, it also has a pain-killing effect.

It is rather incredible that the gospel of John provides us with this information, and even details the enormous amounts of myrrh and aloe that were used. One certainly gains the impression that the author is trying to tell us something. An alternative explanation would be that he has got information of which he himself does not understand the implications. He does actually write, "following Jewish burial customs." Whether this is written for the purpose of confusing the reader, or because John really does believe that a Jewish burial custom requires seventy-five pounds of myrrh and aloe, is impossible to know.

Another piece of information that seems strange, although not as astonishing, is that about the "strips of linen cloth" in which the body of Jesus is wrapped. The Greek word is ὀθόνιον (othonion). It is difficult to find these strips or bands in a Jewish burial ritual. They do, however, remind us of what the Egyptians wrapped around the bodies of the dead when preparing them for burial. Since the gospel of John so clearly states the body of Jesus is wrapped "with the spices," one interpretation of these strips is that they served as bandages. It is, however, possible that *othonion* is a misleading translation of the Hebrew *tachrichim* which is the garment in which the dead person is dressed for a Jewish burial. The root of the word (כרך) actually means "to bind," "to enwrap," or "to surround."

So, what happens after the burial? Yet again, it depends on which gospel we read. According to the gospel of Matthew, the high priests and Pharisees are worried, as Jesus has predicted that he shall rise up from the dead after three days. So they go to Pilate and ask him to order that the grave shall be guarded for three days, "otherwise his disciples may come and steal the body, and then tell the people that he has been raised from the dead; and the final deception will be worse than the first." So Pilate orders a guard to be posted, and the stone to be sealed.[32] There is no such story in any of the other three gospels.

What is, however, described in various forms in all the gospels, is that Mary Magdalene and "Mary, mother of James" (or "the other Mary," or "the women from Galilee"; note that James, too, is one of the brothers of Jesus) buy pleasant-smelling spices and oils in order to return to the grave after the Sabbath—and according to the gospel of Mark their purpose is to anoint Jesus (despite the fact that he has already been buried!). In Mark there is a further description of what then happens:

> *And very early on the first day of the week, just after sunrise, they came to the tomb. They were wondering among themselves who would roll away the stone for them from the entrance to the tomb, when they looked up and saw that the stone, huge as it was, had been rolled back already. They went into the tomb, where they saw a young man sitting on the right-hand side, wearing a white robe; and they were dumbfounded. But he said to them, "Do not be alarmed; you are looking for Jesus of Nazareth, who was crucified. He has been raised; he is not here."* [33]

Yet again, we meet the young man in the white robe.

The gospel of John describes a relatively similar (though not identical) episode that can be interpreted to mean that the young man in the tomb is the "disciple that Jesus loved": in the version in the gospel of John, Mary Magdalene does not enter the tomb, and she does not see a young man, but she does see the stone that has been rolled away, and out of fright she runs off to find Peter (something that, in the gospel of Mark, she is urged to do by the young man in the tomb). Then, in the gospel of John, it is written:

> *And [Mary Magdalene] ran to Simon Peter and the other disciple, the one whom Jesus loved. "They have taken the Lord out of the tomb," she said, "and we do not know where they have laid him." So Peter and the other disciple set out and made their way to the tomb. They ran together, but the other disciple ran faster than Peter and reached the tomb first. He peered in and saw the linen wrappings*

lying there, but he did not enter. Then Simon Peter caught up with
him and went into the tomb. He saw the linen wrappings lying
there, and the napkin which had been round his head, not with the
wrappings but rolled up in a place by itself. Then the disciple who
had reached the tomb first also went in, and he saw and believed.[34]

As regards "the disciple whom Jesus loved," he has traditionally also been given another identity. It is an old notion that this disciple is identical to the apostle John. There are two reasons for this: "The disciple whom Jesus loved" is only mentioned in the gospel of John, but that gospel never mentions the disciple John (also called John, son of Zebedee), despite the fact that in the synoptic gospels he seems to be one of the most important disciples (at one place in the gospel of John there is mention of "the sons of Zebedee"[35]). And secondly, the gospel of John ends with a story about "the disciple whom Jesus loved," which is followed by the words, "It is this same disciple who vouches for what has been written here, and we know that his testimony is true."[36]

According to these lines, then, "the disciple whom Jesus loved" is not only the *disciple* John, but perhaps also the *gospel writer* John. Many people, however, regard this last chapter as a later interpolation.

The gospel of John is in many ways a mystifying gospel. It was probably written later, it is different, and it gives us new information. But it is not always so easy to dismiss this new information.

In the above quote about the tomb, there is, for example, yet another piece of information that the gospel writer John is evidently anxious to convey: "He saw the linen wrappings lying there, and the napkin which had been round his head, not with the wrappings but rolled up in a place by itself." Why is it so important that the napkin is not together with the wrappings? The information is difficult to interpret; what is obvious, however, is that John wants to emphasize something with this. One possible interpretation is, of course, that the body of Jesus had been wrapped, together with the enormous amount of myrrh and aloe, but that his head had been left free, because he was alive, and was breathing.

But now, when the women arrive, the tomb is seen to be empty and Jesus has disappeared without trace. All that is left are the strips of linen. So where is Jesus? And is he dead, or is he alive?

Let us look at the stories of the gospel writers—and of the apostle Paul. Because when it comes to what happened to Jesus after the crucifixion, Paul, our earliest source of information, has a lot to say. And according to him, there was no doubt whatsoever that Jesus, after being crucified and laid in the tomb, had risen again from the dead. In the First Letter to the Corinthians, he writes:

> First and foremost, I handed on to you the tradition I had received: that Christ died for our sins, in accordance with the scriptures; that he was buried; that he was raised to life on the third day, in accordance with the scriptures; and that he appeared to Cephas [Peter], and afterwards to the Twelve. Then he appeared to over five hundred of our brothers at once, most of whom are still alive, though some have died. Then he appeared to James, and afterwards to all the apostles. Last of all he appeared to me too; it was like a sudden, abnormal birth.[37]

Paul has no doubts at all as to the fact that Jesus rose up from the dead. And that is not all: Paul regards this event as absolutely essential for the raison d'être of Christian teaching: "and if Christ was not raised, then our gospel is null and void, and so too is your faith." And he goes on, even more rashly: "and if Christ was not raised, your faith has nothing to it and you are still in your old state of sin. It follows also that those who have died within Christ's fellowship are utterly lost."[38]

Why does Paul stake everything on the resurrection, at least in this letter? For a person who does not say particularly much about the life of Jesus otherwise, there is an almost forced element in the way he hammers in the total meaning of the resurrection. Because this is how Paul reasons here: Jesus' deeds may be good, his ethics may be right, his predictions may be correct, he can even be the messenger of God. *But if he has not risen from the dead, then all of the rest is worthless.* Why? Because it is the resurrection that gives proof that Jesus is who he claims to be. That is how Jesus reasoned. And that is evidently how Paul reasons, too.

Does Paul have support for this from the gospel writers—and from the disciples? It was, after all, the disciples who regularly had expressed doubt about Jesus.

Let us begin with the gospel writers. All four writers are in agreement on this point: Jesus rose up from the dead, and he showed himself to his disciples. The only question mark is in the gospel of Mark. The last verses in the gospel (16:9–20), where Jesus actually shows himself, do not seem to be present in some early manuscripts. But even in the verses before these, there is *mention* that Jesus has risen, and the disciples are asked to make their way to Galilee to meet him there.

The gospel of Matthew, in turn, ends with the disciples actually going to Galilee, and there meeting Jesus. Before that, Mary Magdalene and "the other Mary" have come across Jesus beside the tomb, and there touched his feet. But this meeting does not seem as real, not least because the women shortly before this have been informed that Jesus is on his way to Galilee.[39]

The gospel of Luke, too, has a first appearance of the resurrected Jesus that seems more dreamlike: Two disciples—one of them is Cleopas (Clopas), the husband of the third Mary beside the cross—are walking along a road when suddenly Jesus joins them. But they do not recognise him. Somewhat later, Jesus shows himself to a large number of followers in Jerusalem, and it is said that he has also previously shown himself to Peter.[40]

In the Acts of the Apostles, too, which as far as we can judge were written by the same person who wrote the gospel of Luke, Jesus shows himself during a meal in Jerusalem, and he shall continue to show himself to the disciples for forty days.[41]

In the gospel of John, finally, Jesus makes his first appearance in front of Mary Magdalene beside the tomb. But she does not recognize him, and when he makes himself known to her, he does not want her to touch him. Later the same evening, Jesus shows himself to the disciples, but they do not seem to touch him either. One week later, however, he asks the doubting Thomas to touch his wounds. In the disputed last chapter of the gospel of John, Jesus shows himself yet again to the disciples, this time in Galilee.[42]

How do the disciples receive the resurrected Jesus? Do they continue to show doubt? In the gospel of Matthew, we can read that when Jesus shows himself to them in Galilee, they "knelt in worship, though some were doubtful."[43] In the gospel of Luke, the description is mainly one of the shock and surprise of the disciples when they suddenly see Jesus in the flesh right in front of them. And in the gospel of John, there is the story of the doubting Thomas, the person who first doubts the resurrection but who when he himself meets Jesus and is invited to touch his wounds, becomes convinced.[44]

It would seem that Jesus has finally succeeded in convincing most of his disciples that he is the person he has claimed himself to be.

What happens next? Strangely enough, the gospel of Matthew ends with Jesus meeting his disciples in Galilee. Nothing is told about his later fate. The story just stops.

Nor does the gospel of John have much more to tell us, even though the last, disputed chapter gives the impression that Jesus is preparing to set off on a journey.

Someone who does have more to tell, though, is the author of the gospel of Luke and the Acts of the Apostles. In the Acts of the Apostles, it is told how Jesus shows himself to the disciples and speaks of the kingdom of God for all of forty days. Then one day they gather together for a meal:

> When they were all together, they asked him, "Lord, is this the time
> at which you are to restore sovereignty to Israel?" He answered, "It is
> not for you to know about dates or times which the Father has set

within his own control. But you will receive power when the holy
spirit comes upon you; and you will bear witness for me in
Jerusalem, and throughout all Judea and Samaria, and even in the
farthest corners of the earth." After he had said this, he was lifted up
before their very eyes, and a cloud took him from their sight.[45]

In the gospel of Luke, the same author tells a similar story.[46]

Thus Jesus disappears by rising up to heaven (just like the prophet Elijah in the Old Testament). In the gospel of Mark, too, this ascension to heaven is described, but that is in the concluding verses, which may not be authentic. The author of Luke is thus the only gospel writer who with certainty gives us an ending, one that explains what happens when Jesus vanishes from the sight of humans. This is remarkable, since the author by his own admission has only collected information from others. But the need for an ending is obvious. Because what would we do without one? How would we explain that there are no more stories about Jesus' words and deeds? The divine miracle has indeed taken place: Jesus has risen up from the dead. But now he must acquire eternal life, and where should this life be lived? The ascension to heaven is one way to solve the dilemma: Jesus continues to live, but he vanishes from the sight of humans.

The question is, where?

* * *

Throughout history, those people who have looked at the stories of the death of Jesus, his resurrection, and ascension to heaven with non-religious eyes have arrived at different conclusions as to what actually happened. As mentioned above, there have been a number of theories. One theory that circulated early on was that Jesus died on the cross but that the body was stolen by the disciples. In his *Dialogue with Tryphon*, Justin Martyr (who died about the year 165 CE) writes that Jews spread rumours across the entire world that "his disciples stole him by night from the tomb," and in the gospel of Matthew the section about the sealing of the tomb seems almost written to disprove this statement ("We request you to give orders for the grave to be made secure until the third day. Otherwise his disciples may come and steal the body.").[47]

Another hypothesis was that those who saw Jesus after his resurrection were hallucinating, or were in some sort of religious ecstasy.[48]

A third common hypothesis was that Jesus never was crucified, but that somebody else suffered that fate. And the fact that a person called Jesus Barabbas ("Jesus, son of the Father") was released by the Romans has been interpreted by some people as meaning that it was actually Jesus of Nazareth who managed to get away. The Gnostic Basilides, who was active in Alexandria at the beginning of the second century, claims that Simon of Cyrene, the man who carried Jesus' cross, was crucified instead of Jesus.[49] This idea is possibly also put forward in one of the Gnostic texts found in Nag Hammadi (written down in the fourth century, but copied from earlier works): "I did not succumb to them as they had planned. But I was not afflicted at all. Those who were there punished me. And I did not die in reality but in appearance. . . . It was another, their father, who drank the gall and the vinegar; it was not I. They struck me with the reed; it was another, Simon, who bore the cross on his shoulder."[50]
It is also worth noting that Judas Iscariot, the man who betrayed Jesus, afterwards "went away and hanged himself."[51] The theory that Judas was crucified instead of Jesus was put forward very directly in the medieval apocryphal gospel of Barnabas.[52]
Also in the Koran, in which Jesus (Isa) is described as a great prophet, it is said—strangely enough—that he was never crucified:

> . . . for their saying, Verily, we have killed the Messiah, Jesus the son of Mary, the apostle of God, . . . but they did not kill him, and they did not crucify him, but a similitude was made for them.[53]

How has this information ended up in the Koran? Is it based on a legend of some sort? And in that case, where does it come from?

That Jesus completely succeeded in avoiding being crucified—whether on account of a Roman citizenship or for some other
reason—is a theory that cannot be dismissed. The story of the released Barabbas is strange, and demands some sort of explanation.

* * *

If one regards the texts of the gospels from a non-religious perspective, one has two choices: one either accepts the concrete elements in the story of the passion—Jesus lived, was crucified,
buried, rose from the dead, ascended to heaven—and tries to find
rational explanations. Or one dismisses the main features of the
story as fiction.

It is of course possible that Jesus was crucified, in the
same way as others who met with this cruel fate, and that he died,
in the same way that almost all those who were crucified died.
And that he then remained dead (whether or not the disciples hid
the body; whether or not anybody hallucinated that they saw
him alive). But what is remarkable is that there is so much in the
stories of the crucifixion and the burial to indicate that something
uncommon has taken place. There is so much that is atypical—
without, perhaps, being intended to be. It is as if the gospel writers wanted to convey the story as it really happened. Why,
otherwise, did they not describe him hanging on the cross for
three days, and dying in the same way that other crucified men
died? Why, in their writing, did they let him give a signal that he
wanted a drink, and when he got this drink let him expire? Why
point out that those who were crucified beside him had their legs
broken, while Jesus did not? And why describe that he was
wrapped in seventy-five pounds of medications—medications
that were used to treat wounds?

It is not difficult to gain the impression that the *purpose* of
the process that Jesus went through was for him to survive. And
because the gospels actually say that Jesus showed himself alive
again, there is reason to believe that he actually did.

*

But what then was the ascension to heaven?

Jesus has several reasons to vanish after having again shown himself alive. We have already raised one of the reasons: it guarantees
him "eternal life" and confirms his divinity.

But there is, of course, yet another reason. Jesus had been
crucified (if he actually was crucified) because the authorities—be
they the Sanhedrin or the Romans—wanted it, or at any rate felt
themselves forced to condemn him to death. So he cannot, after
this, simply go wandering about as if nothing has happened!
Whether Jesus has survived through the attentions of the authorities, or purely with the help of some close accomplices—or a combination of both—he must now disappear. Presumably he must
leave the country.

In all probability, it is this which has come to be called the
"ascension" in the gospel of Luke. And which came to be left without comment in the gospels of Matthew and John. The story of
Jesus comes to an end when the gospels come to an end, quite simply because Jesus vanishes from sight.

It is perhaps worthwhile to end this chapter by again mentioning
the story of a fairly successful aspiring messiah, a man whom Flavius Josephus describes in not just one, but two of his books, *Jewish
Antiquities* and *War of the Jews*:

> *Moreover, there came out of Egypt about this time to Jerusalem one
> that said he was a prophet, and advised the multitude of the com-
> mon people to go along with him to the Mount of Olives, as it was
> called, which lay over against the city, and at the distance of five fur-
> longs. He said further, that he would show them from hence how, at
> his command, the walls of Jerusalem would fall down; and he
> promised them that he would procure them an entrance into the city
> through those walls, when they were fallen down. Now when Felix
> was informed of these things, he ordered his soldiers to take their*

weapons, and came against them with a great number of horsemen and footmen from Jerusalem, and attacked the Egyptian and the people that were with him. He also slew four hundred of them, and took two hundred alive. But the Egyptian himself escaped out of the fight, but did not appear any more.[54]

CHAPTER 9

WHAT HAPPENED ON THE ROAD TO DAMASCUS?

*So when they had come here with me I lost no time, but took my
seat in court the very next day and ordered the man to be brought before me. When his accusers rose to speak, they brought none of the
charges I was expecting; they merely had certain points of disagree-
ment with him about their religion, and about someone called Jesus,
a dead man whom Paul alleged to be alive.*

Acts of the Apostles, 25:17–19

The first time I came across the claim that Jesus did not die on the
cross was twenty-five years ago—an acquaintance casually put
forward the theory during a dinner party. The statement immediately led to what could be called an "aha reaction." Pieces fell into
place: the reluctant Pontius Pilate who did not want to crucify Jesus,
the unusually short time on the cross, the resurrected Jesus, once
again alive. And the complicated construction *life-death–resurrection-
ascension* now had a rational explanation: the ascension was of
course the flight abroad that the Romans demanded of Jesus in exchange for letting him live.

But within a minute, a question arose: What happened next? A person with such strong visions as Jesus; a person who seems to have planned for—and evidently succeeded—surviving a death sentence; a person who was driven so strongly to want to spread his teachings throughout the world. He cannot simply disappear after this.

The question as to what happened next has naturally been asked by all those who, in one form or another, have come to the conclusion that Jesus did not die on the cross, or was never crucified. And although they might agree on that point—that Jesus survived—they strongly disagree when it comes to the theories about what happened afterwards. There is, after all, no biblical text to base theories on—at least, nothing that is immediately obvious.

There are, effectively, two main trains of thought: some authors, including Schonfield and Derrett, envisage that Jesus, despite having survived a crucifixion, died shortly afterwards of the wounds he had suffered.

Most commentators, however, picture that Jesus leaves the country, or in some way or another keeps out of the way. D. H. Lawrence lets the resurrected Jesus embark upon a long journey and end up in an Egyptian temple where he is seduced by an Isis priestess, while the authors of Holy Blood, Holy Grail let Jesus have a child with Mary Magdalene, the descendants of whom give rise to the Merovingian dynasty in France. Donovan Joyce puts forward the hypothesis that Jesus dies later during the Jewish war against the Romans, as one of the warriors at Masada. Linderholm and the authors of Jesus in Rome claim that Jesus must have continued to missionize, and journey around in different countries, while Karl Bahrdt, perhaps the earliest proponent of Die Scheintod-Hypothese, suggested that Jesus withdrew and lived in isolation with the Essenes.[1]

One of the most stubborn theories has it that Jesus, after having said farewell to his disciples, travels to India—first spending time in some other countries, such as Turkey and Persia. This theory is based upon some actually existing legends. In 1932, India's first prime minister, Jawaharlal Nehru, wrote a letter to his daughter Indira Gandhi: "All over Central Asia, in Kashmir and Ladakh and Tibet and even farther north, there is still a strong belief that Jesus or Isá travelled about there."[2] Holger Kersten is one of the authors who describe the theory of Jesus' travels eastward in his book *Jesus Lived in India*.[3]

But are there then no rumors that were spread *within* Christian circles? Yes, a rather unexpected source of information with regard to the fate of Jesus after the crucifixion and resurrection can actually be found in the works of Irenaeus, one of the foremost church fathers.

Irenaeus, who was bishop in Lyons, was born in Asia Minor and lived until about the year 200 CE. With his work *Adversus haereses* he became known as one of the strongest opponents of "heretical ideas." Nevertheless, in this very work, Irenaeus writes as follows:

> *On completing His thirtieth year He* [Jesus] *suffered, being in fact still a young man, and who had by no means attained to advanced age. Now, that the first stage of early life embraces thirty years, and that this extends onwards to the fortieth year, every one will admit; but from the fortieth and fiftieth year a man begins to decline towards old age, which our Lord possessed while He still fulfilled the office of a Teacher, even as the Gospel and all the elders testify; those who were conversant in Asia with John, the disciple of the Lord, [affirming] that John conveyed to them that information. And he remained among them up to the times of Trajan* [Author's note: Roman emperor, 98–117 CE]. *Some of them, moreover, saw not only John, but the other apostles also, and heard the very same account from them.*[4]

In other words, church father Irenaeus does actually seem to convey the information that Jesus lived to old age. One can interpret the text as meaning that he who "remained among them up to the times of Trajan" was John, rather than Jesus. But all the same, Irenaeus does claim that Jesus reached "old age" (which begins "from the fortieth and fiftieth year"), and he refers to testimony from the disciples. In the following paragraph, Irenaeus himself interprets Jesus' high age as meaning that he was in his fifties when he was crucified, and that he had been active for twenty years prior to that! But a more reasonable interpretation, if one is to follow the chronology of the gospels and at the same time believe the testimony of the disciples as to his high age, is that Jesus is still alive a number of years after the period that is described in the gospels.

But in that case, where? What does a person do who has shown such a powerful and absolute vision as Jesus has? How would he behave in order to realize it? Would he hide? Would he reappear in a new guise?

On that occasion, twenty-five years ago, one name soon came to my mind: Saint Paul.

At that time I did not know much about him. But I did know that it was Paul who took over the spreading of the faith, that it was he who completed Jesus' vision. And that he did so with extraordinary passion.

* * *

The Roman Empire, in the decades following the birth of Jesus: Now about 50 million people live here. And the emperor ensures that he can keep track of his subjects by the regular censuses. During the reign of Emperor Augustus, between four and five million of the inhabitants in the empire held full citizenship—primarily people who lived on the Italian peninsula. The number of citizens increases to between six and seven million by the year 47 CE. The others, more than 85 percent of the population, belong to nations that the Romans have conquered, or they are slaves and others.[5] There are Celts and Italians, there are Germans and Berbers and Egyptians and Greeks. And there are Jews. There are surprisingly many Jews. It is estimated that the total number of Jews at the time of Flavius Josephus amounted to eight million, and most of these lived in the Roman Empire.[6] This was admittedly after the destruc-

tion of Jerusalem and the resulting mass emigration, but even before that the Jewish population outside the borders of Judea and
Galilee was surprisingly large. And one of the reasons was the
large number of converts. Flavius Josephus describes the situation,
as it appeared during a time of calm, in the town of Antioch in
what was then Syria.

> For as the Jewish nation is widely dispersed over all the habitable
> earth among its inhabitants, so it is very much intermingled with
> Syria by reason of its neighbourhood, and had the greatest multi-
> tudes in Antioch by reason of the largeness of the city, wherein the
> kings, after Antiochus [Epiphanes], had afforded them a habitation
> with the most undisturbed tranquillity . . . and granted them the en-
> joyment of equal privileges of citizens with the Greeks themselves; and
> as the succeeding kings treated them after the same manner, they both
> multiplied to a great number, and adorned their temple gloriously by
> fine ornaments, and with great magnificence, in the use of what had
> been given them. They also made proselytes of a great many of the
> Greeks perpetually, and thereby after a sort brought them to be a por-
> tion of their own body.[7]

The Roman era was a dynamic one. New ideas were spread with
the mixing of nations in the empire; even new gods were absorbed,
and there was often a general feeling of movement and instability.
This was an era when many—especially, perhaps, Greeks and Romans—started to look beyond their pantheon. And Judaism, with
its partly new ethics but perhaps above all with its single, omnipo-
tent, ever-present God, became of interest to many. Besides, the Old
Testament already existed in Greek translation, called the *Septuaginta*,
and the holy texts of the Jews were thus accessible to all in the
Greek-speaking parts of the world. People who were not Jews now
started to be drawn to the synagogues.

The Jewish congregations seem to have encouraged converts at this
time, probably as a counterweight to the powerful Hellenist influ-
ences, which greatly affected Jewry. But one of the problems for

many of those Gentiles who were attracted to Judaism were the demands that were made upon them if they were to be accepted as proselytes: they had to observe the Sabbath and the kosher rules (i.e., what sort of food one could eat), and males had to be circumcised. And the last requirement, circumcision, was usually seen as the hardest to fulfil.

For this reason, large groups of "God-fearers" were formed (they were called *theosebeis* in Greek, and were probably the same groups that were called *sebomenoi* or *phoboumenoi*—*hoi phoboumenoi ton theon*, "those who fear God"—in the Acts of the Apostles). These were non-Jews who in virtually all respects had joined Judaism—they went to the synagogue, prayed to the only God, followed Jewish traditions—but they did not go through a complete conversion. And what primarily prevented them was the demand for male circumcision.

According to an inscription that was found in 1976 in a synagogue in Aphrodisias, in southwestern Turkey, more than half of those who contributed to the upkeep of the synagogue were *theosebeis*.[8]

That it was primarily in the eastern, more Greek, part of the Roman Empire that people came to be attracted to Judaism, has its explanations. Firstly, it was here that the large Jewish populations were concentrated. But probably, too, it was here that there was the most interest—positive as well as negative. The Greeks were a cultured people, they had a history that more than well matched that of the Romans, their language was the *lingua franca* of the entire region—even the Romans used Greek when they wanted to reach out to the largest reading public. But the Greeks, like the Jews, were a conquered people. The relation between Greeks and Jews was charged—there was competition as well as animosity, which could sometimes lead to violence—but there was also an ever-present interaction, and a not-inconsiderable mutual attraction.[9]

It was in these areas, around the eastern parts of the Mediterranean, that Judaism would gain most of its converts.

And it was in these areas that the apostle Paul would start his journeys. The apostle Paul, author of the earliest writings that have survived within Christianity—earlier even than the gospels.

PAUL:	JESUS:
"Call down blessings on your persecutors—blessings, not curses."	"Bless those who curse you, pray for those who treat you spitefully."
Romans 12:14	*Luke 6:28*

There is something mysterious about Paul, or Saul as he was called from the beginning. There is a sort of zero point in his life, a point when he seems to be born again (he does actually say of his experience at this time that "it was like a sudden, abnormal birth"[10]). And it is perhaps at this point we should begin:

One day in the early part of the fourth decade (between 31 and 36 CE, according to most chronologies[11]) a man is travelling on the road to Damascus. He is in his thirties, and his journey has only one purpose: to find and arrest supporters of Jesus Christ and take them to Jerusalem. At least, that is how he later describes the purpose of his journey.

By this time, Jesus has been dead perhaps one year, or possibly two, and according to the man's story he has himself spent this time persecuting Christians. The man is called Saul. Saul, who is a Jew, says he has been a Pharisee all his life. But even though he is an "Israelite"—"a Hebrew born and bred; in my practice of the law a Pharisee"[12]—he says that he was born outside Judea and Galilee. His hometown is instead said to be Tarsus in Cilicia—in present-day Turkey—which is also a part of the Roman Empire. Interestingly, though, it is only in one place in the Acts of the Apostles that it says that Saul was *born* in Tarsus—but in several places that he *came from* Tarsus.[13] What makes it interesting is that—in another source—there is information that Saul was born somewhere completely different.

The church father Jerome tells us that Saul's parents and Saul himself were born in the town of Gischala in Galilee, but that they moved to Tarsus when Saul was still very small.[14] Gischala lay less than twenty miles north of Jesus' hometown of Nazareth—and was, as opposed to Nazareth, a town that we know existed at the time of Jesus. The town is named in many contexts, not least in the works of Flavius Josephus.

It is not clear where Jerome got his information about the birthplace of Saul. Paul does not himself name a hometown in any of his letters.

It is, however, Paul himself who tell us something else about his background, something that indicates that he was a man with certain privileges. Paul has been honored with something very unusual for a Jew at this time: a Roman citizenship. In the Acts of the Apostles, there is a description of him telling a Roman commandant how he acquired this citizenship:

> The commandant came to Paul and asked, "Tell me, are you a Roman citizen?" "Yes," said he. The commandant rejoined, "Citizenship cost me a large sum of money." Paul said, "It was mine by birth."[15]

Nowhere is there any explanation why Paul should have acquired Roman citizenship at birth. It is, of course, implied that his father too is a Roman citizen. But how would a Jew with a fairly modest background (Saul himself has trained as a tentmaker) be able to acquire something so desirable? Besides, for a Pharisee it would mean a conflict, as a Roman citizen was expected to take part in the Roman religious cult. Many Bible scholars have commented upon this citizenship with surprise. And few have given any good answers.

What else do we know about Saul's earlier life? Not much. From the texts, we understand that he has some sort of wound or illness, though it is unclear which. He returns to this several times, in his later letters to the Christian congregations. To the congregation in Galatia he writes:

It was bodily illness, as you will remember, that originally led to my bringing you the gospel, and you resisted any temptation to show scorn or disgust at my physical condition; on the contrary, you welcomed me as if I were an angel of God, as you might have welcomed Christ Jesus himself. [16]

And for the congregation in Corinth, he tells thus:

To keep me from being unduly elated by the magnificence of such revelations, I was given a thorn in my flesh, a messenger of Satan sent to buffet me; this was to save me from being unduly elated. [17]

Another fact that is remarkable about Saul/Paul is that he lives in celibacy, and seems to have done so all his life. At any rate, there is no mention of a wife or children. And as he himself says: "To the unmarried and to widows, I say this: it is a good thing if like me they stay as they are." [18] This contrasts strongly with the norm among Pharisees, who as a rule entered into marriage at a very young age. And Saul has been a Pharisee all his life.

It was also Saul's upbringing as a Pharisee that brought him to Jerusalem the first time. It is he himself who describes how he came there: "'I am a true-born Jew', he began, 'a native of Tarsus in Cilicia. I was brought up in this city, and as a pupil of Gamaliel I was thoroughly trained in every point of our ancestral law.'" [19] Gamaliel the Elder is one of the great rabbis of the era, so if one should take Paul's words (as they are quoted in the Acts of the Apostles) as the truth, his religious schooling has been decidedly thorough.

From Paul's own words, too, we understand that he has been a very committed, indeed one could say fanatic, Jew. As he writes: "In the practice of our national religion I outstripped most of my Jewish contemporaries by my boundless devotion to the traditions of my ancestors." [20]

What is worth noting is that if one reads the original Greek text of the Acts of the Apostles and the Letter to the Galatians, Paul describes himself, in both places, with a word that we recognize.

The word is ζηλωτής—*zelotes*. And it means just what it seems to mean: zealot. But in most translations, the translators have decided to see the word as an adjective or an adverb. In the Revised English Bible, the sentence in the Acts of the Apostles reads: "I have always been ardent in God's service, as you all are today." But a literal translation from the Greek is: "I have been a zealot in the service of God to the same degree that you all are today."[21]

The text in the Letter to the Galatians, in the same English translation, is as follows: "I outstripped most of my Jewish contemporaries by my boundless devotion to the traditions of my ancestors." But a literal translation from the Greek is: " To a higher degree than my Jewish contemporaries I was a zealot for the traditions of our ancestors."[22]

There are a few other places, too, in the New Testament where the word "zealot" or "zealots" is used, but in those instances where it refers to a particular person, this person is either Paul or Simon the Zealot.[23] Even though one can of course translate the adjective of the word "zealot," i.e., "zealous," as "fanatic/keen," we can in at least some of these cases not disregard the possibility that there is here a reference to the Zealots, the Jewish rebels. We are, after all, in an era and an environment where the Zealots were active. Besides, the word in the text is not an adjective or an adverb. It is a noun.

The Zealots were not just rebels; they were also extremely rigid in a religious sense. If Paul had actually been a Zealot earlier, then he would presumably at some time later have ended up in conflict with them, at least on the religious plane.

The question of Saul/Paul's possible early connection with the Jewish rebels, the Zealots, has been brought up by several scholars.[24]

But with regard to actual events in Saul's early life, the texts have remarkably little to say. As one can read in the *Catholic Encyclopedia*: "He was still very young when sent to Jerusalem to receive his education at the school of Gamaliel. . . . From that time it is absolutely impossible to follow him until he takes an active part in the martyrdom of St. Stephen."[25]

The stoning of Saint Stephen (Stephanus, or Stefanos, as he is called in the original Greek) is a key scene in the Acts of the Apostles—and, so it would seem, in Saul's life. It is this scene that would appear to be the starting point for Saul's frantic hunting of Christians.

Who then was this Stephen? In the Acts of the Apostles, we can read that he helped Jesus' disciples in Jerusalem. It was he who looked after the Greek-speaking members of the congregation. The reason Stephen was to be stoned to death, according to the same source, was that the Sanhedrin had accused him of blasphemy.

The martyrdom of Stephen thus took place in Jerusalem, or rather outside Jerusalem, because as it says in the Acts they "threw him out of the city, and set about stoning him."[26] Saul is present, and we are told that "Saul was among those who approved of his execution." The stoning of Stephen, the man who is sometimes called the "protomartyr," becomes—according to the Acts of the Apostles—the starting point for "a time of violent persecution for the church in Jerusalem."[27]

Is this Stephen mentioned in any other contemporary sources, outside the New Testament? No, at least not so that we recognize him.

But Flavius Josephus does actually mention a person who has the same name. In fact, in all of Josephus' works, there is only one person by this name: Stephen (or Stephanus). Josephus' Stephen is not a Christian. He is "a servant of Caesar." What does agree, however, is that this Stephen also is attacked, on a road about ten miles outside Jerusalem. And those who attack him are Zealots, *leistai*, who, according to Josephus, plunder him. This is a significant event in the existence of the rebel movement. Because as a result of the attack upon Stephen, the Roman procurator Cumanus (48–52 CE) is furious, and he immediately orders the Roman troops to attack the surrounding villages (Josephus does not mention whether Stephen dies, but to judge by Cumanus' reaction that would seem a probable outcome). During the Roman attack on the villages, one of the soldiers takes a Torah, a scroll with the five books of Moses, and tears it into pieces in front of the villagers. This leads to a great tumult among the Jews, and the threat of an uprising, which Cumanus only succeeds in stopping by having the guilty soldier beheaded.[28]

Both of these attacks upon men by the name of Stephen will come to be starting points: in one case for Saul/Paul's persecution of Christians, in the other for Zealot rebel activity. Because Josephus' story about Stephen marks the beginning of the sudden frequent use of the word *leistai* in the year 48 CE.

So we are now yet again talking of an event that takes place fifteen to twenty years later than what seem to be similar events in the New Testament. Whether the tale of the Roman Stephen has any relevance at all in this context is of course impossible to say.

What we can say is that the name Stephen, as against the names of most of Jesus' disciples, is not a Hebrew or an Aramaic name. What we also can say is that it was the Zealots who attacked "the other" Stephen—and Paul might possibly have been a Zealot. We can further note that in the New Testament there is only one person with the name Stephen (Stephanus). And in the collected works of Josephus there is also only one person by the name of Stephen (Stephanus). And both of these are attacked on a road outside Jerusalem.

Yet another coincidence—if such it is—is worth mentioning. Immediately after Josephus describes the attack upon Stephen, he tells about the conflict that arises between the Jews and the Samaritans sometime between 48 and 52 CE. And Josephus introduces this with the following words:

> It was the custom of the Galileans, when they came to the holy city at the festivals, to take their journeys through the country of the Samaritans; and at this time there lay, in the road they took, a village that was called Ginea, which was situated in the limits of Samaria and the great plain, where certain persons thereto belonging fought with the Galileans, and killed a great many of them.

This leads, according to the accounts in Josephus' books, to *leistai* going to the attack against the Samaritans and burning down their villages.[29]

Compare that with the following lines from the gospel of Luke:

> *As the time approached when he was to be taken up to heaven, he set his face resolutely towards Jerusalem, and sent messengers ahead. They set out and went into a Samaritan village to make arrangements for him, but the villagers would not receive him because he was on his way to Jerusalem. When the disciples James and John saw this they said, "Lord, do you want us to call down fire from heaven to consume them?" But he turned and rebuked them, and they went on to another village.*[30]

There are fifteen to twenty years between these episodes. And there are fifteen to twenty years between the implied conflict between Jews and Samaritans in the New Testament and the evident conflict between Jews and Samaritans described in Josephus' works.[31]

* * *

"The witnesses laid their coats at the feet of a young man named Saul. As they stoned him Stephen called out."[32] How has Saul come to be present at the stoning of Stephen? We do not know, because Saul turns up as if from nowhere. The Acts of the Apostles do not mention him at all before he suddenly stands there as a part of the lynch mob. But from this point on, Saul seems to be a participant in the persecution of Christians, and a very active participant. "Saul, meanwhile, was harrying the church; he entered house after house, seizing men and women and sending them to prison."[33]

So how long had Saul been in Jerusalem before the stoning of Stephen? From the Acts of the Apostles, chapter 22, it is hard to come to any other conclusion than that he has been there a long time. Here, Paul describes the period in his youth when he studied under Gamaliel, and then he goes directly—without mentioning having left the city in between—on to describe how he becomes known as a persecutor of the supporters of Jesus.[34]

This conclusion is not, however, really supported by his own lines in the letter to the Christians in Galatia. In this letter, Paul describes a journey to Jerusalem three years after his own conversion, and says: "I [Paul] was still unknown by sight to the Christian congregations in Judea."[35]

Whatever the circumstances, the story of Saul/Paul, like that of Jesus, shows a great emptiness in the middle of life—an emptiness between early youth and when he is in his thirties, when he suddenly enters the story.

And we soon find ourselves on the road to Damascus.

There are several descriptions of Saul's conversion, his experience of meeting Christ on the road to Damascus.[36] But the only descriptions that convey the experience in detail are those that are told by somebody else, namely the author of the Acts of the Apostles. This author quotes Paul, for example in the following manner:

> "What happened to me on my journey was this: when I was nearing Damascus, about midday, a great light suddenly flashed from the sky all around me. I fell to the ground, and heard a voice saying: 'Saul, Saul, why do you persecute me?' I answered, 'Tell me, Lord, who are you?' 'I am Jesus of Nazareth whom you are persecuting,' he said. My companions saw the light, but did not hear the voice that spoke to me. 'What shall I do, Lord?' I asked, and he replied, 'Get up, and go on to Damascus; there you will be told all that you are appointed to do.' As I had been blinded by the brilliance of that light, my companions led me by the hand, and so I came to Damascus."[37]

In his letters, on the other hand, Paul seldom tells of the past, whether it be about his own life or about the life of the person whose message he is conveying: Jesus. He is thus much less concrete when he describes his conversion in the letters: "But then in his good pleasure

God, who from my birth had set me apart, and who had called me through his grace, chose to reveal his Son in and through me, in order that I might proclaim him among the Gentiles."[38]

Sometimes, some small oddments seem to crop up in Paul's letters, and the above quote definitely contains such an oddment. Why "from my birth"? After all, it was Jesus who was appointed in the womb, while Paul does not portray himself as anything other than a faithful Pharisee up to the time of his conversion.

There is no reason to doubt that what occurs is indeed a conversion, that Saul does undergo some sort of "rebirth" there on the road to Damascus. In fact, in his second letter to the Corinthians, chapter 12, Paul speaks of a man, evidently himself, who at this time was "caught up to the third heaven" (once again an odd reminder of Jesus, this time his ascension to heaven). The question one perhaps may ask oneself is: Who was Saul before this conversion?

The experience outside Damascus would not only be a turning point in Saul's life, it would also come to mark the beginning of the spread of Christianity across the world. Because it is Saul, who shall be Paul, who, almost single-handedly and with extreme dedication, comes to build up the new religion, at least outside the borders of Iudaea. The letters he later will write to his newly established congregations—which he tries to keep alive during his long absences—are testimony to a determination bordering on desperation:

> I should like you to bear with me in a little foolishness; please bear with me. I am jealous for you, with the jealousy of God; for I betrothed you to Christ, thinking to present you as a chaste virgin to her true and only husband. Now I am afraid that, as the serpent in his cunning seduced Eve, your thoughts may be corrupted and you may lose your single-hearted devotion to Christ.[39]

One has good reason to ask oneself where Paul got his enormous drive. He did not know Jesus; he had not been one of his disciples. He came from nowhere, straight into the red-hot core of the story.

PAUL:	JESUS:
". . . when the command is given, when the archangel's voice is heard, when God's trumpet sounds, then the Lord himself will descend from heaven; first the Christian dead will rise, then we who are still alive shall join them, caught up in clouds to meet the Lord in the air." *I Thessalonians 4:16– 17*	". . . and they will see the Son of Man coming on the clouds of heaven with power and great glory. With a trumpet-blast he will send out his angels, and they will gather his chosen from the four winds, from the far-thest bounds of heaven on every side." *Matthew 24:30– 31*

There would be some delay, however, before Saul started his preaching—quite a number of years. What does he do after the conversion experience outside Damascus? The answer depends on which source we read. If we read the letters, he journeys more or less immediately to "Arabia" where he stays a long time.[40] The Jewish Bible scholar Leo Baeck has suggested that the correct word may be "Araba" (instead of "Arabia"), which is a part of the Negev desert, and that Saul thus lived in the vicinity of the Essenes. On the other hand, the area that was known as *Arabia Petrea* is not very far from there. From Arabia, he then returns to Damascus. This undocumented period in Arabia and Damascus lasts all of three years.[41]

If, however, we read the Acts of the Apostles, there is nothing about any journey to Arabia. Instead, it is told that Saul stayed on in Damascus and "Without delay he proclaimed Jesus publicly in the synagogues, declaring him to be the Son of God."[42]

In both sources, it is however apparent that Saul for as long as possible avoids showing himself in Jerusalem. In the Letter to the Galatians, one can read:

> *Three years later I did go up to Jerusalem to get to know Cephas [Peter], and I stayed two weeks with him. I saw none of the other*

apostles, except James, the Lord's brother. What I write is plain truth; God knows that I am not lying! Then I left for the regions of Syria and Cilicia. I was still unknown by sight to the Christian congregations in Judea.[43]

In the Acts of the Apostles, one can instead read: "On reaching Jerusalem he tried to join the disciples, but they were all afraid of him, because they did not believe that he really was a disciple."[44] After this, there is a description of how Saul's friend Barnabas manages to convince the disciples to allow Saul to preach in the congregations in the city, but when some Greek-speaking Jews "planned to murder him," the disciples quickly sent Saul back to Tarsus.

In another place, Paul is quoted as follows: "After my return to Jerusalem, as I was praying in the temple, I fell into a trance and saw him there, speaking to me. 'Make haste,' he said, 'and leave Jerusalem quickly, for they will not accept your testimony about me.'"[45]

According to the Letter to the Galatians, Saul/Paul was not to return to Jerusalem for fourteen years.[46]

Why is Saul's presence in Jerusalem so sensitive? The Acts of the Apostles are not really clear on that point. What is clear is that his life is threatened by Jews, but it is not really explained why. Is it because he preaches Christianity? But the disciples in Jerusalem do that too, and besides they are building up congregations. It even says in the text, just after the disciples have sent Saul back to Tarsus, "Meanwhile the church, throughout Judea, Galilee, and Samaria, was left in peace to build up its strength, and to live in fear of the Lord. Encouraged by the Holy Spirit, it grew in numbers."[47]

So, is the problem instead that Saul has made himself known as a persecutor of Christians in Jerusalem, and is thus threatened with death by other Christians? It is, of course, conceivable, but is it likely? Here comes Saul as a newly saved Christian, ready to do everything for the Christian congregations. It would seem to be unreasonable that these congregations would threaten his life because they could not forget his old sins. And besides, this would not explain why the church "was left in peace" after Saul was sent back to Tarsus. It is as if they need to send him away in order to be left in peace by outsiders. The threat, then, would come from some outside source, rather than the church.

That Saul/Paul then continues to avoid Jerusalem for many years is even more remarkable. After all, it is there that the disciples and their congregations are to be found. It is in Jerusalem that the faith he preaches has its spiritual center.

There must reasonably be something else that makes him afraid to return to Jerusalem. And something else that causes him to actually be arrested on his last visit to Jerusalem, some years later. But more about that further on.

So, what happens after the first, abruptly terminated, visit to Jerusalem? As mentioned, the disciples send Saul to Tarsus in Cilicia, and there he seems to live quietly for quite a number of years—as many as fourteen years according to the Letter to the Galatians.[48] This letter (which is not always consistent with the Acts of the Apostles) thus provides the adult Saul/Paul with seventeen years that are not accounted for—three years directly after his conversion, fourteen years after the first visit to Jerusalem. What did he do all this time? Was he doing nothing? That does not seem to be really like him.

It is deserving of mention that *if*, for some reason, the authors of the writings in the New Testament felt compelled to artificially place all the historical events (i.e., everything that happened before Paul begins his great missionary work) in an earlier period than when they really happened, the Letter to the Galatians gives room for this—as much as seventeen years.

It is a staggering idea. Because a deliberate placing of events in an earlier time would mean that Paul in actual fact was active for a much shorter period than we believe. And that the activities of Jesus, and his crucifixion, took place much later than we think.

It need not have happened like this; it is not a necessary adjustment of history. But it would actually help us to explain a number of peculiar features. And it is doable—with just a few strokes of a pen, the names of a couple of emperors, a couple of Jewish kings, a Roman procurator and a couple of high priests could easily be exchanged.

What is remarkable is that if you put the New Testament beside part two of Flavius Josephus' *War of the Jews* and part twenty of *Antiquities of the Jews*, and then carry out the simple operation of transferring everything in the gospels fifteen to twenty years later in time, then you will notice after a while that it is as if one can read parts of the New Testament almost like a roman à clef! A roman à clef in which several stories in the gospels seem to be poetic and religious retellings of historical events described by Josephus.

* If Jesus is arrested in the 50s CE, rather than the 30s, it is suddenly understandable how he could be crucified together with "robbers" (*leistai*) the Zealot rebels who (in the works of Josephus) are conspicuous by their total absence between the years 6 and 44 CE, but become very frequent after the year 48.

* If Jesus is arrested in the 50s, it is no longer strange that his disciples have names like Simon the Zealot and Judas Iscariot.

* If Jesus is arrested after the year 52, the story of Jesus of Nazareth is suddenly very like Josephus' prominent story about "the Egyptian"; particularly if it is correct, as the gospel author John writes, that one thousand soldiers were needed to arrest Jesus, there on the slopes of the Mount of Olives.

  Thus, a problem that has long occupied Bible historians–that a person who according to the New Testament arouses such attention in his time nevertheless is invisible in contemporary historical accounts–could have a plausible answer. And Jesus is, in that case, a well-documented historical person.

* If Jesus is arrested after the year 52, instead of in the 30s, it is possible to explain why the Sanhedrin is said to have two high priests ruling together, because the high priests Jonathan and Ananias (son of Nebedaios) really did rule together. There is, however, no indication in Josephus that Annas and Caiaphas did so.

* If it is Felix (52–c. 59 CE) and not Pilate (26–36 CE) who is the Roman governor at the time of Jesus' arrest, this would explain both the personal animosity between the governor and the Jewish king ("That same day, Herod and Pilate became friends; till then there had been a feud between them."[49]) and the mention of the governor's wife ("While Pilate was sitting in court a message came to him from his wife: 'Have nothing to do with that innocent man; I was much troubled on his account in my dreams last night.'"[50]). The tetrarch Agrippa II (53–66 CE) had married off his sister Drusilla to King Azizus, after the king had agreed to be circumcised. When Felix meets Drusilla, he falls passionately in love with this Jewish princess, and persuades her to leave her husband and marry him, against the "laws of her forefathers" as Josephus writes.[51] Josephus does not have anything to say about the wife of Pilate.

* If Jesus is arrested and crucified after the year 52, it is no longer surprising that in the Acts of the Apostles Rabbi Gamaliel claims that Theudas, who died about the year 45 CE, is already dead.

* If John the Baptist started to gather people together by the River Jordan at the beginning of the 40s, instead of around the year 28, the story about him suddenly becomes startlingly similar to the story of Theudas, the man who "persuaded a great part of the people to take

their effects with them, and follow him to the River Jordan" and who was later beheaded ("They also took Theudas alive, and cut off his head, and carried it to Jerusalem.") Josephus uses similar words when he describes Theudas and when he describes "the Egyptian."

* If the king at the time of the birth of Jesus was Herod Antipas (tetrarch of Galilee, 4 BCE–39 CE), and not Herod the Great (42 BCE–4 BCE), we have the explanation for how Jesus, according to the gospel of Matthew, could return from Egypt both "after Herod's death" and "in the course of time" when John the Baptist appeared in the Judean wilderness.[52] And in that case, Jesus was not a child when he returned from Egypt, but an adult man—just like Celsus said. This would explain why people in his hometown did not at first recognize him.

* With regard to the second birth story, that in the gospel of Luke, the reference to the tax census under Quirinius could possibly have a symbolic content: the only known historically significant result of this tax census was that it was the starting shot for the establishment of the Zealots.

* If Jesus was active at the end of the 40s and the beginning of the 50s, we have an explanation for the conflicts, implied in the gospels, between Jews and Samaritans (something that is completely absent in the Acts of the Apostles). The conflict between the Jews and the Samaritans was triggered and then went on in the period 48–52 CE, and ended when procurator Felix came to Iudaea in the year 52 CE.

* If we delay the stories in the gospels by about fifteen to twenty years, the description in Luke about how

Jesus and his disciples journey through a village in Samaria becomes decidedly like Josephus' description of the events in the Samaritan village of Ginea ("Gêman" in *Antiquities of the Jews*), i.e., the events that triggered the conflict between Jews and Samaritans.

*   If Paul's conversion takes place in the 50s, instead of in the 30s, there really is an historical Stephen. And *if* the Stephen in the gospels is the same as the Stephen in Josephus, Paul's earlier life can be seen in a completely different light. Then the target of his earlier hostility was not the Christian community.

With regard to Paul's activities, the possible time shift shrinks, or ceases, in the mid–50s (by the adding of seventeen "empty" years in the Letter to the Galatians; the same thing is possibly accomplished in the Acts of the Apostles by placing "later" events "earlier" in the story.) But this is not necessarily the case. The Acts of the Apostles are often rather difficult to harmonize with Paul's letters, because the chronology sometimes seems to be jumbled.

Some of the apparent parallels between the New Testament and the books of Josephus can be coincidences. But all of them? It is hard to escape the feeling that there really is a pattern here. Nothing in the gospels or the Acts of the Apostles seems to be there by chance. Even what seem to be the most pictorial or metaphorical phrases, like "call down fire from heaven," appear to have equivalents in Josephus in concrete events. Of course, in Josephus we can only find a small portion of what is described in the New Testament, and vice versa. But what we can find does fit amazingly well, at least with regard to the gospels. It is sort of like when you are solving a part of a jigsaw puzzle in one place, and another part in another place, and then try to get the two parts to fit together. They will only fit at one given point. And this particular puzzle will fit if we shift the stories in the gospels fifteen to twenty years forward in time. Not otherwise.

The question one must ask is: why? And *if* there actually has been a deliberate time shift—and this, I would nevertheless emphasize, is only one of several possible hypotheses—then there really can only be one reasonable explanation: Flavius Josephus was a known person in Rome, according to church father Eusebius "the most famous Jew of his time," and his books were, according to Jerome, deposited in the Library of Rome.[53] In the 70s and the 90s, Josephus had published his version of what had taken place during the decades leading up to the Jewish War (and he was presumably not the only one). Luke, at least, seems to have read Josephus. Maybe it was not in the interest of the gospel writers, or the original editor, that comparisons should be made.

* * *

PAUL:	JESUS:
"God gave me the privilege of laying the foundation like a skilled master builder; others put up the building. Let each take care how he builds." *I Corinthians 3:10*	"He is like a man building a house, who dug deep and laid the foundations on rock. When the river was in flood, it burst upon that house, but could not shift it, because it had been soundly built." *Luke 6:48*

After Saul has lived many years in Tarsus, the man called Barnabas comes to him from Jerusalem. Barnabas takes Saul to Antioch, in Syria. They stay there together for a year "and gave instruction to large numbers."[54]

Who, then, is this Barnabas? He is a central person, who is first introduced in the Acts of the Apostles with the words, "For instance, Joseph, surnamed by the apostles Barnabas (which means "Son of Encouragement"), a Levite and by birth a Cypriot, sold an estate which he owned; he brought the money and laid it at the apostles' feet."[55] So Barnabas is based in Jerusalem, but at the same time he seems to have been with Saul already at the time of the conversion, outside Damascus. Because when Saul returns to Jerusalem the first time, it is Barnabas who calms the nervous disciples: "Barnabas, however, took him and introduced him to the apostles; he described to them how on his journey Saul had seen the Lord."[56]

Barnabas thus seems to have known the disciples earlier; he has their confidence. And he will now come to be Saul's most important associate. One can wonder why we have not read about this Joseph Barnabas in the gospels. Perhaps he is mentioned there, but under a different name.

Saul then, after having lived in obscurity in Tarsus for quite a number of years, is now fetched by Barnabas, and together they travel to Antioch. After spending a year there, Barnabas and Saul hear from a prophet about an impending "severe and world-wide famine." The disciples in Antioch then decide to contribute money and "sent it off to the elders, entrusting it to Barnabas and Saul." We can read this in the Acts of the Apostles.[57] According to this source, Saul thus suddenly dares return to Jerusalem. Is this the same visit that Paul himself says takes place "fourteen years later"?[58] If one reads the Letter to the Galatians, it is hard to see any decent agreement. This is one of the cases where the Acts of the Apostles and the letters of Paul do not really agree with each other, at any rate in their inner chronology. And in such cases, most commentators tend to place greater trust in the letters.[59]

But regardless of whether this visit to Jerusalem actually takes place (and in that case, when?), what is described as the reason for the visit—to send money "to the elders" in Judea—will come to form a pattern. Because Paul's future letters to the Christian congregations he founds will in considerable part come to be about collecting money for the Christian congregation in Jerusalem:

> I have been longing for many years to visit you on my way to Spain
> . . . But at the moment I am on my way to Jerusalem, on an errand
> to God's people there. For Macedonia and Achaia have resolved to
> raise a fund for the benefit of the poor among God's people at

Jerusalem. They have resolved to do so, and indeed they are under an obligation to them.

Romans, 15:23–27

Now about the collection in aid of God's people: you should follow the instructions I gave to our churches in Galatia. Every Sunday each of you is to put aside and keep by him whatever he can afford, so that there need be no collecting when I come. When I arrive, I will give letters of introduction to persons approved by you, and send them to carry your gift to Jerusalem.

I Corinthians, 16:1–3

We must tell you, friends, about the grace that God has given to the churches in Macedonia. The troubles they have been through have tried them hard, yet in all this they have been so exuberantly happy that from the depths of their poverty they have shown themselves lavishly open-handed. Going to the limit of their resources, as I can testify, and even beyond that limit, they begged us most insistently, and on their own initiative, to be allowed to share in this generous service to their fellow-Christians. . . . This is not meant as an order; by telling you how keen others are, I am putting your love to the test.

II Corinthians, 8: 1–8

"In point of fact," says Raymond Collins, "all seven epistles in the canonical corpus which contemporary scholarship unanimously deems to be the genuine work of Paul, somehow address themselves to financial considerations."[60]

It is remarkable that Paul devotes so much effort to collecting money for Jerusalem, and evidently for the leadership of the congregation (why, otherwise, would he call them "God's people" or, as it is more often translated, "the saints"?) How can we explain this? Are they poorer than other congregations? Of course, the people in

Jerusalem will have political, and perhaps economic, difficulties, but would this make them poorer than, for example, the congregations in Macedonia, which in "the depths of their poverty have shown themselves lavishly open-handed"?

Either Paul is collecting money for the organizational work that is required in Jerusalem, or there is some other explanation. And it is difficult to avoid the feeling that he is in some way solving a problem he has with the Jerusalem congregation by sending them money. As Paul writes in the Letter to the Romans: "Be my allies in the fight; pray to God for me that I may be saved from unbelievers in Judea and that my errand to Jerusalem may find acceptance with God's people [the saints]."[61]

So who then are the people who govern the congregation in Jerusalem?

Jesus' closest disciple, Peter, quite clearly has a very important role, and is described as one of the most prominent. Besides, we can follow his activities in quite considerable detail in the Acts of the Apostles. But the person who seems to have perhaps the greatest power in Jerusalem is a man of whom we have read nothing at all in the gospels—except in connection with Jesus' unsuccessful visit to his home town of Nazareth—namely his brother James. After the crucifixion of Jesus, James has evidently stepped forth as a leading person among the Christians in Jerusalem. And one sometimes gets a clear impression that it is James who decides what Peter should do.[62] That we are dealing with James, the brother of Jesus, and not James, the brother of John, is, however, based on rather scanty evidence.[63]

For Saul, however, Barnabas seems to be the most important associate, now when he finally—after all the years in passive exile—embarks upon his work. And the two of them shall soon acquire more associates:

> ... and Barnabas and Saul, their task fulfilled, returned from Jerusalem, taking John Mark with them.[64]

Who is this "John Mark," or "John who calls himself Mark" in other translations? According to one of Paul's letters, he is the cousin of Barnabas.[65] And the newcomer seems to be someone who shall follow Paul on a part of his missionary travels. Paul also mentions Mark in several letters that he writes later in imprisonment.[66] Whether this John Mark is identical to the gospel writer Mark is an open question. Whether he is identical to the gospel writer John, and possibly thus also the "disciple whom Jesus loved," is also an open question (his mother is called Mary[67]). One thing that is expressed clearly is, at least, that John Mark is a person that Saul, after many years of absence, fetches from Jerusalem.

Barnabas and John Mark are, however, not the only ones who shall follow Saul on his journeys. He gathers around him a number of fellow travelers—or disciples. Some of the names that are given later are Silas, Titus, Timothy, Aquila, Demas, and Luke.

It is now that Saul's missionary activity really starts. He shall be transformed from Saul to Paul. And Barnabas will be his most important colleague.

> *These two, sent out on their mission by the Holy Spirit, came down*
> *to Seleucia, and from there sailed to Cyprus. Arriving at Salamis,*
> *they declared the word of God in the Jewish synagogues.[68]*

"Are they Hebrews? So am I. Abraham's descendants? So am I." Thus writes Paul to one of the congregations he shall come to found.[69]

If Jesus can be said to have had a complicated relation to his own Jewish people, and above all to its establishment, this is even more pronounced in the case of Paul. But despite this, Paul, just like Jesus, directs his missionary work above all to the Jews. Wheresoever he journeys, it is to the synagogue he makes his way—and to the Jews that he presents his message of the resurrected Christ.[70]

And to start with, it seems to go quite well. Barnabas and Paul visit Pisidian Antioch, and "on the sabbath they went to synagogue and took their seats." When the officials of the synagogue after the reading of the Torah ask if anyone in the congregation has anything to say, Paul stands up and preaches about Christ to the Jews.

This seems to fall in fertile ground, because "as they were leaving the synagogue they were asked to come again and speak on these subjects next sabbath; and after the congregation had dispersed, many Jews and gentile worshippers went with Paul and Barnabas, who spoke to them and urged them to hold fast to the grace of God."

But soon, problems seem to arise. Because a few lines later in the text, it says about the next Sabbath that "almost the entire city gathered to hear the word of God" from Paul, and "when the Jews saw the crowds, they were filled with jealous resentment, and contradicted what Paul had said with violent abuse."[71]

Very early on, it would seem, Paul discovers that he does not really get through to the Jews. With the so-called "God-fearers"—non-Jews who are attracted to Judaism—he does however appear to have greater success with his preaching: "When the Gentiles heard this, they were overjoyed and thankfully acclaimed the word of the Lord . . . But the Jews stirred up feeling among those worshippers who were women of standing, and among the leading men of the city."[72]

Similarly at the next place: "At Iconium they went together into the Jewish synagogue and spoke to such purpose that Jews and Greeks in large numbers became believers. But the uncon-

PAUL:	JESUS:
"'A little leaven,' remember, 'leavens all the dough.'" *Galatians 5:9*	"It is like yeast which a woman took and mixed with three measures of flour till it was all leavened." *Luke 13:21*
"So we who observe the festival must not use the old leaven, the leaven of depravity and wickedness, but only the un-leavened bread which is sincerity and truth." *I Corinthians 5:8*	"Be on your guard, I said, against the leaven of the Pharisees and Sadducees." *Matthew 16:11*

verted Jews stirred up the Gentiles and poisoned their minds against the Christians."[73]

The tone in the Acts of the Apostles, and above all in the letters that Paul will soon write, shall come to be more and more about the Jews' rejection of him. It seems as if Paul is unable to get over this. Though he is obviously pleased with the large crowds that he succeeds in attracting, it becomes all the more painful for him that he is not able to convince his own people:

> I tell you that there is a great grief and unceasing sorrow in my heart. I would even pray to be an outcast myself, cut off from Christ, if it would help my brothers, my kinsfolk by natural descent. They are descendants of Israel, chosen to be God's sons; theirs is the glory of the divine presence, theirs the covenants, the law, the temple worship, and the promises. The patriarchs are theirs, and from them by natural descent came the Messiah. May God, supreme above all, be blessed for ever! Amen.[74]

Paul's relation to the Jews will become all the more problematic. Because, as in the case of Jesus, Paul's original intention was probably to preach mainly to the Jewish people, and quite simply try to convince them that the prophecy of the coming Messiah, he who would save them, was fulfilled. Paul, like Jesus, was bound to his Jewish people with ties that he never really succeeded in breaking— however filled with conflict these ties were, and above all would come to be.

But with the "God-fearers" and other Gentiles he meets with increasingly greater success on his journeys. And as far as traveling is concerned, it is as if nothing can prevent the frantic pace, not even Paul's physical weakness:

> At the games, as you know, all the runners take part, though only one wins the prize. You also must run to win. Every athlete goes into strict training. They do it to win a fading garland; we, to win a garland that

*never fades. For my part, I am no aimless runner; I am not a boxer who
beats the air. I do not spare my body, but bring it under strict control, for
fear that after preaching to others I should find myself disqualified.*[75]

During the years directly after this, Paul and his associates will visit
many towns around the eastern part of the Mediterranean. They
preach and they even heal, as Jesus once did. In the Acts of the
Apostles, it is told, for example, how Paul and Barnabas in Lystra
come upon a man who has been lame since birth: "Paul fixed his
eyes on him and, seeing that he had the faith to be cured, said in a
loud voice, 'Stand up straight on your feet'; and he sprang up and
began to walk."

That Paul is regarded as more than just a human being is
seen from the reactions this healing of the lame man brings forth:
"When the crowds saw what Paul had done, they shouted, in their
native Lycaonian, 'The Gods have come down to us in human
form.'" People call Barnabas Zeus, and Paul Hermes, "because he
was the spokesman." But the two apostles protest wildly at this, and
only after a great effort did they persuade the people to refrain from
making sacrifices to them.[76]

Paul's powers are not, however, restricted to healing the
sick. On at least one occasion, he raises someone from the dead.[77]

Eventually, Paul and Barnabas return to their base in Antioch in Syria.

But soon, something decisive happens. Paul has realized
that those who are most susceptible to his message are the "God-
fearers" and the heathens, not the Jews. And he has started to ad-
just the message accordingly:

*I am free and own no master; but I have made myself everyone's ser-
vant, to win over as many as possible. To Jews I behaved like a Jew, to
win Jews; that is, to win those under the law I behaved as if under the
law, though not myself subject to the law. To win those outside the
law, I behaved as if outside the law. . . . To them all I have become
everything in turn, so that in one way or another I might save some.*[78]

And one of the things that Paul has started to preach is that to be saved you do not at all need to go through the rituals that a conversion to Judaism demands.

PAUL:	JESUS:
"All that I know of the Lord Jesus convinces me that nothing is impure in itself; only, if anyone considers something impure, then for him it is impure." *Romans 14:14*	"Nothing that goes into a person from outside can defile him; no, it is the things that come out of a person that defile him." *Mark 7:15*

Paul shall thus come to break with an important principle that the disciples—and possibly Jesus—had kept up, namely that one stayed within the Jewish law, at any rate in certain decisive respects. As one can see from the description in the gospels of the crucifixion, the disciples respected the Sabbath. It is true that Jesus, before this (at any rate as it is described in the gospels) made several statements indicating that he did not think one always had to follow the Sabbath rules in every detail,[79] and that perhaps one did not need to follow the kosher rules, but he did not seem to have made "breaking the rules" into a principle. At any rate, he had not given any such principle to his disciples. In the Acts of the Apostles, namely, it is told how the foremost disciple, Peter, after the death of Jesus, is given an offer to eat something "unclean," and how he reacts:

He grew hungry and wanted something to eat, but while they were getting it ready, he fell into a trance. He saw Heaven opened, and something coming down that looked like a great sheet of sailcloth; it was slung by the four corners and was being lowered to the earth, and in it he saw creatures of every kind, four-footed beasts, reptiles and birds. There came a voice which said to him, "Get up Peter, kill and eat." But Peter answered, "No, Lord! I have never eaten anything profane or unclean."[80]

But where Jesus possibly had had a tendency to "soften up" the law—and come into confrontation with Pharisees and Sadducees about this—Paul now goes all the way. And he not only declares that the kosher rules no longer need apply, but he also breaks perhaps the most inviolable law: the one that says that all Jewish boys must be circumcised. As he writes in a letter: "That is the rule I give in all the churches. Was a man called with the marks of circumcision on him? Let him not remove them. Was he uncircumcised when he was called? Let him not be circumcised. Circumcision or uncircumcision is neither here nor there; what matters is to keep God's commands."[81]

The implication of this is greater than it might seem at first. Paul not only puts aside a fundamental Jewish law, he also gets rid of the greatest obstacle that all the Greeks who are attracted to the synagogues experience. Had it not been for the demand that they be circumcised, probably the greater part of those who call themselves "God-fearers" would have converted fully. And now a man comes and says to them that they do not need to be circumcised. They can believe in the only God, they can read and believe in the Jewish Bible, they can absorb the ethics. But they do not need to undergo this operation. All they need to do is recognize that the Messiah prophesied in the Bible has come, in the form of Jesus Christ, Son of God.

It is not only those who are already convinced, the "God-fearers," that Paul reaches with his new message. With his brilliance and intensity he soon reaches large numbers of people outside the synagogues too. All those who long to leave the old religion, and its many gods. All those who are attracted to the message about the only God, just and all-powerful, the Father, he who has sent his only son to the earth.

There are, however, some who become wary. And they are not just the Jews in the congregations that Paul visits. They are also the Jews in Jerusalem—those who were, and are, Jesus' disciples:

> Some people who had come down from Judea began to teach the
> brotherhood that those who were not circumcised in accordance with

Mosaic practice could not be saved. That brought them into fierce
dissension and controversy with Paul and Barnabas, and it
was arranged that these two and some others from Antioch
should go up to Jerusalem to see the apostles and elders about
the question.[82]

Finally, Paul thus returns to Jerusalem, for the decisive meeting that
has come to be called the Council of Jerusalem (most people understand this to be the meeting that Paul refers to in the Letter to
the Galatians, when he writes: "Fourteen years later, I went up again
to Jerusalem with Barnabas"; possibly, this interpretation means
that some of the missionary journeys around the Mediterranean
that have already been described actually take place *after* the Council of Jerusalem, since in the Letter to the Galatians, Paul only says
that he had previously visited "Syria and Cilicia."[83]).

Is Paul afraid to return to Jerusalem? From the text, this is hard to
determine. When we read the Acts of the Apostles it seems that this
time he shows his face to most of the apostles ("When they reached
Jerusalem they were welcomed by the church and the apostles and
elders."). In Paul's own letter, the Letter to the Galatians, this is not
as clear. There it simply says: "I explained, at a private interview
with those of repute, the gospel which I preach to the Gentiles."
Who are "those of repute"? Some lines further on, there is mention
of "sham Christians, intruders who had sneaked in," and then come
three other names: "James, Cephas [i.e., Peter], and John." Again,
roughly the same persons that Paul had had contact with on his
visit fourteen years earlier. In neither the Acts of the Apostles nor
the Letter to the Galatians, however, does Paul show himself to the
public, or go out onto the streets to preach.[84]

So what takes place at this meeting with the leadership of the congregation in Jerusalem? What actually happens is the beginning of
the separation between Judaism and Christianity. The apostles in
Jerusalem cannot conceive of receiving uncircumcised men into
their congregation—they have always been directed towards Jews,

and they shall continue to be so. But, strange though it may seem, they are evidently prepared to accept that Paul acts differently. As he himself writes:

> . . . they saw that I had been entrusted to take the gospel to the Gen-
> tiles as surely as Peter had been entrusted to take it to the Jews; for the
> same God who was at work in Peter's mission to the Jews was also
> at work in mine to the Gentiles.[85]

This willingness to compromise that Jesus' foremost disciples show is remarkable, and an indication as good as any of the importance they accord to Paul. They evidently accept that the church is divided into two: one part that is directed towards Jews, one part that is directed towards non-Jews. But Paul must actually give something in exchange: "All they asked was that we should keep in mind the poor, the very thing I have always made it my business to do."[86] It is thus possibly implied here that the work of collecting money was started *after* the Council of Jerusalem, and not the other way around, as it is stated in the Acts of the Apostles.

Paul and his fellow travelers now return to Antioch, and there start their new activity, liberated from the demands that the Jerusalem church had previously made upon them. And the split soon becomes even more distinct. Peter comes on a visit to Antioch, and shortly after that some more guests come from Jerusalem, sent out by James, the brother of Jesus. A confrontation soon takes place, which Paul describes:

> But when Cephas came to Antioch, I opposed him to his face, because
> he was clearly in the wrong. For until some messengers came from
> James, he was taking his meals with gentile Christians; but after they
> came he drew back and began to hold aloof, because he was afraid of
> the Jews. The other Jewish Christians showed the same lack of princi-
> ple; even Barnabas was carried away and played false like the rest.[87]

Paul solves the problem by yet again setting out on a journey. And now he and Barnabas go different ways. Paul appoints Silas as his companion, and travels to Syria and Cilicia. In Lystra they pick up another fellow traveler, Timothy. These three shall now travel around and start congregations in Asia Minor. It is during these journeys that Paul writes most of his famous letters.

Thus, as opposed to the case with Jesus, when it comes to Paul we have the text that he himself has put down in writing. These letters—thirteen or fourteen in number, of which seven are regarded as "authentic," i.e., written by Paul himself—give a clear picture of this man's character, his driving force and modus operandi. They are sometimes brilliant, sometimes extremely down-to-earth, sometimes irritated. And there is no doubt at all that Paul is a man with an enormous will. He praises, he curses, he begs, and he threatens. Anything to get the congregations he is trying to keep afloat—many congregations at great distance—not to abandon him and his faith during his long absences from them.

PAUL:	JESUS:
"I am jealous for you with the jealousy of God; for I betrothed you to Christ thinking to present you as a chaste virgin to her true and only husband."	"When the day comes, the kingdom of Heaven will be like this. There were ten girls, who took their lamps and went out to meet the bridegroom."
II Corinthians 11:2	Matthew 25:1

And Paul spreads an irresistible message, a message that embraces everyone—Jew and Greek, sinner and seeker:

But now, quite independently of law, though with the law and the prophets bearing witness to it, the righteousness of God has been made known; it is effective through faith in Christ for all who have such faith—all, without distinction.[88]

But in his relation to the Jews that do not accept his message, Paul now comes to be radicalized. In his first letter to the Christians in the letter that is considered to be the earliest of the preserved letters, he writes about:

> . . . the Jews, who killed the Lord Jesus and the prophets and drove us out, and are so heedless of God's will and such enemies of their fellow-men that they hinder us from telling the Gentiles how they may be saved. All this time they have been making up the full measure of their guilt. But now retribution has overtaken them for good and all! [89]

And about circumcision, he writes: "Those agitators had better go the whole way and make eunuchs of themselves!" and "Be on your guard against those dogs, those who do nothing but harm and who insist on mutilation—'circumcision' I will not call it." [90]

We have cause to see these words as weapons in a war, or in a competition, a running race as Paul himself calls it, a race where "only one wins the prize." [91] For what Paul is competing against is the other great religion that attracts all the Greeks and Romans who have tired of their gods, namely Judaism. And really they are more or less the same religion, with the decisive difference that Christianity has found its Messiah. Paul is driven by an enormous zeal to win this competition. The question is whether, in the history of the world, there is a better example of a person who single-handedly has transformed a world, almost without using others to help him. We have many examples of leaders whose private will governs an entire country; warriors who take over an entire continent, too. But they have the help of an army, a government, a police force. Paul has only himself, and some disciples he has personally chosen. His pathos, burning enthusiasm, and ability are without comparison, and quite astonishing.

Paul journeys around and preaches for some more years—in Macedonia and Greece, in Syria and Asia Minor. During this time, he has the city of Ephesus as his base.

But, finally, he does actually return to Jerusalem.

The year is 57 or 58 CE when Paul again makes his way to Jerusalem (The Acts of the Apostles mention an additional earlier visit, which is not, however, supported in the letters). He is on a journey in the Mediterranean, obviously in the company of Luke, among others. The group lands at Tyre, in present-day Lebanon. Luke himself writes in the Acts of the Apostles (and he writes "we"):

> *We came in sight of Cyprus and, leaving it to port, we continued our voyage to Syria and put in at Tyre, where the ship was to unload her cargo. We sought out the disciples and stayed there a week. Warned by the spirit, they urged Paul to abandon his visit to Jerusalem. But when our time ashore was ended, we left and continued our journey.*[92]

The travelers end up in Caesarea. And yet again Paul is warned against going to Jerusalem. But he answers: "Why all these tears? Why are you trying to weaken my resolution? I am ready, not merely to be bound, but even to die at Jerusalem for the name of the Lord Jesus."[93]

This is almost like a repeat of Jesus' decision to enter into Jerusalem, many (or perhaps just a few) years earlier.

Why does Paul want to go to Jerusalem? He has, after all, come to an agreement with the apostles there about leaving the conversion of Judea to them. But obviously he is unable to refrain from going to those people he most of all wants to save: the Jews in Jerusalem. Because this time, Paul is not going to hide himself when he arrives.

The first people he meets when he arrives in Jerusalem are James and "all the elders." And he is immediately given a warning. "You observe, brother, how many thousands of converts we have among the Jews, all of them staunch upholders of the law [Greek original: all are Zealots when it comes to the law]. Now they have been given certain information about you; it is said that you teach all the Jews in the gentile world to turn their backs on Moses, and tell them not to circumcise their children or follow our way of life. What is to be done, then? They are sure to hear that you have arrived." The apostles advise Paul to go through an official ritual of purification, and shave his head, "then everyone will know there is nothing in the reports they have heard about you."[94]

Again, some people are said to be a threat to Paul, but this time it seems as if they are the "converts," the Jewish-Christians, those who believe in Christ but wish to continue to follow the Jewish law. Or, if one wants to interpret the Greek text in another way, they are the Zealots.

This may be an appropriate time to yet again bring up the books of Flavius Josephus. Because it is not entirely impossible that also the "Jerusalem congregation"—the apostles remaining in Jerusalem— is mentioned in Josephus' books, even though the analogies are less clear, and less tied to a certain interval of time. Some of the stories in the Acts of the Apostles—particularly perhaps in chapter 5— about the work of Peter and the other apostles, after the crucifixion of Jesus, seem to have a certain echo in *Antiquities of the Jews* and *War of the Jews*, but somewhat later, just prior to and at the beginning of the Jewish uprising.[95] It is, however, as previously stated, not as clear as in the case of the gospels. But if there is something behind these parallels too, one has cause to ask whether some—or even all—of the disciples are actually leading Zealots (and whether, perhaps, we see traces of Menahem in Peter). If so, their role as "disciples" in the gospels would be a symbolic one.

* * *

If it really is to calm the converts that Paul shaves his head—or if it is so that he shall not be recognized—we can only speculate. But what he does now is to show himself publicly in Jerusalem for the first time since his own conversion. And he does so by going to the most holy place of Judaism. He goes to the Temple—just like Jesus once did. He goes to the Temple several times, for seven days—just like Jesus once did. And in the end he is recognized:

> But just before the seven days were up, the Jews from Asia saw him
> in the temple. They stirred up all the crowd and seized him, shouting,

*"Help us, men of Israel! This is the fellow who attacks our people,
our law, and this sanctuary, and spreads his teaching the whole
world over. What is more, he has brought Gentiles into the temple
and profaned this holy place."*[96]

The crowd takes Paul and drags him out of the Temple. This is
turning into a lynch mood, but a Roman commandant hears word
of what is happening and rushes to the Temple with his soldiers.
When he arrives, the crowd stops beating Paul. The commandant,
who at first does not understand who Paul is, has him arrested
nevertheless, and taken to the barracks.

Once there, Paul introduces himself as a "Jew from Tarsus
in Cilicia, a citizen of no mean city. May I have your permission to
speak to the people?"[97]

Strangely enough, the commandant lets Paul speak to the
crowd that has gathered. Paul now, thus, has definitely made his
presence public in Jerusalem, and he is going to take the opportunity to reach out to the assembled crowd here too.

But while Paul has been successful in Thessalonica and
Corinth, in Antioch and Athens, Jerusalem continues to elude him.
The crowd listens for a while, but then they start shouting: "'Down
with the scoundrel! He is not fit to be alive!' And as they were
yelling, and waving their coats and flinging dust in the air, the commandant ordered him to be brought into the barracks and gave instructions that he should be examined under the lash, to find out
what reason there was for such an outcry against him."

This is when Paul comes out with his revelation:

*But when they tied him up for the flogging, Paul said to the centu-
rion who was standing there, "Does the law allow you to flog a
Roman citizen, and an unconvicted one at that?" When the centurion
heard this, he went and reported to the commandant; "What are you
about? This man is a Roman citizen." The commandant came to
Paul and asked, "Tell me, are you a Roman citizen?" "Yes," said he.
The commandant rejoined, "Citizenship cost me a large sum of
money." Paul said, "It was mine by birth."*[98]

The commandant immediately cancels the flogging. But as he still is not really sure why the crowd is so hateful towards the prisoner, he has him taken to the Sanhedrin the following day. There, a debate breaks out, and Paul manages to set the Pharisees in the council against the Sadducees. "In the mounting dissension, the commandant was afraid that Paul would be torn to pieces, so he ordered the troops to go down, pull him out of the crowd, and bring him into the barracks." [99]

The Romans simply do not know what to do with Paul. According to the Acts of the Apostles, the Jews want to kill him. But the commandant does not consider he is able to either release Paul or punish him (and for what?). In the end, he decides to send him to the Roman procurator in Caesarea, who at this time is called Felix (52–c. 59 CE). The commandant writes:

> From Claudius Lysias to His Excellency the Governor Felix. Greeting. This man was seized by the Jews and was on the point of being murdered when I intervened with the troops, and, on discovering he was a Roman citizen, I removed him to safety. As I wished to ascertain the ground of their charge against him, I brought him down to their Council. I found that their case had to do with controversial matters of their law, but there was no charge against him which merited death or imprisonment. [100]

Felix finds it just as difficult to know what to do, and he too summons the Sanhedrin to a meeting. The high priest comes to Caesarea, and explains to the procurator that they have found Paul "to be a pest, a fomenter of discord among the Jews all over the world, a ringleader of the sect of the Nazarenes. He made an attempt to profane the temple and we arrested him." [101]

The irresolute Felix does not know what to do with Paul. And yet again we are confronted with a Roman governor who behaves in an atypical manner. Because this is the Felix that the Roman historian Tacitus will describe in the following way: "indulging in every kind of barbarity and lust, [Felix] exercised the power of a king in the spirit of a slave."[102]

Felix quite simply lets Paul stay in prison for the rest of his period in office—two years.

Felix is succeeded by Porcius Festus, in the year 59 or 60 CE. And Festus is no less indecisive than his predecessor with regard to Paul. According to the Acts of the Apostles, the Sanhedrin continues to insist that the prisoner be put on trial. It even says that they ask Festus to have Paul transferred to Jerusalem, "for they were plotting to kill him on the way."[103] Just as earlier under Felix (and in a similar manner as with Jesus under Pilate), there follows a tug-of-war between the Sanhedrin and the Roman governor, in which the Jews want to try the prisoner, while the Romans do not really know what they should do with him. In the end, Festus asks Paul: "Are you willing to go up to Jerusalem and stand trial on these charges before me there?" Paul refuses, which he seems capable of doing. And he says to Festus: "If I am guilty of any capital crime, I do not ask to escape the death penalty; if, however, there is no substance in the charges these men bring against me, it is not open to anyone to hand me over to them. I appeal to Caesar!"

Then Festus answers: "You have appealed to Caesar; to Caesar you shall go!"[104]

It is amazing how awkwardly the Roman authorities conduct themselves when it comes to dealing with their prisoner, the man who on the basis of his Roman citizenship demands an audience with the emperor. And now there is yet another parallel to what happened during the trial against Jesus—at least according to the gospel of Luke: in his indecisiveness, the Roman representative in Iudaea calls in a Jewish king. In the case of Jesus, it was Herod Antipas, tetrarch of Galilee. In the case of Paul, it is Agrippa II, who has been tetrarch of the small states north of Galilee since the year 53 CE (and the person whose sister, Drusilla, had married Felix). And just like in the case of Jesus and Herod Antipas, the Jewish king refrains from putting Paul on trial, and sends him back to Festus with the words: "The fellow could have been discharged, if he had not appealed to the emperor."[105]

At his own request, thus, Paul shall now be taken before the emperor in Rome, who at this time bears the name Nero. And he shall be put upon a ship that will take him across the Mediterranean. Luke writes:

> *When it was decided that we should sail for Italy, Paul and some other prisoners were handed over to a centurion named Julius, of the Augustan cohort. We embarked in a ship of Adramyttium, bound for ports in the province of Asia, and put out to sea.*[106]

What sort of trip are Paul and his fellow travelers engaged on? It is indeed full of hardships, and the tale reads almost like an adventure story. The travelers meet with storms and they are shipwrecked. Strange though it may seem, the journey lasts for many months, and despite Paul being a prisoner he does seem for the most part to be fairly free to go and do as he wishes.

After some time at sea, the company manages to get to Malta to spend the winter there. Paul makes an impression upon his new environment, and it is told in one episode in the Acts of the Apostles how the people on the island react when he is bitten by a viper:

> *The natives, seeing the snake hang on to his hand, said to one another, "The man must be a murderer; he may have escaped from the sea but divine justice would not let him live." Paul, however, shook off the snake into the fire and was none the worse. They still expected him to swell up or suddenly drop down dead, but after waiting a long time without seeing anything out of the way happen to him, they changed their minds and said, "He is a god."*[107]

On Malta, despite being a prisoner, Paul is received as a celebrated guest:

> In that neighbourhood there were lands belonging to the chief magis-
> trate of the island, whose name was Publius. He took us in and en-
> tertained us hospitably for three days. It so happened that this man's
> father was in bed suffering from recurrent bouts of fever and dysen-
> tery. Paul visited him and, after prayer, laid his hands on him and
> healed him; whereupon the other sick people on the island came and
> were cured. They honoured us with many marks of respect, and when
> we were leaving they put on board the supplies we needed.[108]

Finally, Paul and his fellow travellers do actually reach Rome. And, as it is written, "Paul was allowed to lodge privately, with a soldier in charge of him."[109]

It is an unusual imprisonment that Paul lives through, and he does not seem to make any visit to the emperor. On the other hand, after only three days in Rome, Paul does call together the "local Jewish leaders." And these—who do not seem to be Jewish-Christians, but, rather, traditional Jews—come in answer to the call. Paul tells them of his movement, and asks to be able to speak to the Jewish congregation. "So they fixed a day, and came in large numbers to his lodging."

In other words, Paul has not wasted a single day. And now he is at the heart of the empire. If he can convince the people in Rome to believe in Jesus Christ, then his movement will indeed have the possibility of becoming exactly what Paul intends: a world movement.

The Jews are thus gathered together at Paul's house in Rome and "From dawn to dusk he put his case to them; he spoke urgently of the kingdom of God and sought to convince them about Jesus by appealing to the law of Moses and the prophets. Some were won over by his arguments; others remained unconvinced."[110]

Then we are not told much more. The Acts of the Apostles just come to an end with the following simple lines:

> He stayed there two full years at his own expense, with a welcome for all
> who came to him; he proclaimed the kingdom of God and taught the
> facts about the Lord Jesus Christ quite openly and without hindrance.[111]

Thus ends the story of Paul, the man who spread the faith in Jesus to the countries around the Mediterranean. We do not get any more information. According to old Christian tradition, however, Paul is said to have met a martyr's death, later during the reign of Emperor Nero, in approximately the year 66 CE.[112] This martyrdom is regarded as more or less fact within Christianity. But there is no support for it in the New Testament. And considering that the Acts of the Apostles were written after the fall of Jerusalem in the year 70 CE (and probably during the 90s), it would be very surprising if the author had not mentioned that Paul died in 66 or 67, if that really were the case. It cannot be ruled out that Paul was still alive when the Acts of the Apostles were written, and, if so, when the gospels of Mark, Matthew, and Luke were put in writing too. Nor can it be ruled out that he was the person who supervised the work. Perhaps it is Paul who is Theophilus, the person for whom Luke writes his gospel.

PAUL:	JESUS:
"Every charge must be established on the evidence of two or three witnesses." *II Corinthians 13:1*	". . . every case may be settled on the evidence of two or three witnesses." *Matthew 18:16*
	"If I testify on my own behalf, that testimony is not valid." *John 5:31*

So the story of Paul ends in a similar way to that of Jesus; completely open.

And yet not. Because this man, Paul from Tarsus, can assume the honor of having carried out one of the greatest and most comprehensive revolutions in the history of the world. Christianity, monotheism, and, not least, the ethics that grew out from the Jewish and Christian traditions, would through his care come to be spread across a great part of the world—a much greater part of the world than Judaism could ever have spread to. And this world would, as a result of this, come to change, fundamentally.

PAUL:	JESUS:
". . . for the whole law is summed up in a single commandment: 'Love your neighbour as yourself'"	"The second is this:'You must love your neighbour as yourself.' No other commandment is greater than these."
Galatians 5:14	*Mark 12:31* [113]

Are there, then, no further sources of information about the apostle Paul?

There are a number of legends about Paul that have been collected together in apocryphal texts, such as The Acts of Paul, but on the whole they do not give us much new knowledge. A possibly interesting source of information are the so-called Ebionites. They were a Jewish-Christian sect that arose in Palestine in connection with the so-called Bar Kochba uprising in 135 CE. The Ebionites stuck to the Jewish law and tradition, but accepted Jesus Christ as the Messiah, although they dismissed the idea of the virgin birth. They settled east of the River Jordan, where they continued to be active for several hundred years.

The Ebionites' own writings have not survived, but they are quoted by Epiphanius of Salamis (315–403 CE) and are also mentioned by some other early Christian theologians. And according to these, the Ebionites, who continued to practice circumcision, were clearly opposed to Paul. When they write about him, they describe him as a Greek who converted to Judaism in order to be able to marry the daughter of the high priest, and then left the religion when she rejected his courtship. [114]

There is also a little information about Paul in the First Letter of Clement, which is considered to have been written by the church father Clement of Rome sometime between 80 and 140 CE (the year 96 CE is often given). In chapter 5, the author says that Paul "came to the extreme limit of the west, and suffered martyrdom under the prefects. Thus was he removed from the world, and went into the holy place, having proved himself a striking example of patience." The "extreme limit of the west" is thought to mean Spain. A journey to Spain is also mentioned in the so-called Muratorian fragment, the oldest known list of the books of the New Testament, the original of which was written in about the year 170 CE. In his letter to the Romans, Paul has also written that he plans to travel to Spain.[115] Perhaps he did make this journey in the end.

What, then, can we find in contemporary non-religious sources?

Remarkably, historians from this time have very little, or nothing at all, to say about Paul. Tacitus and Suetonius touch upon what seems to be the early Christian movement in Rome, at the beginning of the second century. But they do not mention Paul, at least not in any obvious way.

What about Flavius Josephus? In *Antiquities of the Jews,* as well as in *War of the Jews,* Josephus does actually write of a man named Saul (Saulus), and the theory has been put forward that this person is Paul.[116] The section in *Antiquities of the Jews* is about King Agrippa II, about how he was disliked by the population because he had spent so much money on building up the town of Caesarea Filippi, and about how the king created violent animosity between the high priests, which led to general tumult. The text then reads:

> *Costobarus also, and Saulus, did themselves get together a multitude*
> *of wicked wretches, and this because they were of the royal family;*
> *and so they obtained favor among them, because of the kindred to*
> *Agrippa; but still they used violence with the people, and were very*
> *ready to plunder those that were weaker than themselves. And from*
> *this time it principally came to pass that our city was greatly disor-*
> *dered, and that all things grew worse and worse among us.*[117]

One of the reasons that "Saulus" has been interpreted as Paul is the privilege he is said to have on account of his belonging to the king's family. It has been proposed that that is the reason why the Roman authorities have difficulties in handling Paul, and why Festus calls in Agrippa. The time almost fits, but not completely—that which Josephus describes takes place under procurator Gessius Florus, who comes to power about five years after Felix resigns and two years after Festus resigns. The name Saul(us) fits of course. But the Saulus named above seems to be a rather high-ranking person in the Jewish establishment, at any rate according to the section in *War of the Jews*.

So much for historians and Paul. Is there, then, information about any *other* person—a person with another name—who might be identical to Paul?

Yes, possibly. Around the year 220 CE, the Greek philosopher Flavius Philostratus wrote a biography of a man who was called Apollonius of Tyana. Philostratus wrote this almost novel-like biography at the instigation of the wife of Emperor Septimius Severus, Julia Domna. She, in turn, had come across notes that had been made by Apollonius' foremost disciple, Damis, and gave these to Philostratus to start with.

Some authors have put forward the theory that Apollonius of Tyana is in fact identical to the apostle Paul.[118]

Apollonius was born around the time of the birth of Christ in the town of Tyana, which is in Cappadocia, in Asia Minor. But according to Philostratus, it was no ordinary pregnancy and no ordinary birth:

> To his mother, just before he was born, there came an apparition of Proteus, who changes his form so much in Homer, in the guise of an Egyptian demon. She was in no way frightened, but asked him what sort of child she would bear. And he answered: "Myself."
> "And who are you?" she asked.
> "Proteus," answered he, "the god of Egypt."[119]

When the mother is then going to give birth, lightning strikes the earth and then rises back up into the air, "and the gods thereby indicated, I think," writes Philostratus, "the great distinction to which the sage was to attain, and hinted in advance how he should transcend all things upon earth and approach the gods." [120]

At fourteen years of age, Apollonius makes his way to Tarsus (the supposed hometown of Paul) in order to study. He is a very gifted pupil and has a remarkable memory. He also has magical talents that shall make him famous. In his philosophic conviction he is a neo-Pythagorean, and he is a pronounced mystic. Philostratus describes Apollonius as a moral and religious ideal. He was an ascetic who lived in celibacy, he refrained from eating meat, and in his twenties he lived for five years in total silence. This period was mainly spent in Cilicia and Pamphylia.

Apollonius would come to do an exceptional amount of traveling (but, as far as is known, never to Judea—although Philostratus does mention a stay in "Arabia"). After he has finished his five years of silence, he sets off to Antioch where he gathers disciples. Later, he travels eastward, Nineve being one of the places he visits—it is there he meets his disciple Damis—and to Babylonia and then on to India. After his return from India, he travels around the Mediterranean, and, for example, spends a lot of time in Ephesus.

During his travels, Apollonius makes a name for himself on account of his talents as a healer. In Babylonia, for example, he heals the king who has fallen ill. And later he shall call a young woman back from the dead. In one later part of Philostratus' description, Apollonius even implies that his own disciple will soon come to regard him too as having been risen from the dead:

> "And when you have saluted Demetrius, turn aside to the seashore where the island of Calypso lies; for there you shall see me appear to you."
>
> "Alive," asked Damis, "or how?"
>
> Apollonius with a smile replied: "As I myself believe, alive, but as you will believe, risen from the dead." [121]

Finally, Apollonius ends up in Rome. The reason is that he has heard that Emperor Nero has started to persecute the philosophers in the city. And Apollonius makes his way there to see what can be done about it. Of his thirty-four companions, only eight dare go ashore on the coast of Italy.[122]

Apollonius refuses to adapt to Nero; rather he tries to create a spiritual revolt in Rome. It ends with his being arrested. But when the roll on which the accusation has been written is to be read out, it is discovered to be blank. So Apollonius is set free, because the Emperor's adviser Tigellinus becomes afraid of the philosopher's supernatural powers.

We may be able to date this episode in the life of Apollonius. Because it is known that in 65–66 CE Emperor Nero, after having discovered a conspiracy against him, clamps down on, among others, philosophers. In any event, it seems likely that the visit of Apollonius of Tyana to Rome takes place at about the same time that Paul is there.

What then happens in Apollonius' life? Well, he goes off to Spain, and then on to Africa and Greece.

As indicated above, nothing is known about Apollonius ever having visited Judea, but it is interesting to note that at this time he is invited by Vespasian to visit the country, to give him advice concerning his plans to try to become emperor. Vespasian is in Jerusalem to quell the Jewish revolt that has just broken out. Apollonius refuses to come, on the grounds that it is a country "which its inhabitants polluted both by what they did and by what they suffered." Vespasian is forced to travel down to Egypt to meet the wise man.[123]

Later in life, Apollonius shall yet again find himself before a court in Rome, this time accused of having conspired against the emperor, who is then Domitian (the tyrannical son of Vespasian). But during the trial a remarkable dialogue unfolds:

> *The emperor . . . confined himself to four questions which he thought were embarrassing and difficult to answer. "What influences you," he said, "to dress differently from everybody else, and to wear this peculiar and singular garb?"*
>
> *"Because," said Apollonius, "the earth which feeds me also clothes me, and I do not like to bother the poor animals."*

> *The emperor next asked the question "Why is it that men call*
> *you a god?"*
> *"Because," answered Apollonius, "every man that is thought to*
> *be good, is honoured by the title of god."* [124]

Apollonius of Tyana is found not guilty this time too—and this time too the trial ends with a miracle: the accused quite simply disappears before everyone's eyes.

Philostratus, whose notes from Damis are said to end before the death of Apollonius, uses other sources toward the end. And he writes: "with regard to the manner in which he died, if he did actually die, there are many stories." [125] One of the stories that Philostratus gives most room to is that Apollonius is said to have disappeared from the earth and humanity by going up to heaven. [126]

A common view, which Philostratus also refers to, is that Apollonius died about the year 97 CE in Ephesus, (i.e. the city where Paul had his base for a number of years). [127]

Although there is much in Philostratus' story that is romanticized, Apollonius is regarded as a real person. There are others who have written about him, before Philostratus or at roughly the same time as him. Origen names a certain Moiragenes who had written about Apollonius of Tyana. [128] Apollonius is also mentioned by Lucian of Samosata (120–180 CE) and by Cassius Dio (155–235 CE) among others.

It is not in any way obvious that Apollonius of Tyana is identical to Paul—there are evident differences: it is not known, for example, that Apollonius spent any time in Judea; and even if he is a mystic and magician, nowhere is it stated that he has any connection with Christianity—or Judaism. At the same time, there are so many similarities that it is not uncommon for the theory to be put forward that they are the same person: they both spend time in Tarsus, Ephesus, and Rome at about the same periods (and Paul names an "Apollo" although this person seems to come from Alexandria[129]); Apollonius is sometimes called "Pol"; Apollonius travels to Spain after leaving Rome; both avoid Judea; both live in celibacy; both are always traveling and with many disciples; both end up in a Roman court but are released.

But just as often as the theory is put forward that Apollonius is identical to the apostle Paul, the hypothesis is put forward that he is identical to another person—namely, Jesus of Nazareth.

As early as at the beginning of the fourth century, Hierocles, who was governor of Bithynia, among other things, wrote a polemical book in which he compared Apollonius and Jesus. This book *Philalethes* (*Lover of Truth*) would come to arouse very strong reactions.[130] And the discussions as to whether Philostratus' story of Apollonius of Tyana was a heathen plagiarism of the stories in the gospels about Jesus of Nazareth, or vice versa, flared up at regular intervals throughout the centuries.[131]

To this one might add the strange lines by Irenaeus, stating that Jesus, according to the testimony of the apostle John, had lived to an old age.[132] Tradition has it that John was in Ephesus. And there is also a church tradition that Mary, the mother of Jesus, was eventually taken—by John—to Ephesus, where she then lived until her death. Ephesus is a city that comes back—in connection with Apollonius, with Paul, with the mother of Jesus. And possibly with Jesus himself.

Whether Apollonius of Tyana is identical to Paul, or to Jesus, is perhaps not so important in this context. There are sufficiently large differences to allow one to dismiss him as being either one or the other. But what is interesting is that Philostratus' story has caused certain authors to draw parallels between Apollonius and Paul, and other (or even the same) authors to draw parallels between Apollonius and Jesus.

Without these authors even having reflected upon the idea of drawing a parallel between Jesus and Paul.

CHAPTER 10

A HYPOTHESIS

Who was Jesus of Nazareth, and what actually happened during and after the crucifixion of this man?

Nobody knows, because all we have is circumstantial evidence. His life and his work have given rise to one of the major religions of the world, a religion that has as one of its foundations that Jesus—the son of God—died on the cross and then arose again from the dead. We can, of course, not exclude the possibility that it happened just like that, and that Jesus really was divine. In the universe in which we live, there are so many unanswered questions that nobody can say with certainty anything about the forces that govern us. Divinity is a concept that one can really only approach with hypotheses.

But if one has as a hypothesis that Jesus was a man of flesh and blood—and that his life was a human life—then one must come to terms with the text that is presented, and interpret this in some way.

I wish to put forward the hypothesis that Jesus of Nazareth was in fact the same person as Paul from Tarsus. It is a provocative idea, and it immediately clashes with our superficial concepts of these men: Jesus as a mild, wise, loving—and beautiful—man; Paul as an intensive, inconstant, often choleric—and, as one often imagines, deformed—man. The very idea that they could be the same person seems astounding, but that is probably on account of the fact that we have all carried with us the picture of Jesus from such a tender age, that this image is almost a reflex, regardless of whether we have been brought up religiously or not.

But, I would suggest, one does not need to scrape away much of the surfaces from these pictures to arrive at the indisputable similarities. I shall try to summarize the circumstances that have led me to this hypothesis—that Jesus of Nazareth and Paul from Tarsus are the same man.

I intend to begin with some of the arguments that could speak *against* the claim that we are dealing with one and the same person. And I shall discuss these, and try to answer them.

1. JESUS AND PAUL ARE PERSONS WITH TOTALLY DIFFERENT TRAITS OF CHARACTER.

When one thinks of Jesus, it is often his message of love that stands out as the most prominent. When one thinks of Paul, it is his stubbornness, and intensity. Add to this the description of the outward appearance of Paul that can be read in the apocryphal *Acta Pauli et Theclae*, which was probably written at the end of the second century: "And he saw Paul coming, a man small in size, with a bald head and crooked legs; in good health; with eyebrows that met and a rather prominent nose; full of grace, for sometimes he looked like a man and sometimes he looked like an angel." That is hardly the way we imagine Jesus.

But the difference between the descriptions we have of Jesus and those we have of Paul, is that our perception of Paul's personality to a considerable degree is based upon how he describes himself; that is, in the letters we have his own words, seemingly uncensored, immediate, unembellished. When it comes to Jesus, he is always described and quoted by others, and after the event.

And yet: if we look closer at the statements attributed to Jesus and those that Paul writes, the carrot and the whip are present in both of them. It is by no means so that Jesus journeys about in Galilee as an embrace personified. There is much love, but also many exhortations, that sometimes turn into direct threats:

> *Jesus continued, "You belong to this world below, I to the world above. Your home is in this world, mine is not. That is why I told you that you would die in your sins unless you believe that I am what I am."*

> *John 8:23–24*

Paul, in turn, can display a loving language just as sincere as that preached by Jesus. In the First Letter to the Corinthians, he writes:

> *I may speak in tongues of men or of angels, but if I have no love, I am a sounding gong or a clanging cymbal. I may have the gift of prophecy and the knowledge of every hidden truth; I may have faith enough to move mountains; but if I have no love, I am nothing. . . .*
> *At present we see only puzzling reflections in a mirror, but one day we shall see face to face. My knowledge now is partial; then it will be whole, like God's knowledge of me. There are three things that last for ever: faith, hope, and love; and the greatest of the three is love.*

> *First Letter to the Corinthians 13*

Jesus is, without doubt, capable of talking like Paul. And just as indisputably, Paul is capable of speaking like Jesus. And as regards Jesus' outward appearance, we actually have no idea at all what he looked like. It is, however, interesting to note that there is at least an intimation that even he was perhaps not so well built. In the gospel of John, it is described how Mary Magdalene stands beside the tomb when the resurrected Jesus turns up. She does not recognize him:

> *Jesus asked her, "Why are you weeping,? Who are you looking for?" Thinking it was the gardener, she said, "If it is you, sir, who removed*

him, tell me where you have laid him, and I will take him away
[Greek original: 'carry him away from there']."[1]

2. JESUS IS A PERSON WHO SHOWS CONSIDERABLY MORE TOLERANCE THAN PAUL.

In several letters, Paul claims that women should not speak in the congregation, and that they should subordinate themselves to men.[2]

Jesus, on the other hand, throughout expresses understanding of and love toward women. Nor can one discern that he belittles women, although his disciples on one occasion express surprise at his speaking to a woman.

It is also explicit that Paul often uses hard words about people whom he regards as "sinners." In the First Letter to the Corinthians, he writes, for example: "I meant that you must have nothing to do with any so-called Christian who leads an immoral life, or is extortionate, idolatrous, a slanderer, a drunkard, or a swindler; with anyone like that you should not even eat."[3]

This seems to strongly contrast with Jesus' message: "I did not come to call the virtuous, but sinners."[4]

But as in the above paragraph, this can to a certain extent be about a difference of degree, rather than a difference in kind. Jesus' words are presumably edited and adapted, while Paul's come to us directly from his letters. And we must not forget that the same hard Paul also writes: "For all alike have sinned, and are deprived of the divine glory; and all are justified by God's free grace alone, through his act of liberation in the person of Christ Jesus."[5]

Nevertheless, the difference in tone is often striking, regardless of whether it is a difference of degree or a difference in kind.

3. JESUS SPOKE ARAMAIC, PAUL SPOKE GREEK.

As far as we can tell, Paul could speak Greek, and his letters are written in Greek. One can reasonably assume that Jesus' mother tongue was Aramaic, which was the language most people spoke in the area where he lived.

We do not, however, know anything about Jesus' knowledge of languages, and nor do we know whether Greek was Paul's mother tongue. It is important to note that Paul was quite obviously able to communicate with Jesus' disciples, and that he spoke to the people in Jerusalem "in Hebrew."[6]

4. JESUS REACHED OUT TO JEWS, PAUL TO NON-JEWS.

"I was sent to the lost sheep of the house of Israel, and to them alone," says Jesus,[7] while it is very clear that Paul appeals to "the uncircumcised." But one has cause to regard this as a process of development that also takes place during Paul's own activity. Paul finds himself in a much more heterogeneous environment than did Jesus. He starts by making for the synagogues, but is rejected, at least by the Jews. And he increasingly comes to turn away from them and direct his mission towards the "heathens" and the God-fearers. Which means to the majority in the environment in which he now finds himself.

Yet Paul will never cease to hope that the "whole of Israel will be saved."[8]

5. PAUL WRITES VERY LITTLE ABOUT JESUS' LIFE.

PAUL:	JESUS:
On the night of his arrest the Lord Jesus took bread, and after giving thanks to God broke it and said: "This is my body, which is for you; do this in memory of me." In the same way, he took the cup after supper, and said: "This cup is the new covenant sealed by my blood. Whenever you drink it, do this in memory of me." *I Corinthians, 11:23–25*	Then he took bread, and after giving thanks he broke it, and gave it to them with the words: "This is my body which is given for you; do this as a memorial of me." In the same way he took the cup after supper, and said, "This cup, poured out for you, is the new covenant sealed by my blood." *Luke, 22:19–20*

Only in a few places in his letters does Paul touch upon concrete events in Jesus' life.[9] One can almost gain the impression that he does not know much about Jesus.

But one can actually say the same about how Paul describes his own earlier life—hardly at all. Not even his conversion on the road to Damascus does he describe in any concrete manner in his letters. It is above all in the Acts of the Apostles that we are told the story of Paul. The letters seem in general to be mainly about the here and now.

6. PAUL MET JAMES AND PETER, AND LATER JOHN TOO, DURING HIS FIRST JOURNEYS TO JERUSALEM.

For me, this was for a long time the most important argument against Paul being able to be identical to Jesus. If Paul met these three men, who after all knew Jesus very well, then they would surely have recognized him. What is tricky about this is that it is hard to imagine that there were a lot of people who were initiated into this plan—if there was actually a plan. If Jesus tries to convince the disciples that he really can perform miracles—and rise up from the dead, and then ascend up to heaven—then there is not really much point in letting them see him in flesh and blood on the streets of Jerusalem again (which does not, on the other hand, contradict his having risen from the dead. . .)

The important question is, however, whether Jesus' role was not as much political as it was spiritual. We may not necessarily need to see a possible escape in connection with a death sentence as a secret plan, at least not as regards the disciples who were closest to Jesus. From the beginning, perhaps it was simply a question of letting Jesus survive and leave the country (as, apparently, "the Egyptian" did).

And when we read the gospels, it is actually obvious that Jesus did not get himself down from the cross, did not roll himself in seventy-five pounds of myrrh and aloe, and did not himself roll the stone away from the tomb. Other people were needed for this, albeit only a few. Paul also writes that the first person that Jesus shows himself to after the resurrection is indeed Peter.[10]

The entire question about what the disciples knew depends to a great extent on what actually happened when Jesus was arrested and the days immediately after this, *when* this actually occurred, and the degree to which his actions at this point in time were mainly religious or political. However much we might read between the lines, many question marks remain with regard to this.

Now let us move to the arguments that, in my opinion, would support the notion of Paul from Tarsus being identical to Jesus of Nazareth:

1. PAUL'S SUDDEN PASSION FOR A PERSON HE HAS NEVER MET, AND WHOSE DISCIPLE HE HAS NEVER BEEN.

Paul's devotion and ardor when it came to spreading the message—that Jesus Christ "was proclaimed Son of God by an act of power that raised him from the dead"[11]—is unique and incomparable. Yet he was not one of those one would have *expected* to be responsible for the spreading of this entirely new faith: a close disciple of Jesus, or at least someone who had met the living Jesus. Paul comes as if from nowhere—absolutely nowhere. And yet he has a passion for the faith equal only to that of Jesus himself.

2A. PAUL'S CONVERSION TAKES PLACE SHORTLY AFTER JESUS IS CRUCIFIED.

2B. PAUL'S CONVERSION TAKES PLACE OUTSIDE JUDEA AND GALILEE, BUT WITHIN THE BORDERS OF THE ROMAN EMPIRE.

Paul appears when Jesus vanishes—most chronologies conclude that Paul's conversion takes place within a year or two after the crucifixion of Jesus. These chronologies are, of course, based on events described in the Acts of the Apostles, and as we have shown, the dates of these events are not necessarily reliable. But Paul's own words, too, make it clear that the conversion takes place after the crucifixion of Jesus, and apparently not very long after.[12] Thus, we may conclude that Paul's conversion is closely linked in time to the disappearance of Jesus, *irrespective of when that actually happened, irrespective of whether we accept the traditional chronology of Jesus' life or not.*

Geographically, Paul's whereabouts then would fit well with where somebody who had been exiled by the Romans might be (but much less well with where someone might be expected to be converted to the Christian faith at that time).

It can of course be a coincidence that Paul appears shortly after the crucifixion of Jesus. And it can similarly be a coincidence that his conversion takes place so far from the setting where Jesus was active, and where his disciples still are active.

It is nevertheless striking.

Furthermore, Paul's own explanation for his journey to Damascus—"to arrest [Christians] and bring them to Jerusalem"[13]— is peculiar. Such a long-distance chase seems not only overzealous but unproductive, since most believers are to be found decidedly closer to home, at least according to the Acts of the Apostles.[14]

3. ACCORDING TO JEROME, PAUL COMES FROM THE SAME AREA AS JESUS.

According to the New Testament, Paul comes from Tarsus in Cilicia. But the church father Jerome (327–420 CE) states that he was born in the town of Gischala—which the church father mistakenly places in Judea, but which is actually situated in Galilee, about eighteen miles north of present-day Nazareth. As opposed to Nazareth, Gischala is also a town that we know existed at the time of Jesus.

If Jerome is correct, and Paul comes from the same area as Jesus, it is remarkable that Paul and the Acts of the Apostles fail to mention this. It is of course possible that Jerome is wrong, but if that is the case it is difficult to find a reasonable explanation for his mistake. Gischala is not mentioned in the New Testament, and the town does not seem to have any special symbolic importance, other than that one of the Jewish rebel leaders, John of Gischala, came from there and that the town was an important stronghold during the war against the Romans, 66–70 CE.

There is also a further intimation, in another work, that Paul comes from Galilee. It is not clear where and when this work, called *Philopatris*, came into being, and who wrote it. At first, the author was thought to be the Greek Lucian (c. 120–180 CE), but the work was presumably written much later and by somebody else. In this work there is reference to a person, apparently Paul, who is described as a "bald, long-nosed Galilean."[15]

4. PAUL—LIKE JESUS?—WAS BORN WITH ROMAN CITIZENSHIP.

At that time it was extremely unusual for a Jew in the areas occupied by the Romans to have Roman citizenship. Besides, it meant a religious conflict.

Yet the tentmaker and Pharisee Paul was born with just such a Roman citizenship—without any explanation being offered for this. Paul will come to make use of this citizenship to avoid being put on trial by the Romans.

In the case of Jesus, too, there is—according to New Testament sources—a remarkable reluctance on the part of the Romans to put him on trial, and—according to other sources—a "privileged position" in relation to the Romans, possibly a relation to a Roman officer.

Although Roman citizenship is a reasonable explanation of why the Romans do not want to try Jesus, it is of course only a hypothesis that Jesus had such a citizenship.

5. PAUL, LIKE JESUS, IS A "A HEBREW BORN AND BRED." YET BOTH
   OF THEM HAVE A DECIDEDLY AMBIVALENT ATTITUDE TOWARDS
   THE JEWS.

Both Jesus and Paul are Jews, and Paul often emphasizes this fact.[16] Yet they both speak of "the Jews" as if they were a people apart from themselves. In the case of Jesus, this is particularly strange, as he lived in a Jewish country where most people, including all his disciples, were Jews. Both Paul and Jesus often talk about Jews—their own people—with obvious animosity (although the animosity in Jesus' case is generally directed towards "Pharisees and Sadducees," i.e., to the main factions within Judaism). And both of them claim, time after time, that the Jews or their leaders want to kill them.

PAUL:	JESUS:
"You, my friends, have followed the example of the Christians in the churches of God in Judaea: you have been treated by your own countrymen as they were treated by the Jews, who killed the Lord Jesus and the prophets and drove us out, and are so heedless of God's will and such enemies of their fellow-men that they hinder us from telling the Gentiles how they may be saved. All this time they have been making up the full measure of their guilt. But now retribution has overtaken them for good and all!"	"Alas for you, scribes and Pharisees, hypocrites! You build up the tombs of the prophets and embellish the monuments of the saints, and you say, 'If we had been living in the time of our forefathers, we should never have taken part with them in the murder of our prophets.' So you acknowledge that you are the sons of those who killed the prophets. Go on then, finish off what your fathers began! Snakes! Vipers' blood! How can you escape being condemned to hell? . . . Truly I tell you: this generation will bear the guilt of it all."
I Thessalonians 2:14–16	Matthew 23:29–36

6. PAUL, LIKE JESUS, TRAVELS TO JERUSALEM AT A YOUNG AGE.
In the case of Jesus, it is described (in Luke, 2:46) how he sat in the temple "surrounded by the teachers, listening to them and putting questions." In the case of Paul, it is said that he came to Jerusalem and became a pupil of Gamaliel the Elder. There is nothing strange about a young Jew travelling to Jerusalem, but what is striking here is that this is all that is told about the childhood and youth of these two men.

7. AFTER THIS, FOR BOTH JESUS AND PAUL, THERE IS A "VACUUM" UNTIL THEY ARE ADULTS.
The New Testament does not have *anything* to say about these men's adult lives before they are thirty years old. Then they suddenly appear.

8. PAUL, LIKE JESUS, IS UNMARRIED.

It was extremely unusual for a man from a Pharisaic family to still be unmarried at the age of thirty. It says in the Talmud that "One who reaches the age of twenty and has not married, he lives all his days in sin," and a man who was unmarried after this age could be forced by a court to get married.[17] The pressure to get married was incredibly strong. The only known rabbi during Talmudic time who lived in celibacy was Shimon ben Azzai, and he did not recommend it to anybody else. In this respect, the little group of Essenes who lived in celibacy (and possibly the similar *Therapeutae*, who lived in Egypt[18]) were unique.

If Paul, as he says, was born into a family of Pharisees, it is exceptional that he was unmarried at the age of thirty.

And this is something he has in common with Jesus.

PAUL:	JESUS:
"To the married I give this ruling, which is not mine but the Lord's: a wife must not separate herself from her husband—if she does she must either remain unmarried or be reconciled to her husband—and the husband must not divorce his wife." *I Corinthians 7:10–11*	"Whosoever divorces his wife and remarries commits adultery against her; so too, if she divorces her husband and remarries, she commits adultery." *Mark 10:11–12*

9. PAUL HAD SOME SORT OF WOUND.

It is clear at various places in the texts that Paul suffers from some sort of injury or illness. It is reasonable to assume that somebody who has been crucified for six hours, and been jabbed with a lance, would suffer some aftereffects. Besides, he writes in the Letter to the Galatians, "In future let no one make trouble for me, for I bear the marks of Jesus branded on my body."[19] But that this has some connection with the crucifixion is, of course, just one of several possible explanations. The "marks of Jesus" upon Paul's body have been interpreted as meaning that Paul had been persecuted, and physically mistreated, because he had preached about Jesus. Another interpretation postulates that he has similar tattoos on his body to the ones Jesus had (after he had come from Egypt).

With regard to other reasons for his handicap, there are possible hints that Paul suffers from poor sight.[20] Krenkel has suggested that he suffered from epilepsy.[21]

10. BOTH FOCUS WHAT MIGHT SEEM TO BE AN INORDINATE AMOUNT OF ATTENTION ON THE RESURRECTION.

One could imagine that it was Jesus' message that was the decisive element when spreading his faith. But for Paul, the resurrection—at any rate if one is to judge from his words in the First Letter to the Corinthians—is that which overshadows everything else: "And if Christ was not raised, then our gospel is null and void, and so too is your faith."[22] Why? That Jesus came to stake so much upon his death and resurrection—something he, according to the gospels, predicts time after time—is one thing. It was, after all, the resurrection that proved that he really was the person he said he was. But it is difficult to understand why somebody else—such as Paul, for example—would consider everything else unimportant, next to the resurrection. It is as if Paul, like Jesus, tries to prove that Jesus really is the person he makes himself out to be.

11. PAUL IS ODDLY UNWILLING TO TRAVEL TO JERUSALEM—WHERE THE "HOME CONGREGATION" IS TO BE FOUND.

The explanations that are given for why Paul avoids Jerusalem—and is hurriedly sent away from there by the other apostles—vary. Sometimes it is other Christians that he is afraid of (they know him as somebody who previously persecuted them), sometimes it is the Jewish-Christians who want to continue to follow the Jewish law (and who have heard that Paul teaches "all the Jews in the gentile world to turn their backs on Moses"), sometimes it is traditional Jews (who consider that Paul desecrates the Temple). And in fact one never really understands why Paul, especially, would be permanently risking his life if he came to Jerusalem—when the other apostles continue to work there undisturbed, and build up congregations. It is even stated that the apostles were "having favour with all the people. The Lord added to the assembly day by day those who were being saved."[23]

When Paul eventually, after a number of years and a number of warnings, again enters the Temple, he does so with his head shaved.

It is obvious that Paul is afraid of something. But none of the above can explain to us why the Romans keep him prisoner for two years.

This Roman imprisonment, as well as Paul's fear of showing himself to Pharisees and Sadducees in the Temple, would be explicable, however, if he had once been a Zealot.

Particularly if he had once been sentenced to death as a Zealot.

12. BOTH HAVE DISCIPLES WITH WHOM THEY JOURNEY AROUND. BOTH HAVE A TENDENCY TO PREACH WHILE TRAVELING. AND BOTH CHOOSE, TO A GREAT DEGREE, TO PREACH IN SYNAGOGUES.

Their lifestyles and their styles of preaching are, in other words, very similar.

13. UNLIKE THE DISCIPLES, PAUL IS A SUBJECT IN THE NEW TESTAMENT.

Through his letters, Paul speaks of himself and describes his own life. He also has the entirely dominating role in the Acts of the Apostles. This gives Paul a considerably more prominent position than any of the disciples, and he becomes a subject in the story. Why Paul gets to play such a prominent role in the New Testament is not explained.

14. THE ARREST AND TRIAL OF PAUL ARE ALMOST AN EXACT REPLICA OF WHAT HAPPENED TO JESUS (BEFORE THE VERDICT), ALBEIT SPREAD OUT OVER A LONGER TIME.

Both Jesus and Paul are arrested after having created a tumult in the Temple in Jerusalem.

Both are taken to the Roman authorities, which—in both instances—do not know what to do with them..

In both cases, there is mention of not only the meeting with the governor, but also of the governor's wife.[24]

Both are taunted by the Jewish crowd.

Both are taken before a Jewish tetrarch.

Both are thrown between Roman authorities, the Sanhedrin and the Jewish royal power. And both are treated in a similar way by the various instances. Even the slap on the face by the high priest, or at any rate the threat of this, is repeated.[25]

It is so similar, that one almost wonders if what is described is the *only* trial.

15. SURPRISINGLY OFTEN, PAUL USES THE SAME TERMINOLOGY AND IMAGERY AS JESUS.

Paul wrote his letters quite a number of years *before* the gospels were written. Yet those letters contain ideas, turns of phrase, and metaphors that are decidedly like those that were *later* ascribed to Jesus in the gospels. And remember, Paul was not one of Jesus' disciples.

Numerous Bible scholars have noted the parallels between the ideas and metaphors of these two men—despite the fact that Paul wrote first.[26] The explanation given for these parallels is that there must have been an oral "Jesus tradition" that Paul supported himself upon. As David Wenham writes:

> Paul cites the Jesus-tradition in various way. Sometimes he quotes the tradition explicitly and almost verbatim (as with his account of the Last Supper). Sometimes he quotes the tradition explicitly, but very freely, retaining relatively few of the ipsissima verba of the tradition (as with the divorce sayings). Most frequently he draws on the tradition freely and incorporates Jesus' teaching into his own teaching without explaining that he is doing so (as with the echoes of the Sermon on the Mount in Romans).[27]

Wenham and others note, perhaps with surprise, that Paul in these instances does not name the source of his ideas, namely Jesus. But

PAUL:	JESUS:
About dates and times, my friends, there is no need to write to you, for you yourselves know perfectly well that the day of the Lord comes like a thief [*kleptes*] in the night. While they are saying, "All is peaceful, all secure," destruction is upon them. *I Thessalonians 5:1–3*	Keep awake, then, for you do not know on what day your Lord will come. Remember, if the householder had known at what time of night the burglar [*kleptes*] was coming, he would have stayed awake and not let his house be broken into. *Matthew 24:42–43*

if, in fact, they are Paul's own ideas, from beginning to end, then there really is no need for him to name a source . . .

The discussion about the similarities between the ideas of Jesus and Paul is an old one—and is sometimes called "The Jesus-Paul Debate." By no means all consider the similarities to be so important—some find about a thousand parallels, others find ten.[28] But those who consider these parallels to be significant often explain them with "Paul's intimate knowledge, and use, of the Jesus tradition."

There are, in my opinion, two other possible explanations for these similarities: one would be that Paul himself was so involved in the editing of the gospels that he has put his own words into the mouth of Jesus.

The other, that the similarities of the ideas can be explained by the fact that they are expressed by one and the same man—only some years in between. That is to say: Jesus and Paul are the same person.

This, of course, is a hypothesis. But a hypothesis that is perhaps worthy of consideration.

* * *

And then there is a little episode, or rather a little exchange of views, something that is told—somewhat casually—in the Acts of the

Apostles. Paul has come to Jerusalem, for the last time. He is in the Temple, and is recognized:

> The whole city was in a turmoil, and people came running from all directions. They seized Paul and dragged him out of the temple, and at once the doors were shut. They were bent on killing him, but word came to the officer commanding the cohort that all Jerusalem was in an uproar. He immediately took a force of soldiers with their centurions and came down at the double to deal with the riot. When the crowd saw the commandant and his troops, they stopped beating Paul. As soon as the commandant could reach Paul, he arrested him and ordered him to be shackled with two chains; **he enquired who he was and what he had been doing. Some in the crowd shouted one thing, some another, and as the commandant could not get at the truth because of the hubbub, he ordered him to be taken to the barracks.** When Paul reached the steps, he found himself carried up by the soldiers because of the violence of the mob; for the whole crowd was at their heels, yelling, "Kill him!"
>
> Just before he was taken into the barracks, Paul said to the commandant: "May I have a word with you?"
>
> The commandant said: "So you speak Greek?"

And then the commandant adds a sentence that in the original Greek reads: οὐκ ἄρα σὺ εἶ ὁ Αἰγύπτιος ὁ πρὸ τούτων τῶν ἡμερῶν ἀναστατώσας καὶ ἐξαγαγὼν εἰς τὴν ἔρημον τοὺς τετρακισχιλίους ἄνδρας τῶν σικαρίων;

"Are you then not the Egyptian who some time ago created turmoil and together with the four thousand sicarii went out into the wilderness?"[29]

Perhaps Luke, the collector of eyewitness accounts and written histories, could not allow that Flavius Josephus' version of events would go down as history. But neither could Luke resist leaving some clues for posterity.

CHAPTER 11

POSTSCRIPT

Writing this book has been an enjoyable as well as an exacting process. I have been spurred on by curiosity—and continual new discoveries—and have been held back by the feeling that I may be violating some sort of taboo, if only imaginary, and by an unwillingness to offend.

But in the end, I have not been able to resist stilling my curiosity. I believe that one, despite everything, must be allowed to seek answers to the questions that arise in life, whatever they might concern.

What is presented in this book is, as I have said before, a hypothesis—a hypothesis that at the start was based on intuition and then, as the journey progressed, was filled out with facts. These facts are not, however, comprehensive. From this text, each and every one can take with them whatever they want—or nothing.

The truth about what really happened two thousand years ago is not something that any of us has special access to.

ACKNOWLEDGMENTS

I would like to thank Annika Lindgren, Per Faustino, and Viveca Ekelund at the Prisma/Norstedts Publishing House, Stockholm, for continuous support and excellent meetings. And thanks to Maureen Graney, editor-in-chief of The Lyons Press, for presenting this book to English-language readers.

NOTES

CHAPTER 1: PROLOGUE

1 John Dominic Crossan, *The Historical Jesus: The Life of a Mediterranean Peasant*, HarperSanFrancisco, 1991, p. xxvii.

2 Albert Schweitzer, *The Quest of the Historical Jesus: A Critical Study of its Progress from Reimarus to Wrede* (John Bowden), Adam and Charles Black, London, 1906/10, p. 4.

3 Schweitzer, p. 4.

4 Craig L. Blomberg, *The Historical Reliability of the Gospels*, Inter-Varsity Press, 1987, p. xv.

5 David Friedrich Strauss, *Ulrich von Hutten* (Preface), quoted by Schweitzer, p. 5.

CHAPTER 2: DID JESUS EVER EXIST?

1 Flavius Josephus, *Antiquities of the Jews*, 18:1:1, 18:2:1. Josephus quotations are from the William Whiston translation, online at http://www.earlychristianwritings.com/text/josephus/josephus.htm (chapter and verse indicated for each book); Greek version (ed. B. Niese) from Perseus Digital Library, Tufts University.

2 F. F. Bruce, *The New Testament Documents: Are They Reliable?*, Eerdmans, 1981 (1943), pp. 86–87.

3 Matthew 15:21. All Bible quotations are from the Revised English Bible with the Apocrypha, Oxford University Press, New York, 1989.

4 Matthew 8:28.

5 Luke 8:26; Origen, *Commentary on the Gospel of John* 6:24. From *Ante-Nicene Fathers, Volume 9*. Edited by Allan Menzies, D.D., American Edition,

1896 and 1897 (all Ante-Nicene, Nicene, and Post-Nicene Fathers online at http://www.newadvent.org).

6   Irenaeus, *Adversus Haereses* 3:11:8. From *Ante-Nicene Fathers, Volume 1* Edited by Alexander Roberts & James Donaldson, American Edition, 1885; Clemens Romanus, *The First Letter of Clemens.*

7   Irenaeus, *Adversus Haereses* 2:22:5, 3:3:4.

8   Irenaeus to Florinus, quoted in Eusebius of Caesarea, *Church History*, 5:20. From *Nicene and Post-Nicene Fathers*, Series Two, Volume 1. Edited by Philip Schaff and Henry Wace, American Edition, 1890.

9   See, for example, Raymond E. Brown, *An Introduction to the New Testament*, Doubleday, 1997; Burnett Hillman Streeter, *The Four Gospels: A Study of Origins*, Macmillan, 1924; Vincent Taylor, *The Gospels, A Short Introduction*, Epworth Press, London, 1930; John A. T. Robinson, *Redating the New Testament*, Westminster Press, London, 1976.

10 Flavius Josephus, *Antiquities of the Jews*, 12:5:4.

11 Flavius Josephus, *Antiquities of the Jews*, 18:1:1, 18:1:6; *War of the Jews* 2:8:1; Acts of the Apostles 5:37.

12 Flavius Josephus, *Antiquities of the Jews*, 18:1:1.

13 Flavius Josephus, *War of the Jews*, 2:17:8–10.

14 Acts of the Apostles 5:36.

15 Flavius Josephus, *Antiquities of the Jews*, 20:5:1.

16 The Book of Joshua 3:14–17.

17 Flavius Josephus, *War of the Jews*, 2:13:5.

18 Flavius Josephus, *Antiquities of the Jews*, 20:8:6.

19 The Book of Joshua 6:20.

20 Zechariah 14:4.

21 Flavius Josephus, *War of the Jews*, 2:13:4.

22 The Book of the Prophet Jeremiah 23:5–6.

23 Matthew 1:1–17; Luke 3:23–38.

24 Zechariah 9:9; Matthew 21:9; Luke 19:38.

25 The First Book of Samuel 16; Micah 5:2.

26 Matthew 2:16.

27 Exodus 1:15–2:6.

28 Matthew 2:13–15.

29 Matthew 2:15; Hosea 11:1.

30 E. P. Sanders, *The Historical Figure of Jesus*, Penguin 1995 (1993), p. 90.

31 John E. Remsburg, *The Christ: A Critical Review and Analysis of the Evidence of His Existence*. The Truth Seeker Company, NY, 1909, p. 18.

32 Flavius Josephus, *Antiquities of the Jews*, 18:1:1, 6.

33 Flavius Josephus, *The Life of Flavius Josephus*, 2.

34 Flavius Josephus, *Antiquities of the Jews*, 18:1:6.

35 E. P. Sanders, *The Historical Figure of Jesus*, p. 30.

36 Flavius Josephus, *War of the Jews*, 3:8:7.

37 Flavius Josephus, *War of the Jews*, 3:8:7.

38 Flavius Josephus, *Antiquities of the Jews*, 20:9:1.

39 Flavius Josephus, *Antiquities of the Jews*, 18:3:3.

40 Eusebius of Caesarea, *Demonstratio Evangelica* 3.5. Translation by W.J. Ferrar, 1920; *Church History* 1:11; *Theophania* 5:44. Translation by Samuel Lee. Online at http://www.tertullian.org/fathers/.

41 Origen, *Contra Celsum*, 1:47. From *Ante-Nicene Fathers, Volume 4*. Edited by Alexander Roberts & James Donaldson, American Edition, 1885; Origen, *Commentary on the Gospel of Matthew* 10:17. From *Ante-Nicene Fathers, Volume 9*. Edited by Allan Menzies, D.D., American Edition, 1896 and 1897.

42 Origen, *Contra Celsum*, 1:47; Origen, *Commentary on the Gospel of Matthew* 10:17.

43 John P. Meier, *A Marginal Jew: Rethinking the Historical Jesus: The Roots of the Problem and the Person, Vol. 1*, Doubleday, 1991, p. 68.

44 John Dominic Crossan, *The Historical Jesus: The Life of a Mediterranean Peasant*, HarperSanFrancisco, 1991, p. 373.

45 Photios, *Bibliotheca*, Cod. 33. Online at http://www.ccel.org/p/pearse/morefathers/photius_03bibliotheca.htm.

46 Cornelius Tacitus, *Annales* 15:44:2–3. Translation by Alfred John Church and William Jackson Brodribb, Macmillan, London, 1864–1877.

47 Cornelius Tacitus, *Historiae* 5:5. Translation by Alfred John Church and William Jackson Brodribb, Macmillan, London, 1864–1877.

48 Gaius Suetonius, *The Lives of the Twelve Caesars*, Claudius 25. Translation by Alexander Thomson, R. Worthington, New York, 1883.

49 Gaius Suetonius, *The Lives of the Twelve Caesars*, Nero 16.

[50] Pliny the Younger to Trajan, 10:96–97. Translation by William Harris. Online at http://community.middlebury.edu/~harris/Classics/plinytrajan.html.

[51] *Mekh., Ba-Hodesh*, 11.

[52] The Book of the Prophet Isaiah 10:34–11:1.

[53] See, for example, R. Travers Herford: *Christianity in Talmud and Midrash*, Williams & Norgate, 1903; F. F. Bruce, *The New Testament Documents: Are They Reliable?*, Willian B. Eerdmans Publishing Co., 1981 (1943) pp. 102–104; Josh McDowell, *Evidence that Demands a Verdict*, Here's Life Publishers, 1972, p. 86.

[54] Sanders, p. xiii, 3.

[55] Matthew 10:5–6.

[56] Luke 1:1–4.

[57] Steve Mason, "Josephus and Luke-Acts," *Josephus and the New Testament*, Hendrickson Publishers, Peabody, Massachusetts, 1992, pp. 185–229; Max Krenkel, *Josephus und Lukas* (1894); Heinz Schreckenberg, "Flavius Josephus und die lukanischen Schriften," *Wort in der Zeit: Neutestamentliche Studien*, 1980, pp. 179–209; Gregory Sterling, *Historiography and Self-Definition: Josephos, Luke-Acts and Apologetic Historiography*, 1992; G. J. Goldberg, "The Josephus-Luke Connection," http://members.aol.com/fljosephus/LUKECH.htm. See also *The Journal for the Study of the Pseudepigrapha 13* (1995), pp. 59–77.

[58] Rudolf Bultmann, *The Gospel of John: A Commentary*. Blackwell, Oxford, 1971 (1941); Craig Blomberg, *The Historical Reliability of the Gospels*, Inter-varsity Press, 1987; S. S. Smalley, *John: Gospel Writer and Interpreter*, Paternoster, London, 1978.

[59] Mark 3:21.

[60] Matthew 13:53–58; Luke 4:16–30.

[61] Mark 6:3.

[62] Matthew 13:55.

[63] See, for example, Mark 6:47–52, 8:14–21, 9:16–19.

[64] Mark 14:51–52.

[65] John P. Meier, *A Marginal Jew: Rethinking the Historical Jesus: The Roots of the Problem and the Person, Vol. 1*, Doubleday, 1991, p. 603.

[66] Mark 1:7; Luke 3:16; Matthew 3:11; John 1:27.

[67] Donald Harman Akenson, *Saint Saul: A Skeleton Key to the Historical Jesus*, Oxford University Press, 2000, p. 191.

[68] John 7:41–42.

[69] The Letter of Paul to the Galatians 1:13–14.

[70] Jewish Encyclopaedia: "Gamaliel I". Funk and Wagnalls, NY, 1906. Online at http://www.jewishencyclopedia.com.

[71] Acts of the Apostles 5:34.

[72] Acts of the Apostles 8:3.

[73] Acts of the Apostles 9:1–2.

[74] Acts of the Apostles 9:4–6.

[75] The First Letter of Paul to the Corinthians 15:8.

[76] Martin Hengel, *Acts and the History of Earliest Christianity*, SCM, London, 1979; Martin Hengel and Anna Maria Schwemer, *Paul Between Damascus and Antioch: The Unknown Years*, SCM, London, 1997; Rainer Riesner, *Paul's Early Period: Chronology, Mission Strategy, Theology*, Eerdmans, 1998.

[77] Galatians 1:18–20.

[78] Letter of Paul to the Romans 1:4.

[79] Galatians 4:4; Romans 1:3.

[80] N. T. Wright, *Jesus and the Victory of God (Christian Origins and the Question of God, Vol. 2)*, Fortress Press, Minneapolis, 1992, p. 90.

[81] Gerd Lüdemann, *Paul, Apostle to the Gentiles: Studies in Chronology*, Fortress Press, Philadelphia, 1984 (1980).

[82] Akenson, p. 9.

CHAPTER 3: BIRTH AND CHILDHOOD

[1] Flavius Josephus, *Antiquities of the Jews*, 17:13:5, 18:1:1, 18:2:1.

[2] Luke 3:1, 3:23; John 2:20.

[3] Matthew 2:13–14.

[4] Matthew 2:15.

[5] R. Travers Herford, *Christianity in Talmud and Midrash*, Williams and Norgate, London, 1903, p. 55.

[6] Peter of Blois, *Contra perfidiam Judaeorum*, ca. 1198.

[7] Allan Temko, "The Burning of the Talmud in Paris," *Commentary Magazine* 17 (5) 1954, pp. 446–455.

[8] *bSanhedrin* 67a. All Babylonian Talmud quotes from Soncino Babylonian Talmud (with comments). Editor: I. Epstein, The Soncino Press, London, 1935–1948.

[9] *bShabbat* 104b.

[10] *jShabbat* 13d; G. R. S. Mead, *Did Jesus Live 100 B.C.?*, Theosophical Publishing Society, 1903, chapter X; Herford, pp. 54–55.

[11] *bShabbat* 104b.

[12] *bKiddushin* 49b.

[13] William Hendriksen, *More than Conquerors: An Interpretation of the Book of Revelation*, Tyndale 1966 (1939).

[14] The Revelation of John 19:12:16.

[15] E. A. Wallis Budge, *Egyptian Magic*, Kegan, Paul, Trench and Trübner, London, 1901, p. 1.

[16] Exodus 7:8–12.

[17] John Dominic Crossan, *The Historical Jesus: The Life of a Mediterranean Jewish Peasant*, HarperSanFrancisco, 1991, pp. 304–310.

[18] Mark 3:22; see also Matthew 12:24.

[19] Luke 11:14–15.

[20] Matthew 11:2–6.

[21] *bSanhedrin* 107b, *bSotah* 47a.

[22] Flavius Josephus, *Antiquities of the Jews*, 17:2:4, 17:3:1, 17:9–13.

[23] Luke 15:11–32.

[24] Matthew 1:19.

[25] John 8:38–41.

[26] John 6:42.

[27] *Mishna Yevamot* 49a.

[28] Herford, p. 44.

[29] *bShabbat* 104b.

[30] *bSanhedrin* 67a.

[31] *bGittin* 90a.

[32] Herford, p. 39.

[33] Ian Wilson, *Jesus: The Evidence*, Pan Books, 1985, pp. 55–56; *Der Gräberfund in Bingerbrück*, http://members.fortunecity.de/bingium/grabstein.html; L. Patterson, "Origin of the Name Panthera," *J Theol Studies* 19, 79–80, 1917.

[34] Susannah Heschel, "Nazifying Christian Theology: Walter Grundmann and the Institute for the Study and Eradication of Jewish Influence on German Church Life," *Church History* 63, 587–605, 1994; Anders

Gerdmar: "En germansk Jesus på svensk botten: svensk-tyskt forskningssamarbete med rasistiska förtecken 1941–1945", Uppsala University, 2004.

35   L. Patterson, "Origin of the Name Panthera," *J Theol Studies* 19, 79–80, 1917.

36   Herford, pp. 37, 38.

37   Origen, *Contra Celsum*, 1:32. From *Ante-Nicene Fathers, Volume 4*. Edited by Alexander Roberts & James Donaldson, American Edition, 1885.

38   Epiphanius of Salamis, *Adversus Haereses (Panarion)* 78:7:5. Translated by Frank Williams. Brill, Leiden, 1987.

39   John of Damascus, *An Exposition of the Orthodox Faith* 4:14. From *Nicene and Post-Nicene Fathers, Second Series, Volume 9*, Edited by Philip Schaff and Henry Wace, American Edition, 1899.

40   Origen, *Contra Celsum*, 1:28.

41   Joseph Klausner, *Jesus of Nazareth: His Life, Times, and Teaching*. Bloch Publishing Company, 1989 (1922), p. 20–23; Herford, p. 345 n.

42   Luke 19:12.

43   Matthew 20:16, 22:10, 18:4; Luke 15:11.

44   E.P. Sanders, *The Historical Figure of Jesus*, Penguin Books, 1995 (1993), p. 194.

45   Matthew 7:7.

CHAPTER 4: ENCOUNTER WITH JOHN THE BAPTIST

1   Luke 2:41–51.

2   Luke 3:23–38.

3   Matthew 3:13; Mark 1:9; Luke 3:21; John 1:29.

4   Flavius Josephus, *Antiquities of the Jews*, 18:3:1.

5   According to one historian, Philo of Alexandria, they were "golden shields" with inscriptions but without images (Philo, *Legatio ad Caium (On the Embassy to Gaius)* 38. Translation by C.D. Yonge, H.G. Bohn, London 1854–1890.).

6   Flavius Josephus, *Antiquities of the Jews*, 18:3:1–2; *War of the Jews*, 2:9:2–3.

7   Akenson, p. 15.

8   *jSanhedrin* 10:6:29C.

9   Philo of Alexandria, *Quod Omnis Probus Liber Sit (Every Good Man is Free)* 12:75. Translation by C.D. Yonge, H.G. Bohn, London, 1854–1890;

Flavius Josephus, *Antiquities of the Jews* 18:1:5. At another place (quoted by Eusebius of Caesarea in *Praeparatio Evangelica (Preparation for the Gospel)* 8:11. Translation by E.H Gifford, 1903) Philo does however say that there were "many thousand" Essenes.

10   John C. Trever, *The Untold Story of Qumran*, Fleming H. Revell Company, Westwood, NJ, 1965, chapter 12; James VanderKam and Peter Flint, *The Meaning of the Dead Sea Scrolls: Their Significance For Understanding the Bible, Judaism, Jesus and Christianity*, HarperCollins, 2002, pp. 3–5.

11   Flavius Josephus, *War of the Jews*, 2:8:2; Pliny the Elder, *Naturalis Historia (The Natural History)*, 5:17. Editors: John Bostock, H.T. Riley. Taylor and Francis, London, 1855. Online at Perseus Digital Library, Tufts University.

12   Eusebius of Caesarea, *Praeparatio Evangelica (Preparation for the Gospel)* 8:11.

13   Flavius Josephus, *War of the Jews*, 2:8:11.

14   IQS, Col. 6:8–11, Col. 7:8–9, 16. Translation by Geza Vermes.

15   Flavius Josephus, *War of the Jews*, 2:8:5.

16   See the discussion in, for example, John P. Meier: *A Marginal Jew: Rethinking the Historical Jesus, Volume Three: Companions and Competitors*. Doubleday, New York, 2001, pp. 495–532.

17   Matthew 3:2, 7–10; Luke 3:7–11.

18   Luke 1:36.

19   Jerome, *Adversus Pelagianos (Against the Pelagians)* 3:2. From *Nicene and Post-Nicene Fathers*, Second Series, Volume 6. Edited by Philip Schaff and Henry Wace. American Edition, 1893.

20   Matthew 3:13–17.

21   Matthew 4:1–11.

22   John 3:22–30, 4:1–3.

23   Matthew 14:3–4; Mark 6:17–19; Luke 3:19–20.

24   Luke 7:18–28; Matthew 11:2–15.

25   Mark 6:17–29.

26   Acts of the Apostles 19:1–4.

27   Flavius Josephus, *Antiquities of the Jews*, 18:5:1, 18:5:4.

28   Flavius Josephus, *Antiquities of the Jews*, 18:5:2.

29   Origen, *Contra Celsum*, 1:47.

30   Christiane Saulnier, "Hérode Antipas et Jean le Baptiste: Quelques remarques sur les confusions chronologiques de Flavius Josèphe," *Revue Biblique* 91:362–376, 1984; G. J. Goldberg, *John the Baptist and Josephus*, http://members.aol.com/FLJOSEPHUS/JohnTBaptist.htm.

31 Flavius Josephus, *Antiquities of the Jews*, 20:5:1.

32 Acts of the Apostles 5:34–37.

33 Flavius Josephus, *Antiquities of the Jews*, 20:5:2.

34 Steve Mason, "Josephus and Luke-Acts," *Josephus and the New Testament*, Hendrickson Publishers, Peabody, Massachusetts, 1992, pp. 185–229; Max Krenkel, *Josephus und Lukas*, 1894; Heinz Schreckenberg, "Flavius Josephus und die lukanischen Schriften," *Wort in der Zeit: Neutestamentliche Studien*, 1980, pp. 179–209; Gregory Sterling, *Historiography and Self-Definition: Josephos, Luke-Acts and Apologetic Historiography*, 1992; G. J. Goldberg, "The Josephus-Luke Connection," http://members.aol.com/fljosephus/LUKECH.htm See also *The Journal for the Study of the Pseudepigrapha 13* (1995), pp. 59–77.

35 Luke 1:80.

CHAPTER 5: THE PREACHER JESUS

1 See, for example, Mark A. Chancey: *The Myth of a Gentile Galilee*, Society for New Testament Studies Monograph Series 118, Cambridge UP, 2002 (also http://assets.cambridge.org/052181/4871/sample/0521814871ws.pdf).

2 Flavius Josephus, *War of the Jews*, 3:3:2.

3 Flavius Josephus, *The Life of Flavius Josephus*, 65.

4 Flavius Josephus, *War of the Jews*, 3:3:2.

5 Flavius Josephus, *The Life of Flavius Josephus*, 72.

6 Jack Finegan, *The Archeology of the New Testament: The Life of Jesus and the Beginning of the Early Church*. Princeton University Press, 1969, p. 27.

7 Luke 4:16–30.

8 Mark 3:20–35.

9 Matthew 12:46–50; Luke 8:19–21, 11:27–28; John 2:3–4.

10 Matthew 10:32–39.

11 Luke 14:26.

12 See, for example, Mark Allan Powell, *Jesus as a Figure in History: How Modern Historians View the Man from Galilee*, John Knox Press, 1998, p. 126.

13 Mark 1:15; Matthew 15:24, 19:28.

14 Sanders, *The Historical Figure of Jesus*, p. 238.

15 Matthew 5:17.

16 Mark 2:23–28; Matthew 12:1–8.

17   Matthew 19:3, 8–9; Mark 10:2.

18   Matthew 4:18–22.

19   Matthew 5:3–5, 41–42.

20   Mark 6:5–6.

21   Mark 5:21–43; Matthew 9:18–26; Luke 8:40–56.

22   Luke 7:11–17.

23   John 11:1–44.

24   Mark 6:36–42, 6:48–52, 8:14–21.

25   Morton Smith, *The Secret Gospel: The Discovery and Interpretation of the Secret Gospel According to Mark*, Harper & Row, New York, 1973, p. 12.

26   Quentin Quesnell, "The Mar Saba Clementine: A Question of Evidence," *Catholic Bible Quarterly*, 37 [1],48–67, 1975.

27   Morton Smith, *Clement of Alexandria and a Secret Gospel of Mark*, Harvard University Press, 1973; Morton Smith: *The Secret Gospel: The Discovery and Interpretation of the Secret Gospel According to Mark*, Harper & Row, New York, 1973.

28   Mark 10:17–31, 14:51; John 11:1–44, 13:23, 19:26, 20:2, 21:20; Luke 18:18–23; Floyd V. Filson, "Who Was the Beloved Disciple," *Journal of Biblical Literature* 68, 83–88, 1949; J. M. Sanders, "Those Whom Jesus Loved," *New Testament Studies* 1:29–41, 1954–55; K. A. Eckhardt, *Der tod des Johannes*, De Gruyter, Berlin, 1961; George O. Stapleton, *Lazarus: The Beloved Disciple*, Booklocker, 2005; Miles Fowler, "Identification of the Bethany Youth in the Secret Gospel of Mark with other Figures Found in Mark and John," *The Journal of Higher Criticism* 5/1, 1998, pp. 3–22, also www.depts.drew.edu/jhc/fowler.html.

29   Smith, *The Secret Gospel*, pp. 113–114.

30   John 11:1–43, 12:1–17.

31   John 13:23, 19:26, 20:2, 21:20.

32   See note 28 above.

33   Luke 8:1–3.

34   Luke 7:37–50.

35   I Corinthians 15:5–6; Luke 9:10–17; Mark 6:31–44, 8:1–10; Matthew 14:13–21, 15:32–39.

36   John 4:27.

37   Mark 1:30; Matthew 8:14.

38   Matthew 27:55; Mark 15:41; Luke 23:55.

[39] See also John 8:1–11.

[40] Mark 3:6.

[41] Mark 8:31, 9:30, 10:32; Matthew 16:21, 17:22, 20:17; Luke 9:18, 9:43, 18:31.

[42] Luke 13:33.

CHAPTER 6: ENTERING JERUSALEM

[1] Mark 11:1–3.

[2] Pliny the Elder, *Naturalis Historia* (*The Natural History*), 5:14.

[3] Jewish Encyclopaedia: "Sanhedrin", "High Priest". http://www.jewishencyclopedia.com; A. Bühler, *Das Synedrion in Jerusalem*, Vienna, 1902.

[4] Flavius Josephus, *War of the Jews*, 6:9:3.

[5] Flavius Josephus, *War of the Jews*, 2:14:3.

[6] E. P. Sanders, *Judaism: Practice and Belief 63 BCE–66 CE*, Trinity Press, 1992, pp. 125–128.

[7] Tacitus, *Historiae* 5:13.

[8] Mark 11:7–10.

[9] Mark 11:15–19.

[10] Mark 12:37–40.

[11] Luke 20:9–19.

[12] Luke 21:5–6; Mark 13:1–2; Matthew 24:1–2.

[13] Mark 13:7–8.

[14] Luke 19:43–44.

[15] Flavius Josephus, *Antiquities of the Jews*, 20:8:6.

[16] Mark 14:3–8.

[17] Mark 14:10.

[18] Mark 14:1.

[19] Mark 14:12.

[20] I Corinthians, 11:23–25.

[21] Luke 22:19–20.

[22] Mark 14:41.

[23] Luke 22:48.

[24] Mark 14:50.

25   Mark 2:1–12, 2:13–17, 2:18–22, 2:23–28, 3:1–6.

26   E. P. Sanders, *The Historical Figure of Jesus*, Penguin Books, 1995 (1993), p. 218.

27   Matthew 26:61; Mark 14:57–58.

28   Mark Allan Powell, *Jesus as a Figure in History: How Modern Historians View the Man from Galilee*, Westminster/John Knox Press, 1998. p. 118.

29   Powell, p. 159; N. T. Wright, *Jesus and the Victory of God (Christian Origins and the Question of God, Vol. 2)*, Fortress Press, Minneapolis, 1996, pp. 553–576.

30   E. P. Sanders, *Jesus and Judaism*, Fortress Press, Philadelphia, 1985, p. 333.

31   Mark 13:24–26.

32   Matthew 8:20; Luke 9:58, 22:48; Mark 8:31.

33   Mark 3:11, 14:61, 15:39; Luke 4:3–9, 4:41, 20:9–19; Matthew 4:3–7, 27:54.

34   John 7:37–38.

35   Matthew 17:12–13.

CHAPTER 7: THE TRIAL

1   Flavius Josephus, *Antiquities of the Jews*, 20:9:1.

2   Flavius Josephus, *Antiquities of the Jews*, 20:10:1.

3   Flavius Josephus, *Antiquities of the Jews*, 13:10:6.

4   Flavius Josephus, *Antiquities of the Jews*, 18:2:1.

5   Flavius Josephus, *Antiquities of the Jews*, 18:2:2.

6   Zvi Greenhut, "Burial Cave of the Caiphas Family," *Biblical Archaeology Review* 18(5), 29–36, 76, 1992; Ronny Reich, "Caiphas Name Inscribed on Bone Boxes," *Biblical Archeology Review* 18 (5), 38–44, 76, 1992.

7   Luke 3:2; John 18:13, 24; Acts of the Apostles 4:6.

8   Flavius Josephus, *Antiquities of the Jews*, 19:6:4.

9   Flavius Josephus, *Wars of the Jews*, 2:12:6.

10   Acts of the Apostles 23:2, 24:1; Jewish Encyclopaedia: "Ananius, Son of Nebedeus". http://www.jewishencyclopedia.com.

11   Flavius Josephus, *Antiquities of the Jews*, 20:8:5; *Wars of the Jews*, 2:13:3.

12   Flavius Josephus, *Antiquities of the Jews*, 18:2:2.

13   Matthew 26:47; Mark 14:43; Luke 22:52.

14   John 18:3, 12.

[15]   F. F. Bruce, *New Testament History*, Doubleday, 1971 (1980), p. 195.

[16]   John 18:12–13.

[17]   Mark 14:56–58.

[18]   Mark 14:61.

[19]   Luke 22:67; John 18:19.

[20]   Luke 23:1–4.

[21]   John 18:31; Luke 23:6–7.

[22]   Mark 15:6–15.

[23]   F. F. Bruce, *New Testament History*, Doubleday, 1971, p. 203.

[24]   Flavius Josephus, *Antiquities of the Jews*, 20:8:5; *Wars of the Jews*, 2:13:3.

[25]   Flavius Josephus, *Antiquities of the Jews*, 20:8:5.

[26]   Flavius Josephus, *Antiquities of the Jews*, 20:8:10.

[27]   Matthew 21:13; Mark 11:17; Luke 19:46.

[28]   Flavius Josephus, *Antiquities of the Jews*, 20:8:5.

[29]   Flavius Josephus, *Wars of the Jews*, 2:13:3.

[30]   Flavius Josephus, *Antiquities of the Jews*, 20:6:1.

[31]   Flavius Josephus, *Wars of the Jews*, 2:13:2.

[32]   Tacitus, *Historiae*, 5:9–10.

[33]   Mark 15:27.

[34]   Matthew 27:38.

[35]   Luke 23:32–33.

[36]   Mark 15:7.

[37]   Matthew 26:55.

[38]   http://en.wikipedia.org./wiki/Makhaira; F. Quesada Sanz, "Máchaira, kopís, falcate," *Homenaje a Francisco Torrent*, Madrid, 1994, pp. 75–94.

[39]   Matthew 26:51–54.

[40]   John 18:10.

[41]   Luke 22:36–38.

[42]   Luke 6:15; Acts of the Apostles 1:13.

[43]   Robert Eisenman: *James, the Brother of Jesus: The Key to Unlocking the Secrets of Early Christianity and the Dead Sea Scrolls*, Viking Penguin, 1997.

[44]   Matthew 27:16–17.

[45]   See, for example, Hyam Maccoby: *The Mythmaker: Paul and the Invention of Christianity*, Barnes & Noble Books, 1998 (1986).

[46] Luke 20:17–18.

[47] Mark 12:10–11.

[48] Philo: *Legatio ad Caium (On the Embassy to Gaius)*, 38(302). Translation by C.D. Yonge, H.G. Bohn, London 1854–1890.

[49] Flavius Josephus, *Antiquities of the Jews*, 18:3:2.

[50] Flavius Josephus, *Antiquities of the Jews*, 18:4:1,2.

[51] Philo: *Legatio ad Caium*, 38.

[52] Matthew 27:24.

[53] Matthew 27:19.

[54] Eusebius of Caesarea, *Church History*, 2:7.

[55] *bSanhedrin* 43a.

[56] Martin Hengel, *Crucifixion in the Ancient World and the Folly of the Message of the Cross*, Fortress Press, Philadelphia, 1977, p. 39.

CHAPTER 8: ON WHETHER JESUS DIED ON THE CROSS

[1] Heinrich Eberhard Gottlob Paulus, *Philologisch-kritischer und historischer Kommentar über das Neue Testament*, 1800–1802; *Das Leben Jesu, als Grundlage einer reinen Geschichte des Urchristentums*, 1828; *Exegetisches Handbuch über die drei ersten Evangelien*, 1830–1833, 1841–1842.

[2] Karl Bahrdt, *Ausführung des Plans und Zwecks Jesu*, 1784–1792; Karl Venturini, *Geschichte des grossen Propheten von Nazareth*, 1800–1801; Friedrich Daniel Ernst Schleiermacher, *Der Christus des Glaubens und der Jesus der Geschichte*, 1832; August Friedrich Gfrörer, *Kritische Geschichte des Urchristenthums*, 1838; David Friedrich Strauss, *Das Leben Jesu*, vol II, 1864; Karl Hase, *Geschichte Jesu*, 1876; Karl Theodor Keim, *Die Geschichte Jesu von Nazara in ihrer Verkettung mit dem Gesamtleben seines Volkes*, 1867–1872.

[3] Frank Harris, *The Miracle of the Stigmata*, Lane, London, 1913; George Moore, *The Brook Kerith: A Syrian Story*, The Macmillan Company, New York, 1916; Ernest Brougham Docker, *If Jesus Did Not Die on the Cross*, Robert Scott, London, 1920; D. H. Lawrence, *The Man who Died (The Escaped Cock)*, Martin Secker, 1931 (1928); Robert Graves and Joshua Podro, *Jesus in Rome*, Cassell, London, 1957; Hugh J. Schonfield, *The Passover Plot*, Hutchinson, London, 1965; Donovan Joyce, *The Jesus Scroll*, Dial Press, 1972; Helmer Linderholm, *Evangelium enligt Pantera* [The gospel according to Pantera], Tiden, Stockholm, 1979; J. D. M. Derrett, *The Anastasis: The Resurrection of Jesus as an Historical Event*, P. Drinkwater, Shipston-on-Stour, England, 1982; Michael Baigent, Richard Leigh, and Henry Lincoln, *Holy Blood, Holy Grail*, Jonathan Cape, 1982; Gérald

Messadié, *L'Homme qui devint Dieu*, Robert Laffont, 1988; Barbara Thiering, *Jesus the Man*, Doubleday, 1992; Holger Kersten and Elmar R. Gruber, *The Jesus Conspiracy: The Turin Shroud & The Truth about the Resurrection*, Element Books 1994 (1992).

4   Pierre Barbet, *Les Cinq Plaies du Christ*, Procure du Carmel de l'Action de Graces, Paris, 1937; Pierre Barbet, *Doctor at Calvary*, P. J. Kennedy, New York, 1953; Frederick T. Zugibe, *The Crucifixion of Jesus: A Forensic Inquiry*, M. Evans Publ., 2005; Frederick T. Zugibe, "Pierre Barbet Revisited," www.shroud.com/zugibe.htm.

5   Flavius Josephus, *War of the Jews*, 5:11:1.

6   Flavius Josephus, *War of the Jews*, 4:5:2.

7   Vassilios Tzaferis, "Jewish Tombs at and near Giv'at ha-Mivtar, Jerusalem," *Israel Exploration Journal* 20(1,2), 18–32, 1970. Vassilios Tzaferis, "Crucifixion: The Archaeological Evidence." *Biblical Archaeology Review* 11, 44–53, 1985; Joseph Zias, "The Crucified Man from Giv'at Ha-Mivtar: A Reappraisal," *Israel Exploration Journal* 35(1), 22–27, 1985.

8   Mark 15:16; Matthew 27:27.

9   Mark 15:21; Matthew 27:32; Luke 23:26.

10   Mark 15:23; Matthew 27:34.

11   H. N. Moldenke and A. L. Moldenke, *Plants of the Bible*, Ronald Press, New York, 1952.

12   *bSanhedrin* 43a.

13   Mark 15:29–30.

14   Mark 15:25, 15:33–39.

15   Mark 15:44.

16   Luke 23:47.

17   William Stroud, *Treatise on the Physical Cause of the Death of Christ*, Hamilton and Adams, 1871.

18   John 19:26–30.

19   Floyd V. Filson, "Who Was the Beloved Disciple?," *Journal of Biblical Literature* 68, 83–88, 1949; J. M. Sanders, "Those Whom Jesus Loved," *New Testament Studies* 1, 29–41, 1954–55; K. A. Eckhardt, *Der Tod des Johannes*, De Gruyter, Berlin, 1961; George O. Stapleton, *Lazarus: The Beloved Disciple*, Booklocker, 2005; Miles Fowler, "Identification of the Bethany Youth in the Secret Gospel of Mark with other Figures Found in Mark and John." *The Journal of Higher Criticism* 5/1, 1998, pp. 3–22, also www.depts.drew.edu/jhc/fowler.html.

[20] John 11:3, 11:5, 11:36, 13:23, 19:26, 20:2, 21:20.

[21] Eusebius of Caesarea, *Church History*, 3:11, 3:32, 4:22.

[22] John 19:31–35.

[23] Kersten and Gruber, *The Jesus Conspiracy*, p. 249.

[24] Flavius Josephus, *The Life of Flavius Josephus*, 75.

[25] Vassilios Tzaferis, "Crucifixion: The Archaeological Evidence," *Biblical Archaeology Review* 11 (1), Jan/Feb 1985, also *Biblical Archaeology Society Online Archive*.

[26] John 19:38; Luke 23:50–51; Mark 15:43; Matthew 27:57.

[27] Mark 15:43–46.

[28] Kersten and Gruber, p. 263.

[29] John 19:38–40.

[30] Psalm 45:8.

[31] Brett Leslie Freese, "Medicinal Myrrh" (newsbriefs), *Archaeology* 49(3), 1996.

[32] Matthew 27:62–66.

[33] Mark 16:2–6.

[34] John 20:2–8.

[35] John 21:2.

[36] John 21:24.

[37] I Corinthians, 15:3–8.

[38] I Corinthians, 15:14–15, 15:17–18.

[39] Matthew 28:6–20.

[40] Luke 24:13–49.

[41] Acts of the Apostles 1:1–4.

[42] John 20:14–29; 21:1–23.

[43] Matthew 28:16–17.

[44] John 20:24–28.

[45] Acts of the Apostles 1:6–9.

[46] Luke 24:50–51.

[47] Justin Martyr, *Dialogue with Trypho*, 108. From *Ante-Nicene Fathers, Volume 1*. Edited by Alexander Roberts & James Donaldson, American Edition, 1885; Matthew 27:64, 28:11–15.

[48] Origen, *Contra Celsum*, 2:59–60.

49 Irenaeus, *Adversus haereses*, 1:24:4.

50 *The Second Treatise of The Great Seth*, Nag Hammadi Library. Translation by Roger A. Bullard and Joseph A. Gibbons. Online at The Gnostic Society Library, http://www.gnosis.org/naghamm/2seth.html.

51 Matthew 27:5.

52 The Gospel of Barnabas, 214–218. Translation by Lonsdale and Laura Ragg, London, 1907.

53 Sura 4:157. The Qur'ân, part I (Sacred Books of the East volume 6), Palmer edition, 1880. Online at http://www.sacred-texts.com/isl/sbe06/004.htm.

54 Flavius Josephus, *Antiquities of the Jews*, 20:8;6.

CHAPTER 9: WHAT HAPPENED ON THE ROAD TO DAMASCUS?

1 Karl Bahrdt: *Ausführung des Plans und Zwecks Jesu*, 1784–1792; D. H. Lawrence, *The Man who Died (The Escaped Cock)*, Martin Secker, 1931 (1929); Robert Graves and Joshua Podro, *Jesus in Rome*, Cassell, London, 1957; Hugh J. Schonfield, *The Passover Plot*, Hutchinson, London, 1965; Donovan Joyce, *The Jesus Scroll*, Dial Press, 1972; Michael Baigent, Richard Leigh, and Henry Lincoln, *Holy Blood, Holy Grail*, Bantam Dell, 1982; J. D. M. Derrett, *The Anastasis: The Resurrection of Jesus as an Historical Event*, P. Drinkwater, Shipston-on-Stour, England, 1982.

2 Jawaharlal Nehru, *Glimpses of World History*, Asia Publishing House, 1965 (1934), p. 86.

3 Holger Kersten, *Jesus Lived in India: His Unknown Life Before and After the Crucifixion*. Shaftesbury, 1986.

4 Irenaeus, *Adversus Haereses* 2:22:5.

5 www.unrv.com/empire/roman-population.php.

6 Paul Kriwaczek, *Yiddish Civilisation: The Rise and Fall of a Forgotten Nation*, Knopf, 2005, p. 32; *Encyclopedia Judaica*: "Population."

7 Flavius Josephus, *War of the Jews*, 7:3:3.

8 Robert F. Tannenbaum, "The God-Fearers: Did They Exist? Jews and God-Fearers in the Holy City of Aphrodite," *Biblical Archaeology Review* 12(5), Sep/Oct 1986, also *Biblical Archaeology Society Online Archive*.

9 Louis H. Feldman, *Jew and Gentile in the Ancient World: Attitudes and Interactions from Alexander to Justinian*, Princeton, 1993; Paul Johnson, *A History of the Jews*, Weidenfeld & Nicolson, 1987.

10 I Corinthians 15:8.

[11]   Martin Hengel, *Acts and the History of Earliest Christianity*, SCM, London, 1979; Martin Hengel and Anna Maria Schwemer, *Paul Between Damascus and Antioch: The Unknown Years*, SCM, London, 1997; Rainer Riesner, *Paul's Early Period: Chronology, Mission Strategy, Theology*, Eerdmans, 1998; Gerd Lüdemann, *Paul, Apostle to the Gentiles. Studies in Chronology*, Fortress Press, Philadelphia, 1984 (1980); John Knox, *Chapters in a Life of Paul*, Abingdon-Cokesbury, New York, 1950.

[12]   Romans 11:1; Philippians 3:5.

[13]   Acts of the Apostles 22:3, 9:11, 21:39.

[14]   Jerome: *De viris illustribus (On Illustrious Men)* 5. From *Nicene and Post-Nicene Fathers*, Second Series, Volume 3. Edited by Philip Schaff and Henry Wace. American Edition, 1892.

[15]   Acts of the Apostles 22:27–28.

[16]   Galatians 4:13–14.

[17]   II Corinthians 12:7.

[18]   I Corinthians 7:8.

[19]   Acts of the Apostles 22:3.

[20]   Galatians 1:14.

[21]   Acts of the Apostles 22:3.

[22]   Galatians 1:14.

[23]   See Luke 6:15; Acts of the Apostles 1:13; Acts of the Apostles 21:20; Acts of the Apostles 22:3; Galatians 1:14; I Corinthians 14:12; First Letter to Peter 3:13; Titus 2:14.

[24]   Mark R. Fairchild, "Paul's Pre-Christian Zealot Associations: a Re-examination of Gal. 1.14 and Acts 22.3," *New Testament Studies* 45(4), 514–532, 1999; Torrey Seland, "Saul of Tarsus and Early Zealotism. Reading Gal 1:13–14 in light of Philo's Writings." *Biblic* 83, 449–471, 2002; J. Taylor, "Why Did Paul Persecute the Church?," *Tolerance and Intolerance in Early Judaism and Christianity* (eds. G. N. Stanton and G. G. Stroumsa) Cambridge, 1998.

[25]   *Catholic Encyclopedia*: "St. Paul." Encyclopedia Press, 1913. http://www.newadvent.org/cathen/index.html.

[26]   Acts of the Apostles 7:58.

[27]   Acts of the Apostles 8:1.

[28]   Flavius Josephus, *Antiquities of the Jews*, 20:5:4; *War of the Jews*, 2:12:2.

[29]   Flavius Josephus, *Antiquities of the Jews*, 20:6:1; *War of the Jews*, 2:12:3.

[30]   Luke 9:51–56.

31 Flavius Josephus, *Antiquities of the Jews*, 20:6:1–3; *War of the Jews*, 2:12:3; John 4:4, 4:9; Luke 9:51–56, 10:25–37. Compare this to the description of Samaria in the Acts of the Apostles 1:8, 8:4, 8:5, 8:9, 8:14, 9:31, 15:3.

32 Acts of the Apostles 7:58–59.

33 Acts of the Apostles 8:3.

34 Acts of the Apostles 22:3–5.

35 Galatians 1:22.

36 Acts of the Apostles 9:1–19, 22:2–16, 26:9–18; Galatians 1:11–12, 1:16–17; I Corinthians 9:1, 15:8.

37 Acts of the Apostles 22:6–11.

38 Galatians 1:15–16.

39 II Corinthians 11:1–3.

40 Galatians 1:17–18.

41 Galatians 1:17–18.

42 Acts of the Apostles 9:20.

43 Galatians 1:18–22.

44 Acts of the Apostles 9:26.

45 Acts of the Apostles 22:17–18.

46 Galatians 2:1.

47 Acts of the Apostles 9:31.

48 Galatians 2:1.

49 Luke 23:12.

50 Matthew 27:19.

51 Flavius Josephus, *Antiquities of the Jews*, 20:7:1–2; Acts of the Apostles 24:24.

52 Matthew 2:19, 3:1.

53 Eusebius of Caesarea, *Church History*, 3:9:2; Jerome: *De Viris Illustribus*, 13.

54 Galatians 1:21, 2:1; Acts of the Apostles 11:25–26.

55 Acts of the Apostles 4:36–37.

56 Acts of the Apostles 9:27.

57 Acts of the Apostles 11:27–30.

58 Galatians 2:1.

59 John Knox, *Chapters in a Life of Paul*, Abingdon, Nashville, 1950; Gerd Lüdemann, *Paul, Apostle to the Gentiles. Studies in Chronology*, Fortress Press, Philadelphia, 1984 (1980); Donald Harman Akenson, *Saint Saul: A*

Skeleton Key to the Historical Jesus, Oxford, 2000; Martin Hengel and Anna Maria Schwemer, *Paul Between Damascus and Antioch: The Unknown Years*, SCM, London, 1997.

[60] Raymond F. Collins, *Letters that Paul Did Not Write: The Epistle to the Hebrews and the Pauline Pseudoepigraphia*. Michael Glazier, 1988, p. 183.

[61] Romans 15:30–31.

[62] See, for example, Galatians 2:11–12.

[63] Acts of the Apostles 12:2; Galatians 1:19.

[64] Acts of the Apostles 12:25.

[65] Letter of Paul to the Colossians 4:10.

[66] Acts of the Apostles 12:12, 12:25, 13:5, 13:13, 15:37, 15:39; Colossians 4:10; II Timothy 4:11; Philemon 1:24.

[67] Acts of the Apostles 12:12.

[68] Acts of the Apostles 13:4–5.

[69] II Corinthians 11:22.

[70] Acts of the Apostles 13:4–5, 13:14, 14:1, 17:1, 17:10, 17:17, 18:4, 18:19, 19:8.

[71] Acts of the Apostles 13:14–45.

[72] Acts of the Apostles 13:48–50.

[73] Acts of the Apostles 14:1–2.

[74] Romans 9:2–5.

[75] I Corinthians 9:24–27.

[76] Acts of the Apostles 14:8–13.

[77] Acts of the Apostles 20:9–10.

[78] I Corinthians 9:19–21.

[79] Mark 2:23–28.

[80] Acts of the Apostles 10:10–14.

[81] I Corinthians 7:17–19.

[82] Acts of the Apostles 15:1–2.

[83] Galatians 1:21–2:10.

[84] Acts of the Apostles 15:4–6; Galatians 2:1–2, 2:4, 2:9.

[85] Galatians 2:7–8.

[86] Galatians 2:10.

[87] Galatians 2:11–13.

88 Romans 3:21–22.

89 First Letter of Paul to the Thessalonians, 2:15–16.

90 Galatians 5:12; Philippians 3:2.

91 I Corinthians 9:24–27.

92 Acts of the Apostles 21:3–5.

93 Acts of the Apostles 21:13.

94 Acts of the Apostles 21:20–22, 24.

95 Compare, for example, Acts of the Apostles 5:1–11 with Flavius Josephus, *Antiquities of the Jews*, 20:9:2, and *War of the Jews*, 2:17:9; cf. Acts of the Apostles 5:17–25 with *Antiquities of the Jews*, 20:9:3.

96 Acts of the Apostles 21:27–29.

97 Acts of the Apostles 21:39.

98 Acts of the Apostles 22:22–29.

99 Acts of the Apostles 23:1–10.

100 Acts of the Apostles 23:26–29.

101 Acts of the Apostles 24:5–6.

102 Cornelius Tacitus, *Historiae*, 5:9.

103 Acts of the Apostles 25:3.

104 Acts of the Apostles 25:9–12.

105 Acts of the Apostles 26:32.

106 Acts of the Apostles 27:1–2.

107 Acts of the Apostles 28:5–6.

108 Acts of the Apostles 28:7–10.

109 Acts of the Apostles 28:16.

110 Acts of the Apostles 28:23, 28:24.

111 Acts of the Apostles 28:30–31.

112 See, for example, Eusebius of Caesarea, *Church History*, 2:25.

113 The commandment that is referred to is at Leviticus 19:18.

114 Epiphanius of Salamis, *Panarion*, 30:16:6–9.

115 Romans 15:24.

116 Flavius Josephus, *Antiquities of the Jews*, 20:9:4; Flavius Josephus, *War of the Jews*. 2:17:4, 2:20:1; Robert Eisenman, "Paul as Herodian," *JHC* 3(1), 110–122, 1996. See also www.depts.drew.edu/jhc/eisenman.html.

117 Flavius Josephus, *Antiquities of the Jews*, 20:9:4.

[118] See, for example, Raymond W. Bernard, *Apollonius the Nazarene: Mystery Man of the Bible*, 1964.

[119] Flavius Philostratus, *Life of Apollonius*, 1:4. Translated by F.C. Conybeare. Online at http://www.livius.org/ap-ark/apollonius/life/va_00.html.

[120] Flavius Philostratus, *Life of Apollonius*, 1:5.

[121] Flavius Philostratus, *Life of Apollonius*, 7:41.

[122] Flavius Philostratus, *Life of Apollonius*, 4:37.

[123] Flavius Philostratus, *Life of Apollonius*, 5:27.

[124] Flavius Philostratus, *Life of Apollonius*, 8:5.

[125] Flavius Philostratus, *Life of Apollonius*, 8:29.

[126] Flavius Philostratus, *Life of Apollonius*, 8:30.

[127] See, among others, Flavius Philostratus, *Life of Apollonius*, 8:30.

[128] Origen, *Contra Celsum*, 6:41.

[129] I Corinthians 3:4–6; Acts of the Apostles 18:24.

[130] Eusebius of Caesarea, *Against Hierocles*. Translation by F.C. Conybeare, Loeb edition, 1912. Online at http://www.tertullian.org/fathers/.

[131] G. R. S. Mead, *Apollonius of Tyana: The Philosopher Explorer and Social Reformer of the First Century AD*, 1901, pp. 28–42; Ferdinand Christian Baur, *Apollonius von Tyana und Christus*, Tübingen, 1832; John Henry Newman, *Historical Sketches, Vol. 1.* "The Apollonius of Tyana," from *Encyclopædia Metropolitana*, 1826, pp. 305–331; Albert Reville, *Apollonius of Tyana, the Pagan Christ of the Third Century* (English translation), London, 1866; Michael Faraday, *Jesus Christ: A Fiction Founded upon the Life of Apollonius of Tyana*, 1883.

[132] Irenaeus, *Adversus Haereses* 2:22:5.

CHAPTER 10: A HYPOTHESIS

[1] John 20:15.

[2] I Corinthians 11:3, 11:7–9, 14:33–35; Colossians 3:18; Ephesians 5:22–24; I Timothy 2:8–15, 5:9–16.

[3] I Corinthians 5:11.

[4] Mark 2:17.

[5] Romans 3:23–24.

[6] Acts 21:40.

[7] Matthew 15:24.

8   See, for example, Romans 11:11–14, 11:25–32.

9   Galatians 1:19, 2:9, 3:1, 3:16, 4:4; Romans 1:3, 15:3, 15:8; Philippians
    2:6–8; I Thessalonians 2:15; I Corinthians 15:4–8, 11:23–25; II
    Corinthians 8:9.

10 I Corinthians 15:3–5.

11 Romans 1:4.

12 I Corinthians 15:8.

13 Acts of the Apostles 9:1–2.

14 Acts of the Apostles 8:1–40.

15 *Philopatris*, 12.

16 Romans 11:1; Philippians 3:5; II Corinthians 11:22.

17 *Kiddushin* 29b; *Shulchan Aruch* 1.c.i.3; *Jewish Encyclopaedia*: "Celibacy."

18 Philo, *De vita contemplativa (On the Contemplative Life)1(2)*. Translation by
    C.D. Yonge, H.G. Bohn, London, 1854–1890.

19 Galatians 6:17.

20 Galatians 4:15, 6:11; Acts of the Apostles 9:3–18.

21 M. Krenkel: *Beiträge zur Aufhellung der Geschichte und der Briefe des Apostels
    Paulus*, 1890, pp. 47–125.

22 I Corinthians 15:14.

23 Acts of the Apostles 2:47.

24 Matthew 27:19; Acts of the Apostles 24:24.

25 John 18:22–23, Acts of the Apostles 23:2–3.

26 David Wenham, "Paul's Use of the Jesus Tradition: Three Samples,"
    Gospel Perspectives vol. 5, *Journal for the Study of the Old Testament*, 1985. pp.
    7–37; Craig Blomberg, *The Historical Reliability of the Gospels*, Inter-varsity
    Press, 1987, pp. 223–230; Peter Stuhlmacher, "Jesustradition in
    Römerbrief?" *Theol.Beitr.*, 240–250, 1983; David L. Dungan, *The Sayings of
    Jesus in the Churches of Paul*, Fortress, 1971, p. 92; D. M Stanley, "Pauline
    Allusions to the Sayings of Jesus," *Catholic Biblical Quarterly* 23, 26–39,
    1961; Victor P. Furnish, "The Jesus-Paul Debate: From Baur to
    Bultmann," *Bull. John Rylands Univ. Libr.* 47, 342–381, 1965; D. R.
    Catchpole, "The Synoptic Divorce Material as a Traditio-Historical
    Problem," *Bull. John Rylands Univ. Libr.* 57, 92–127, 1974; David Wenham,
    Paul: Follower of Jesus or Founder of Christianity?, 1995; Harald Riesenfeld,
    The Gospel Tradition, Fortress Press, 1970, pp. 172–204; Dale C. Allison, Jr.,
    "The Pauline Epistles and the Synoptic Gospels: The Pattern of the
    Parallels," *New Testament Studies* 28, 1–32, 1982; J Bernard Orchard:

"Thessalonians and the Synoptic Gospels," *Biblica* 19, 19–42, 1938; William David Davies, *Paul and Rabbinic Judaism: Some Rabbinic Elements in Pauline Theology*, SPCK, London, 1948; R.V.G. Tasker, "St. Paul and the Earthly Life of Jesus," *Expository Times* 46, 557–562, 1934–35; B. Fjärstedt, *Synoptic Traditions in 1 Corinthians, Themes and Clusters of Theme Words in 1 Corinthians 1–4 and 9*. Uppsala University, Dept. of Theology, 1974.

27   David Wenham, "Paul's Use of the Jesus Tradition: Three Samples," *Gospel Perspectives* vol. 5, *Journal for the Study of the Old Testament*, 1985, p. 28.

28   A. Resch, *Der Paulinismus und die Logia Jesu in ihrem gegenseitigen Verhaltnis untersucht*. Hinrichs, Leipzig, 1904; James D. G. Dunn, "Jesus Tradition in Paul," *Studying the Historical Jesus: Evaluations of the State of Currents Research* (eds. B. Chilton, C.A. Evans), Brill, Leiden, 1994; V. P. Furnish, *Theology and Ethics in Paul*, Nashville, 1968, pp. 51–59.

29   Acts of the Apostles 21:30–38.

INDEX

WEST END